Scripturalizing Educational Elitism

*Social Formation, Mythmaking, and Symbolic Labor
in Origen*

Scripturalizing Educational Elitism

Social Formation, Mythmaking, and Symbolic Labor in Origen

Kevin McGinnis

Claremont Studies in New Testament
and Christian Orgins 4

Scripturalizing Educational Elitism
Social Formation, Mythmaking, and Symbolic Labor in Origen
©2018 Claremont Press
1325 N. College Ave
Claremont, CA 91711

ISBN: 978-1-946230-20-1

Library of Congress Cataloging-in-Publication Data

Scripturalizing Educational Elitism: Social Formation, Mythmaking, and Symbolic Labor in Origen by Kevin McGinnis

> xiii + 220 pp. 22 x 15 cm. –(Claremont Studies in New Testament and Christian Orgins 4) Includes bibliographical references and index.
> ISBN: 978-1-946230-20-1

BR 65 068 M34 2018
    1. Origen

Cover picture: by Biljana Jovanovic

For Jillian, Erin, Ben, and Sarah

Table of Contents

Introduction	1
Background to the Project	5
Recent Scholarship on Identity in Early Christianity	15
Scope, Aim, and Structure of This Study	30
What is Scripturalizing?	35
Practices and the Nature of Social Existence	40
The Place of Narrative Identity in a Practice Ontology	52
The Task of the Interpreter	57
What Scripturalizing Is: An Initial Response	65
Situating Origen in the Greek Philosophical Field	67
Analyzing Fields of Cultural Production	73
The Philosophical Field in the Third Century C.E.	76
Origen the Philosopher	100
Conclusion: Mapping the Philosophical Field	122
Origen the Mythmaker	125
Prolegomena to Studying Origen's Mythmaking	128
The Pedagogical Structure of Origen's Christian Mythology	131
Conclusion: A Christian Ideology in Narrative Form	150

Origen's Symbolic Labor	151
Origen the Scholar and Presbyter	154
The Use of Analogy in Origen's Symbolic Labor	159
Conclusion: Symbolic Labor	175
Conclusion	177
Bibliography	183
Index	201
General Index	207

Abbreviations

The Works of Origen

CCels	*Contra Celsum*
EpistAfr	*Letter to Africanus*
EpistGreg	*Letter to Gregory*
ExhMart	*Exhortation to Martyrdom*
HomGn	*Homilies on Genesis*
HomEx	*Homilies on Exodus*
HomLev	*Homilies on Leviticus*
HomNum	*Homilies on Numbers*
HomJos	*Homilies on Joshua*
HomJd	*Homilies on Judges*
HomJr	*Homilies on Jeremiah*
HomEz	*Homilies on Ezekiel*
HomLc	*Homlies on Luke*
PArch	*Peri archon*

General Abbreviations

ANF	*Ante-Nicene Fathers*
ATR	*Anglican Theological Review*
BJOS	*British Journal of Sociology*
CH	*Church History*
CultStud	*Cultural Studies*
CSR	*Comparative Social Research*
JAAR	*Journal of the American Academy of Religion*
JECS	*Journal of Early Christian Studies*
JSNTSup	*Journal for the Study of the New Testament Supplement Series*
HE	*Historia ecclesiastica*
LCL	*Loeb Classical Library*
MTSR	*Method & Theory in the Study of Religion*

SecCen	*The Second Century*
SC	*Sources Chrétiennes*
SociolRelig	*Sociology of Religion*
USQR	*Union Seminary Quarterly Review*
WTJ	*Westminster Theological Journal*
WUNT	*Wissenschaftliche Untersuchungen zum Neuen Testament*
VG	*Vigiliae Christianae*

Acknowledgments

The topic of this study is Origen of Alexandria and how he fits within a world of intellectuals in the third century. While reflecting on Origen's place within this field, I often thought of where and how I fit into the modern field of scholars of religion. This book is an expression of much of my accumulated cultural capital, but it is my social capital that helped get me to this point and that sustained me over years of self-doubt, economic struggle, and personal, psychological and medical ups and downs. These few words cannot communicate how much I appreciate what these people (and many others) have meant to me especially in regards to the completion of this project.

Since this book is basically my 2014 Claremont Graduate University dissertation, I would like to begin by thanking my committee for their support and flexibility. Vincent Wimbush, whose work through the Institute for Signifying Scriptures greatly shaped the project, helped to solidify my orientation to the study of religion as the study of human practices intrinsically engaged in political forces of oppression and liberation. He stepped in to chair the committee in its final stages for which I am extremely grateful. Until that time, Karen Torjesen had been my chair, but she was forced to step down for personal reasons. Her scholarship on Origen had helped me to see the social hierarchies that pervaded his theology and I was fortunate to work with her throughout the early stages of this project. She encouraged me to pursue this somewhat unusual approach to Origen, which gave me the confidence to continue with a topic I had first conceived in my second year of graduate school. Andrew Jacobs gave me great suggestions throughout the entire process on both minute details of the work and on the bigger themes and theoretical issues. He has been a supportive, encouraging voice throughout this process and continues to be someone whose positive valuation of my work makes me trust that I must be doing something right. In the eleventh hour, Arthur Urbano, for whom I TA'd my first class at Brown University in 2002, stepped in as the third member of my committee. His familiarity with the theoretical aspects of the project and with the approach to religion as a field of competition was a helpful and inspiring addition. He continues to be a significant conversation partner and friend and I look forward to working with him in studying Christianity and its relationship to Greek philosophy in Late Antiquity for many years to come.

I would be remiss if I did not acknowledge the significant contributions of other faculty members in my development as a scholar, all of whom had some influence on this project. During my undergraduate years at the University of California, San Diego, Arthur Droge helped me to see the importance of studying religion as a social phenomon and advised me on the first research paper I wrote investigating Christian-Roman relations in light of Stoic philosophy. During my first years of graduate study at Brown University, Stanley Stowers introduced me to a number of theorists whose work is at the heart of this project. I cannot imagine having stayed in the field at all if not for having been drawn to the perspective he advocated for in the study of religion. His work has been extremely influential in my work and I continue to look to him for advice on my work, which he continues to be generous enough to comment on. I first studied Origen in an independent study I did with Susan Ashbrook Harvey who helped me appreciate his significance in the history of Christianity and who, more than anyone, made me feel that it was not only okay to go beyond the New Testament, but would actually be much more enjoyable for me. Lastly, Ross Kraemer made me a better reader and writer than I ever could have imagined. She also helped me to understand the importance of always keeping in mind matters of oppression and marginalization, especially in matters of gender and class.

Whenever I write anything, I think about the standard that she set for me and hope that I at least approach it.

Some of my best conversation partners have been friends and colleagues that I have known over the years, many of whom I have worked with in relation to our program unit on Religious Competition within the Society of Biblical Literature. For their feedback, encouragement, and friendship, I would especially like to thank Nathaniel Des Rosiers, Daniel Ullucci, Jordan Rosenblum, Debra Scoggins Ballentine, Gail Armstrong, Steve Larson, Gregg Gardner, and Lily Vuong, who generously read an earlier draft of this project. Through this unit, I have also benefited from conversations and debates with Heidi Marx, Andrew McGowan, Catherine Chin, Todd Krulak, and Emma Wasserman. I also benefited greatly from discussions with fellow students at Claremont, most notably Richard Newton, Chris Zeichmann, Nathan Bennett, Tyler Gillet, Alonzo Huntsman, Ryan Carhart, Caleb Webster, Katie Van Heest, Simon Joseph, Jacqueline Hidalgo, Melissa Reid, and Robert Mason. The bulk of this book was written while teaching at University of the Pacific from 2011 to 2014 and I am grateful to my colleagues and friends there, George Randels, Alan Lenzi, and Carrie Schroeder.

Lastly, I want to thank my family for supporting me and for helping give me a sense of purpose without which this project might not ever have seen the light of day. For raising me and shaping me into the person I am, I am forever grateful to my mother, Cecilia, and father, Patrick, who unfortunately passed long before I began work on this. Thanks are also due to my brother, Brian, who always pushed me to think more clearly and to avoid making claims I could not support. This book is dedicated to my wife, Jillian, and three step-children. While teaching full-time and having suffered a stroke in 2013, I easily could have let this process drag out even longer, but wanting to finish and be a bigger part of their lives is what drove me to finish. Their love continues to sustain me and push me forward. I could not, and would not want to, do any of this without them.

INTRODUCTION

With his 1971 article, "The Study of Religion and the Study of the Bible," Wilfred Cantwell Smith fired a shot across the bow of biblical studies and, more broadly, the study of religion.[1] As Smith noted, the study of scripture has predominantly been the study of the history leading up to the creation of a scriptural text and its meaning in a historical critical sense. With this focus on the text and its original intended meaning, scholars have generally neglected the sorts of questions that are more important for a social historical study of religion. From this social historical perspective, scriptures come to have meaning and significance through their reception and use, and communities that make use of scriptures do so in a variety of ways and for a variety of purposes. Scholars, Smith argued, should concern themselves with the forward trajectory of a text as it comes to be considered scripture and comes to influence people in different times and locations. Smith continued this trajectory of studying scripture culminating in his 1993 monograph *What is Scripture?*. In this comparative analysis of scriptures in the major "world" religions, Smith further developed this orientation toward scriptures by examining them not simply as texts but as products of human reception and imaginative manipulation. In his conclusion, Smith claims, "*There is no ontology of scripture. The concept has no metaphysical, nor logical, reference; there is nothing that scripture finally 'is'.*"[2] To study scripture should thus be to study people and the varying ways in which they engage artifacts (usually, though not necessarily, textual in

---

[1] Wilfred Cantwell Smith, "The Study of Religion and the Study of the Bible," *JAAR* 39.2 (June 1971): 131-40.
[2] Wilfred Cantwell Smith, *What is Scripture? A Comparative Approach* (Minneapolis: Fortress Press, 1993/2005), 237.

nature) such that those artifacts become central to a group's self-understanding and come to be seen as scripture.

Smith's call to this reorientation in the study of religion has perhaps best been answered by one of his former students, Vincent Wimbush, whose Institute for Signifying Scriptures has encouraged and supported a number of scholars taking just such an approach to scriptures.[3] In the introduction to the Institute's first publication, *Theorizing Scriptures*, Wimbush issues a similar call to arms:

> We must collect ourselves as a larger, more complexly constituted group and orient ourselves so as to begin (in some cases, perhaps, begin *again*) to fathom how "scriptures" developed, what work we make them do

---

[3] A similar approach to scriptures has developed under the label "canonical criticism," but there are important differences between canonical criticism and the approach to scripture advocated by Smith and Wimbush. Canonical criticism developed as a reaction against historical criticism in large part in order to demonstrate the continuing importance of scripture for communicating divine truths to later communities, thus defending the ongoing theological significance of texts that had been relegated to the past through the predominant focus on their original meaning. Canonical criticism remains focused on the text of scripture, while recognizing the multiplicity of meanings that have been read out them. Smith and Wimbush, as I read them, are encouraging scholars to focus more on people and the dynamics of social existence that incorporate, reference, or play off of scriptures. Such an approach is less concerned with what a text means in the context of the canon or even what it is taken to mean as a whole and is instead interested in techniques of meaning-making that make use scripture in more creative ways. The focus is therefore on those who use scriptures and the authority accorded to scriptures and not on the content of scriptures and their supposed inherent power. The approach of Smith and Wimbush, unlike that of canonical critics, is a purely anthropological one that makes no claims to theological truths or divine meanings. For an overview of canonical criticism, see James A. Sanders, *Canon and Community: A Guide to Canonical Criticism* (Philadelphia: Fortress Press, 1984); *The New Testament as Canon: A Reader in Canonical Criticism* (ed. Robert W. Wall and Eugene E. Lemcio; JSNTSup 76; Sheffield: Sheffield Academic Press, 1992); Robert W. Wall, "Canonical Criticism" in *A Handbook to the Exegesis of the New Testament* (ed. Stanley E. Porter; Boston: Brill, 2002), 291-312; and James A. Sanders, *Torah and Canon* (2d ed.: Eugene: Cascade Books, 2005).

> within and across the societies and cultures, and with what historical and perduring political consequences…We must together engage in the sociology, anthropology, the cultural history, the psychosocial logics, the performance-expressive, the material and political criticism of "scriptures." With this different orientation or agenda, the primary focus should be placed *not upon texts* per se (that is, upon their content-meanings), but upon textures, gestures, and power – namely the signs, material products, ritual practices and performances, expressivities, orientations, ethics, and politics associated with the phenomenon of the invention and use of "scriptures."[4]

If Smith raised the question of scriptures, Wimbush and his associates are attempting to provide answers, focusing especially on scriptures amongst subordinated peoples and questions of political and cultural domination and subversion.[5] Their work helps us to see, among other things, that to study scriptures is to study people and how they shape and express their self-understandings in relation to scriptures, and to examine the power dynamics created, sustained, and challenged through those meaning-making activities.

In this book, I apply this approach to the reception of scripture in early Christianity through an analysis of the scripturalizing practices and rhetoric in the works of Origen of Alexandria. The central focus throughout is not on scripture in Origen, but on scripturalizing – how he attempts to shape Christian life and self-understanding in relation to scriptures. It

---

[4] Vincent L. Wimbush, "Introduction: TEXTures, Gestures, Power: Orientation to Radical Excavation," in *Theorizing Scriptures: New Critical Orientations to a Cultural Phenomenon* (Signifying (on) Scriptures 1; New Brunswick: Rutgers University Press, 2008), 3.

[5] In addition to *Theorizing Scriptures*, this approach can also be seen in the second publication in the Signifying (on) Scriptures book series: James S. Bielo, *The Social Life of Scriptures: Cross-Cultural Perspectives on Biblicism* (Signifying (on) Scriptures 2; New Brunswick: Rutgers University Press, 2009).

is thus a study of Christian identity formation insofar as the focus is not on the "original" meaning of scripture, or even on its meaning as interpreted by Origen, but on the ways in which a particular Christian social formation is advocated for, defended, and asserted to be divinely sanctioned by drawing on scriptures. By "identity" I do not mean simply how Christians understood themselves as different from their non-Christian neighbors. While this is a significant component of identity formation, I prefer to focus instead on the public narratives (what I will be referring to as myths for reasons that will become clear in Chapter One) that Christians shared, which helped justify and explain their particular social practices and the internal hierarchies which developed within Christian communities. The focus on the internal dynamics of social identity is important since matters of power and symbolic violence *within* groups, especially early Christian groups, has generally not been the subject of scholarly analysis. Rounding out the focus on scripturalizing is an analysis of the ways in which these narratives and hierarchies are made to seem authoritative, natural, and even divine in nature, processes that Pierre Bourdieu has called symbolic labor. As I will explain in detail in Chapter One, I see scripturalizing as a dynamic process of social formation, mythmaking, and symbolic labor, which, I will argue, is an expansive way for talking about the complex of activities that contribute to identity formation in relation to scriptures.

Applying this orientation towards scriptures in a study of Origen provides us with an ideologically critical understanding of how Origen's theology is tightly bound to his own social location. It also helps us to see how Origen attempts to sanction with divine authority a hierarchy that situates Origen and other intellectuals at the top, a hierarchy reflective of certain traditional class dynamics in the ancient Mediterranean world. Although I will be drawing heavily on the excellent work that has already been done on Origen, my presentation of him and his work should alter how we see Origen, his theology, and his hermeneutical method while also providing us with a historical case study for this model of scripturalizing. This project thus has three goals: (1) to lay out a sociological model of scripturalizing that will be applicable in other cultural contexts in which scriptures are employed, (2) to contribute to the study of early Christian identity, and (3) to provide an ideologically critical reading of Origen and his work.

Background to the Project

Academic projects such as this one are all too often presented as falling only within a particular history of scholarship on a given problem or question. The practice of providing such a context for a study alerts readers to the contributions made by the work to the field as a whole and explains the questions and problems that the work is meant to shed light on or solve. While this project is also similarly situated, such a presentation glosses the ways in which I myself arrived at these questions and where I position myself as a scholar. It is important to acknowledge my own positionality as a scholar and the circumstances of my personal and academic development that have contributed to the questions asked herein, the approaches taken, and the conclusions at which I arrive. As Russell McCutcheon notes, such peeks behind the authorial curtain in all its opacity typically appear in prefaces and epilogues, but they are rarely intended to be used to understand the main body of the work which is presented as a self-sustaining piece of knowledge, free from the trappings of social, political, gender, and other such dynamics.[6] Pierre Bourdieu advocated for a reflexive sociology in order to make sociological analysis more objective and scientific, but I offer up these self-reflections as an acknowledgement of my own situatedness and of the possible limitations on my project and analysis that may result from my necessarily limited perspective. As an act of self-historicizing, it is an admission to the subjectivity present in this study, not so as

---

[6] Russell T. McCutcheon, *The Discipline of Religion: Structure, Meaning, Rhetoric* (London: Routledge, 2003), 220.

to encourage others to dismiss my work because of my biases, but in order to invite others to engage with my ideas and conclusions in a manner that will supplement this work and contribute to an ongoing dialogue. Such an approach to scholarship is based on the belief that published works are meant to be part of an ongoing and interpersonal educational process, to the extent that they can be, and I would hope for this project to encourage further discussion and exchange.

The connection between an individual scholar's personal background and his or her intellectual interests or insights may at times feel arbitrary or inexplicable, but they are, of course, indicative of histories, both communal and individual, that have shaped that scholar and have provided the social and intellectual context within which that scholar works. I first came to this particular constellation of questions about the formation of early Christian identity through an engagement with the works of Russell McCutcheon, Bruce Lincoln, and Burton Mack. But it is not by chance that I was reading these scholars in the early years of my graduate studies at Brown University, nor was it by chance that I found their works compelling and the questions they raised for me worth pursuing.

My self-positioning covers both my social location as an individual and my location within the field of religious studies. I am the son of an Irish-American father and a Colombian mother who moved to the United States in her twenties. My multi-racial self-identification in a country where racial categories are so important left me feeling dislocated socially in many ways. Feeling neither Colombian nor Irish, and feeling like it was never enough to be simply 'American', I came to be highly attuned to the ways in which people impose definitions of what it means to have membership in such groups. I often resisted simple classifications of myself and resented those who would exclude or include me in either ethnic group for what I considered to be problematic markers of identity such as language, names, or even biological ancestry. These experiences led me to be sympathetic to those who were marginalized or excluded even while I continued to struggle with what I thought it meant to be part of a group, racial or otherwise.

Although much of my early struggles with matters of identity dealt with ethnic identity, my nebulous relationship to religion, particularly in the form of Roman Catholicism, is also significant for understanding my approach to this particular academic field of study. Both of my parents were Catholic, but we did not attend church often in my youth and I barely identified religion as an aspect of my life. That said, I do attribute to my Catholic background, at least in part, certain aspects of my intellectual interests, such as a respect for non-canonical texts in the formation of Christian communities, and a healthy interest in martyrdom and the cult of the saints. It also, I believe, contributed to my acknowledgement of the importance of the reception of scripture and of authoritative figures in shaping Christian communities and in shaping others' understanding of scriptures, as opposed to just wanting to focus on the original meaning of canonical texts. As religion was a marginal aspect of my youth, neither the church nor a belief in God was a significant part of my identity, nor something I spent much time thinking about until my college years, even though I had a sense as a teenager that I did not take to religion or a religious community the way most of my friends did. I came to see myself as standing outside of important communities (ethnic, racial, and religious) and I became critical of the ways in which people drew boundaries between themselves and others on the basis of these markers. I also came to see religious identity primarily as yet another way in which social, and not theological or philosophical, distinctions were made, which would have significant implications for my development as a scholar.

I majored in Classical Studies and religious studies at the University of California, San Diego, where I took several classes with Arthur Droge, whose approach to religion as a purely social phenomenon struck a chord with me. In his courses and in discussions with him, I developed a belief that the scientific study of religion, especially within the context of a public university, should be carried out in an interdisciplinary, humanistic manner. Taking this approach necessarily limited my options when I chose to pursue an advanced degree in religious studies. I earned a master's degree at Brown University, a private, non-affiliated institution, where my understanding of the use of method and theory in the study of religion was shaped primarily by Stanley Stowers and several like-minded students with whom I was fortunate enough to matriculate. When I decided to complete my doctorate in religious studies, I was drawn to Claremont Graduate University as another non-affiliated graduate program in religion with scholars whose work demonstrated a similar understanding of religion. All of my training as a scholar of religion has been carried out in the context of elite institutions of higher education where religion has been studied as something social and not as something reflective of transcendent truths. At these institutions, I have been encouraged to approach religion in terms of social identity and the contestation over power and authority.

Between my years at Brown and Claremont, I earned a Master of Science degree in counseling with an emphasis on student development in higher education at California State University, Long Beach. During this time, I came to think of identity in terms of buying into (i.e., identifying with or internalizing) certain shared narratives. During my course of study there, I was exposed to a variety of racial and ethnic identity models that were prominent in student development theory. I was struck by the normative assumptions made in these models, especially those structured as stages in which one progressed to an 'ideal' manner of identifying with one's racial or ethnic community in the context of the United States.[7] I was also alarmed by the manner in which my professors and fellow

---

[7] For examples of such theories and discussion of past work on this topic, see *New Perspectives on Racial Identity Development: A Theoretical and Practical Anthology* (ed. Charmain L. Wijeyesinghe and Bailey W. Jackson III; New York: New York University Press, 2001).

students felt so comfortable with the notion that such social identities were somehow biological in nature, that our genetic make-up should tell us what we need to identify with in order to be healthy, whole individuals. As I had come to understand identity, it involved sets of practices and beliefs and an affective sense of belonging to a group whose (hi)story was told and retold, not just to educate, but to incorporate. None of this was necessarily tied to blood, however, and I came to reject, at least in large part, the notion that identity was necessarily tied to biology.[8]

Meanwhile, I was also exploring the philosophy of higher education in the United States, both in terms of pedagogy within the classroom and also in terms of co-curricular experiences outside the classroom. Working out my own philosophy of education, I came to realize that I found educational experiences most compelling when they helped to expose as constructed, provisional, *ad hoc*, or otherwise 'fictive' those narratives (myths, histories, traditions) that are so often presented as given, normative, and not to be questioned, i.e., the narratives that give shape to various forms of identity. In other words, I find education to be especially effective when it helps one to make sense of various forms of violence, both real and symbolic, that everyone experiences as they are brought up, in order to come to terms with one's place in the world with greater understanding and thus, hopefully, with less discomfort and even pain. I found the writings of bell hooks on pedagogy to express this best when she describes the possibility of theoretical discourse to be "healing, liberatory, or revolutionary" though "only when we ask that it do so and direct our theorizing towards this end."[9]

---

[8] It is important to note that one's biology may greatly affect the way she is viewed by others and comes to view herself, and to this extent biology may be quite significant in closing off options in terms of what narratives one is likely to identify with, but that is different from claiming that identity is somehow written into one's DNA.

[9] bell hooks, *Teaching to Transgress: Education as the Practice of Freedom* (New York: Routledge, 1994), 61.

hooks suggests that the process of educating, not just in person but also in writing, can and should be directed toward engaging one's audience to reflect critically on their own experiences and to participate actively in other liberatory practices. Given my interest in education as potentially liberating, it is not a coincidence that the theorist whose work I most draw on for my theory of scripturalizing is Pierre Bourdieu, who pointed to sociological analysis as a potential tool in the liberation of peoples from various forms of domination. I, too, see this as the most important goal, at least for my own work, for the creation of knowledge and for the education of others, and this book is so directed, especially to the extent that it provides ways to reconceptualize the manner in which groups are formed and the ways hierarchies are legitimized and enforced.

While the majority of my interests in the theory of religion might be explained, in large part, by my struggles with religious and ethnic identity, I cannot ignore the importance of class in helping me to see the value of Pierre Bourdieu's social theory and in making me sensitive to the aspects of social class that consistently come up in the works of Origen. My father had long been unemployed by the time I went to college, so I was acutely aware of differences in access to both real and symbolic capital. I was most attuned to such differences during my time at Brown University, so much so that I doubted that I belonged in academia and ultimately left the Ivy League institution and returned home to California. This was also the time that I first read Origen and noticed how important access to higher education is to his soteriology. The fact that I have stuck with this project over the course of the past decade is indicative of just how important it is to me that I point out the class hierarchies that are reflected in Origen's theology.

I have presented the aspects of my development as an individual that have led me to down a particular educational path. It is due in part to my particular perspective and to the places in which I have been trained that I have found certain scholarly works particularly compelling. These works have been influential in shaping my view of the nature of religion and of religious studies, and have also been critical in the formation of the present study. Although many scholars could be addressed here, four stand out as particularly significant: Russell McCutcheon, Vincent Wimbush, Bruce Lincoln, and Burton Mack.

The first two scholars have been particularly influential in suggesting a way of approaching religion (McCutcheon) and scripture (Wimbush). I read McCutcheon's *Critics Not Caretakers* in my first graduate level theory class at Brown in 2001. I found McCutcheon's arguments for an approach to religion that was purely social and available to public critique and analysis to be compelling and in line with my own values and beliefs about religion and the field of religious studies. As McCutcheon puts it:

> As is probably clear by now, I favor developing a social definition and social theory of religion. Despite the promise of other equally interesting theoretical frameworks, it is on the level of constructing, legitimizing, and contesting power and privilege that I find so-called religious systems to be of most interest. Therefore, for me, on the redescriptive level religion turns out to be but one subspecies of larger sociohistorical, ideological systems. The challenge, then, is to develop a coherent, theoretically based vocabulary capable of placing religion firmly within the social world, with no leftover residue that prompts supernaturalistic speculations.[10]

Despite the feathers McCutcheon's criticisms of the field have often ruffled, I have found him to be clear in advocating a particular approach to religion based on his interests and goals, which he also offers up for debate and critique. I share his goals of studying religion from a critical, liberatory perspective, which lays bare the oppressive and sometimes violent aspects of

---

[10] Russell T. McCutcheon, *Critics Not Caretakers: Redescribing the Public Study of Religion* (Albany: State University of New York Press, 2001), 24.

religious formation. While I do not believe these are the *only* questions we can ask about religion, I find them to be the most compelling *to me*, and my questions and approaches in this present study are shaped by said interests. With McCutcheon, then, I hold religion to be a purely human, social phenomenon open to scrutiny and critique, admitting, with McCutcheon, to a methodological reductionism, though not necessarily a metaphysical reductionism.

This perspective is parallel to that advocated by Vincent Wimbush in his ongoing promotion of a research agenda that asks questions about scriptures and their uses that are radically different from those that have typically been asked. Wimbush has articulated a radical shift in the scholarly disposition towards scriptures, one that aims not at an interpretation or their 'original meaning', but at the processes by which scriptures are pressed into service in doing work in a community. The study of scriptures, so construed, entails a focus on the "phenomenology of social-cultural formation and the creation and uses of sacred texts."[11] This move away from the lexical meaning of scriptures to their social uses is a significant departure from traditional analyses of sacred texts and it is one that opens up new questions about how scriptures are deployed in the formation of social identity both in terms of defining boundaries between groups and also in terms of delineating hierarchies within groups. Wimbush encourages us to study scriptures almost as tactics and not just as texts that need to be unpacked or interpreted. In this view, scriptures become radically powerful artifacts that can be employed in a multiplicity of ways when it comes to the formation and maintenance of religious communities. Wimbush's work, both in print and in the classroom, have helped me to frame my analysis of Origen as an interpreter of scripture, as one actively engaged in the employment of scriptures as a

---

[11] Vincent L. Wimbush, introduction to *African Americans and the Bible: Sacred Texts and Social Textures* (New York: Continuum, 2000), 14.

tactic, rather than getting caught up in questions of the meaning and application of the scriptures themselves.

The works of Bruce Lincoln and Burton Mack have led more directly to the series of questions I bring to the study of Origen, though still from a theoretical and methodological perspective. I found Lincoln, whose *Theorizing Myth* I read in the same class in which I was introduced to McCutcheon's work, to be appealing because of his insight into how issues of power and identity are imbedded in the myths we so often study as dislocated tales that are somehow detached from local socio-political concerns. I was also appreciative of his recognition that the production of scholarly works, such as this current project, are also implicated in such local socio-political concerns, and that we as scholars are most honest when we historicize and contextualize ourselves in relation to our work. In his study of myths, I noted a similar strategy of mythologizing social hierarchies at play in the works of Pindar, Empedocles, and Plato as I found in the works of Origen whom I studied the following year.[12] This recognition pushed me to explore what an ideologically critical study of Origen might look like and what questions might be raised in such a study.

The final inspiration for this project came from the work of Burton Mack whose ongoing project of theorizing religion, carried out, at least in part, in order to redescribe the history of early Christianity, has greatly influenced my development as a scholar of religion. The most significant notion I have borrowed from Mack is that mythmaking and social formation go hand in hand; that is, the production and re-production of mythic narratives is part and parcel of the creation and maintenance of social structures, communities, and the social practices of those communities, especially in the context of religion. In his writings, I find a recognition of the narrative nature of social identity as well as an ongoing interest in unraveling issues related to power

---

[12] Bruce Lincoln, *Theorizing Myth: Narrative, Ideology, and Scholarship* (Chicago: University of Chicago Press, 1999), 151-59.

in the history of early Christianity. Mack's work was significant in helping me to demystify the history of early Christianity and it set me on a path of investigating the relationships between myths and social formation.

This brief overview of the scholarship that led me to ask the questions of Origen that are raised in this book is not presented in order to situate this project within a line of scholarship, which follows below, but to reveal the types of perspectives that raised these issues for me specifically, and to draw a line connecting these perspectives with my own personal background and social location. My struggles with identity and my questioning of authority in matters of defining group membership led me to scholarly works that reflected how I felt and thought about identity. In this project, I look at the hierarchy that is implicit in Origen's cosmology, theology, and ecclesiology. The manner in which I situate his mythology within a social, competitive contest over types of authority in the communities of which Origen was a member is reflective of the work of these scholars and of my own suspicion of assertions of authority, especially in the context of identity formation, as something not meant to be questioned. This project is also reflective of my belief that education and the production of knowledge ought to be subversive and critical of the ideologies that too often go unrecognized and are thus unwittingly transplanted into scholarly works that re-present the sources we study without adequately problematizing them. Furthermore, my goal in wanting to explore the methods through which such claims are made is meant to explain religious identity formation in sociological and psychological (and thus public) terms.

Finally, and especially so given my focus on matters of power and symbolic violence, it is important to state that I do not mean to imply any judgment on Origen in terms of the sincerity of his belief or the depths of his conviction or even of his care and concern for the members of his church. I do not regard a study of the ideological nature of Origen's work to necessitate a condemnation of his work as intentionally manipulative, but simply as reflective of his particular social location. I *do* believe his works are interested and strategic but not in a way that is meant to imply that Origen was disingenuous or did not wholeheartedly believe in the truth of the theology he communicated. After all, ideologies are most effective when they are unrecognized as ideologies even by those who benefit from them, not when they are invented and manipulated by self-conscious puppet masters.

In this section, I have tried to explain how I came to this project and why I have come to interrogate these Origenian texts in the manner I do. The purpose of this was not to lay claim to an objective, scientific perspective, but, as Denise Kimber Buell puts it, "not only to acknowledge the specificity and limitations of [my] interpretation, but also to advocate for it – even provisionally – on the basis of its particular, contingent implications for the present and future."[13] Although I do not put forth my analysis and conclusions in order to mend some problem in theological discourse or church politics, I do offer it as part of an ongoing discussion about the nature and exercise of power in the development and perpetuation of communities of all shapes, sizes, and affiliations in the hope of providing a wedge for democratizing the processes of mythmaking and social formation, processes which we cannot do without since, in many ways, they define the human condition. These personal reflections aside, I will now go on to situate my project in a line of scholarship, however secondarily construed by myself, on the nature of early Christian identity and the methods which we use to analyze identity.

Recent Scholarship on Identity in Early Christianity

While Origen is the historical figure under scrutiny here, I have carried out this analysis primarily in order to understand the nature of religious identity formation. Identity is a common

---

[13] Denise Kimber Buell, *Why This New Race? Ethnic Reasoning in Early Christianity* (New York: Columbia University Press, 2005), xii.

topic in scholarship on early Christianity, though it is rarely conceived of in an explicitly theoretical manner. As a category of social analysis, however, religious identity ought to be conceived of in terms drawn from social, psychological, and anthropological approaches to human social existence. One of the most influential proponents of such an approach in the field of Biblical Studies is Burton Mack, whose theorizing on religion gave this present study its impetus. Although Mack does not use "identity" in his work, the concept of "mythmaking and social formation" is reflective of an interest in the ways Christians lived, understood, and justified their practices as well as how they differentiated themselves from others.

The concepts which Mack would later develop more fully in later works shaped his 1995 *Who Wrote the New Testament? The Making of the Christian Myth*. In this introductory book, Mack presents a series of analyses of the texts making up the New Testament as well as those that he thinks best shed light on its development (e.g., Q and the Gospel of Thomas) and those which reflect the ongoing battles that established the dominant myth of Christian identity in the first four centuries (e.g, the Didache, 1 Clement, and the writings of Ignatius, Marcion, and Valentinus among others). Mack's concern was to explain the birth of Christianity as an event that makes sense in terms of social history, a task which he sees as undermining the dominant model of Christian origins, which is itself dependent upon what he calls the Lukan-Eusebian myth. His presentation of the various texts he covers in this work is framed by his emphasis on the social structures of Christian communities and the stories they told to justify and explain those structures. Theoretically, however, Mack offers little to work with here, simply stating that mythmaking and social formation go together "in a kind of dynamic feedback system," the former being an intellectual activity situating a community within the grander scheme of things, the latter being the social dynamics of that community.[14] We will return to *Who Wrote the New Testament?* in short order, but for now it is important to understand that he came to this concept of mythmaking and social formation in his efforts to establish a social-historical, non-theological understanding of how Christianity came to be and how orthodox Christianity came to establish itself as the dominant religion of the Roman Empire.

Mack's theories began to coalesce and develop over the next several years, as evidenced in *The Christian Myth*. Here Mack more explicitly describes the problems he finds in New Testament scholarship. For example, he laments the failure of most scholars trained in textual criticism to engage in the fields of comparative religions, cultural anthropology, and religious studies, a failure he sees as contributing to their inability to move beyond an understanding of Christian origins that is dependent on the Christian myth itself.[15] Mack even uses the term 'myth' here in a way that seems to reflect the Platonic disparagement of *mythos* as false and *logos* as true. Without explicitly saying so, Mack seems to suggest that the social historical approach he suggests would offer a trustworthy account (*logos*) of Christian origins that would be independent of the explanations deriving from the myth, explanations which he sees as currently dominating the field of New Testament studies.

Mack offers an approach to religion which consists of five basic features, which are perhaps better understood as presuppositions rather than as theoretical statements with explanatory power. First, he takes religion to be a purely social construct, one that is created by people interacting amongst themselves, not reacting to some divine realm. Second, Mack states that social formation, understood here as the collective work of constructing societies, "defines the human enterprise."[16]

---

[14] Burton L. Mack, *Who Wrote the New Testament? The Making of the Christian Myth* (San Francisco: HarperSanFrancisco, 1995), 11.

[15] Burton Mack, *The Christian Myth: Origins, Logic, and Legacy* (New York: Continuum, 2001), 65.

[16] Mack, *The Christian Myth*, 83.

Third, myths are more than just fun stories; they also create a space for thinking about the present by thinking through the mythic past. Fourth, rituals have social effects through their focused attention on particular activities and should not be understood in terms of engaging with the divine. Finally, Mack asserts again that mythmaking and social formation go together. These five features suggest a frame for understanding religion and offer a metatheoretical base from which applicable social theories can be developed.

Much of what Mack proffers here is constrained by his focus on Christian origins. Mack seeks to explain how this new religion had its beginning, so mythmaking for him is about the creation of new myths (understood as new *texts*) which justify social experimentation by ascribing their practices and values to a foundational figure or by resignifying an existent myth. Mack seems to take for granted the nature of myth itself, although he does allude to myths being stories about divine beings that members of a community use for their self-understanding, for the justification of their way of life, and for situating themselves in the world. In looking at Christian origins, Mack ignores the subsequent influence these myths had in their reception and the ways in which new myths were attached to or read into and out of them.

If mythmaking is specifically about the creation of new myths (or new meanings for old myths) for novel communities, then social formation is also about the creation of these communities. Mack suggests a focus on the ways in which people experimented with new forms of social existence. This experimentation is carried out because of people's "social interests," a term Mack uses simply to say that people, as social beings, are interested in being social. Experimentation implies novelty, the creation of something new through trial and error. As these communities continue to take shape, however, experimentation gives way to perpetuation and conservation as well as resistance, subversion, and alteration. Again, Mack's focus on Christian origins leads to an emphasis on the ways new groups are created, but a comprehensive theory of religion or scripturalizing would need to move beyond this early phase of group formation.

In an earlier article in the *Guide to the Study of Religion*, Mack explains that social formation emphasizes "the complex interplay of many human interests that develop systems of signs and patterns of practice, as well as institutions for their communication, maintenance and reproduction."[17] It is not clear how exactly social formation points to this interplay or what is included within "social formation." At this stage in the development of his theories, Mack had presented compelling arguments for an *approach* to religion, but little in the way of theories that could be employed in historical or anthropological analysis.

This became problematic when Mack's mythmaking and social formation were taken up as the rationale that would help explain the emergence of Christianity in a multi-year project that sought to redescribe Christian origins in a purely social-historical manner. The Society of Biblical Literature's Seminar on Ancient Myths and Modern Theories of Christian Origins structured its work on Mack's mythmaking and social formation and on J. Z. Smith's comparative methodology. William Arnal was perhaps the most critical of Mack's use of the term "social formation" and the understandings and assumptions that he saw driving Mack's analysis.[18] Arnal argues that Mack leans too far toward an idealist approach in which myths are created by individuals who shape social formations. Arnal suggests returning to the Marxist, materialist roots of the concept of social formation. For Arnal, a better approach would be to focus on the extradiscursive, especially the economic forms of production, as these are more

---

[17] Burton Mack, "Social Formation," in *Guide to the Study of Religion* (ed. Willi Braun and Russell T. McCutcheon; London: Cassell, 2000), 283.

[18] William E. Arnal, "Why Q Failed: From Ideological Project to Group Formation," in *Redescribing Christian Origins* (ed. Ron Cameron and Merrill P. Miller; Society of Biblical Literature Symposium Series 280; Atlanta: Society of Biblical Literature, 2004), 67-87.

important for understanding the shape of social life. This also means, for Arnal, that mythmaking needs to be understood not in terms of the creation of new myths from whole cloth, but in terms of people working within traditions in which they are already situated. Arnal and Willi Braun would go on to present a series of theses on mythmaking and social formation in an effort to bring some theoretical clarity to the term, but also to suggest that the definition of the terms should not be determined, at least not within the context of the seminar, thus leaving unanswered the questions they saw as constantly plaguing the work of the Seminar in its early years.[19]

In Mack's 2008 monograph, *Myth and the Christian Nation: A Social Theory of Religion*, he foregoes defining myth and refers the reader to Russell McCutcheon's chapter in the aforementioned *Guide to the Study of Religion*.[20] McCutcheon rejects several common approaches to myth, such as it reflecting a pre-scientific mentality, or as it being an expression of a collective unconscious, or as it being a narrative bearing some eternal truth. Instead, McCutcheon argues that myths are very common strategies for legitimizing social identities, which is reminiscent of Lincoln's definition of myth as "ideology in narrative form."[21] In this sense, myths are more like rhetorical

---

[19] William E. Arnal and Willi Braun, "Social Formation and Mythmaking: Theses on Key Terms," in *Redescribing Christian Origins* (ed. Ron Cameron and Merrill P. Miller; Society of Biblical Literature Symposium Series 280; Atlanta: Society of Biblical Literature, 2004), 459-67.

[20] Russell T. McCutcheon, "Myth," in *Guide to the Study of Religion* (ed. Willi Braun and Russell T. McCutcheon; London: Cassell, 2000): 190-208.

[21] Lincoln, *Theorizing Myth*, 147. The concept of ideology plays a major role in this conception of mythology and is an important term for this project. Ideology, is a slippery concept. In the present work, I consider ideology to be a system of beliefs, values, and practices that are unconsciously internalized by people, thus making them active and willing participants within a culture that is structured hierarchically such that they help replicate those same structures of power and oppression for later generations. For more on this understanding of ideology, see Louis Althusser, *On Ideology* (Radical Thinkers 26; London: Verso, 2008); Terry Eagleton, *Ideology: An Introduction* (London:

techniques rather than genres of narrative. Truth, then, is not found in myths, McCutcheon states, but myths are used to make things seem true, and mythmaking is "a species of ideology production, of ideal-making, where 'ideal' is conceived not as an abstract, absolute value but as a contingent, localized construct that comes to represent and simultaneously reproduce certain specific social values *as if* they were inevitable and universal."[22] The study of myth should therefore be a study of mythmaking, of the active methods by which things are made to seem true and the way these interact with forms of social existence. This definition of mythmaking moves beyond Mack's earlier understanding of mythmaking as the creation of new myths for novel communities, and instead defines it as an ongoing process of deploying myths in the service of social legitimization.

In *Myth and the Christian Nation*, Mack presents his theory as a response not just to a tradition of scholarship overly influenced by a tradition that accepts that religion is a response to some transcendent, divine realm, but also to a tradition of scholarship that emphasizes individual experience as the locus of religious truth. His social theory of religion is social insofar as it focuses on communities, not individuals, and insofar as it is purely social, i.e., anthropological, in nature. In this presentation of his theory, Mack clarifies his notion of social formation, using it as a more specific term than *society*, in that society fails to emphasize aspects of human interplay that goes into the construction of a given form of social existence. The form or

---

Verso, 1991), esp. pages 125-58; and David Hawkes, *Ideology* (2d ed.; The New Critical Idiom 26; London: Routledge, 2003), esp. pages 117-47.

[22] McCutcheon, "Myth," 203. McCutcheon suggests that mythmaking is a subtype of social formation, which he defines as "the activity of experimenting with, authorizing or combating, and reconstituting widely circulated ideal types, idealizations or, better put, mythifications that function to control the means of and sites where social significance is selected, symbolized and communicated." This formulation does not link mythmaking and social formation as parallel processes, but as hierarchical ones. Here he seems either to misunderstand Mack or to part ways from him.

structure, he says, can also be called a social formation. Mack has thus moved away from using the term strictly in regards to novel creations allowing it to take on a diachronic sense that was missing in his earlier work.

Mack also expands his notion of myth by linking it more directly with rituals, presenting them as discursive and non-discursive tools for producing narratives that include an "imaginary world; fantastic features; powerful agents."[23] Here, again, myth has a rather standard definition, but his reliance on McCutcheon suggests that there is more at play in mythmaking than just the creation of fanciful stories. Mack expands upon myths, suggesting that they contribute to an imagined world or worldview that provides a framework for a community's sense of identity.[24] He also suggests that myths work by connecting contemporary matters to an epic or mythic past and by providing a structure for understanding and making judgments about social situations. Mythic systems provide, he says, "a grammar that makes possible the social logic of the thinking and mentality of a people."[25] Mack's conceptions of both myth (making) and social formation have grown in complexity and explication. Combined with social interests and ritual, mythmaking and social formation are also now part of a larger theoretical landscape.

This landscape still bears some of the problems that were pointed out in the Redescribing seminar, however, and the addition of social interests (which is itself under theorized) and rituals does little to compensate. First, the question of how myths are generated has not been addressed. In *Who Wrote the New Testament?*, Mack variously posited the creation of myths by communities, as if they acted and produced texts as a group, and by individuals, such as Paul, who seemed to have considerable

---

[23] Mack, *Myth and the Christian Nation*, 76.

[24] Mack, *Myth and the Christian Nation*, 120-21. This is one of the rare instances where Mack employs the term identity, and it is clearly not equivalent to myth, mythmaking, or social formation as he uses it.

[25] Mack, *Myth and the Christian Nation*, 142.

more ability to construct myths on their own.[26] Both Arnal and Stanley Stowers draw attention to this lacuna in Mack's theory, Arnal suggesting that myths are not really ever created from scratch, and Stowers suggesting that groups do not act in such a manner because texts are produced by individuals.[27] Second, how myths are effective – how they do their work – is also unclear. After all, myths can be created, written down, and copied, but that does not guarantee their efficacy. Third, we need some clarity as to just what we mean by social formation. Even if we go along with Mack in accepting that social formation can be used to define the structures of social life, we get only a hint of what Mack means by this. The hints Mack does provide would seem to lean toward a wholist ontology, which Stowers rightfully criticizes as being inappropriate for understanding how individuals and their communities relate. The advances Mack has made in developing his approach to religion still leave us with much room for theorizing religion and religious identity formation.

From Mack's impressive body of work, we have come to important decisions about how religion ought to be studied and what processes we might focus attention on for understanding how mythic narratives function and how those narratives relate to forms of social existence. First, we can see that there is value in taking a sociological approach to religion that eschews appeals to divine realms or a focus on individual experience. Second, we have learned that identity is formed through processes that are dynamic and ongoing. Identity is not stable; it is constantly up for renegotiation, both in terms of the practices that go along with it and the narratives that explain and justify those practices.

---

[26] For a critique of this problematic connection between a text and its community, see Stanley K. Stowers, "The Concept of 'Community' and the History of Early Christianity," *MTSR* 23 (2011): 238-56.

[27] Arnal, "Why Q Failed," 73-74; Stanley K. Stowers, "Mythmaking, Social Formation, and Varieties of Social Theory," in *Redescribing Christian Origins* (ed. Ron Cameron and Merrill P. Miller, Society of Biblical Literature Symposium Series 280; Atlanta: Society of Biblical Literature, 2004), 489-96.

Third, we are agreed that discursive and non-discursive (myths and social formations) components of identity must be taken in tandem. Studies of religious identity that focus on ideas, beliefs, or theologies only offer a partial understanding of identity as do those studies that only focus on rituals, social practices, or ethics. The two need to be brought into conversation with each other if we are to understand how one influences the other and is influenced in turn. Finally, and as I will develop further in Chapter One, we can make use of mythmaking and social formation for designating the ongoing, fluid negotiations of social existence and social identity that are constantly being carried out, having no visible originating point nor any likely teleology.

While Mack has attempted to formulate a social theory of religion, other scholars have been more narrowly focused on identity in particular. One New Testament scholar who has employed social psychological identity theories in a thorough manner in the explication of biblical texts is Philip Esler. In *Conflict and Identity in Romans*, Esler summarizes various components of social identity theory and argues that the formation of group boundaries is a central concern in Paul's epistle to the Roman church.[28] Building especially off the work of Henri Tajfel and John C. Turner, Esler approaches identity primarily as it concerns one's membership within a group distinct from other groups, i.e., the establishment of boundaries between groups. This is accomplished through the enculturation of group norms, through the use of stereotypes for outsiders, and through a shared understanding of the group's past. Esler also looks at the internal dynamics within groups, mostly in order to understand how internal schisms are mediated by recategorizing the divisions within a superordinate category, thus reinforcing the characteristics that are shared within the group. Lastly, Esler looks at theories of leadership from a social identity perspective.

---

[28] Philip Francis Esler, *Conflict and Identity in Romans* (Minneapolis: Augsburg Books, 2003), 19-39.

Leaders are effective in shaping the understandings and actions of other group members because they are recognized as prototypical figures who represent the shared values of the group. The leaders, whom Esler calls "entrepreneurs of identity," are effective to the extent that they are able to distinguish and elevate their group in relation to others.

Esler's work is theoretically sound and internally consistent, leading to a fruitful analysis of the importance of group identity to *Romans*. As Bengt Holmberg points out, however, Esler's focus on Paul as an "entrepreneur of identity" forces the question of whether or not Paul's Roman audience accepted his leadership and his arguments. Holmberg states, "It is easy to be blinded by the sheer power of Paul's person and presentation and thus to overlook the vital role of the recipients in enabling such a change in their social identity."[29] In other words, while Esler's use of social identity theory may help us understand Paul's rhetoric in *Romans*, it does not help us know if or how that rhetoric was effective in the community. This is precisely the type of problem we are faced with when taking a historical critical approach to texts that only hopes to understand the text in its initial composition. In other words, Esler's approach helps us to understand Paul better, but does little for helping us to understand the ongoing and dynamic process of Christian identity formation. In order to do this, we must be able to look at the reception of a text such as *Romans* in different communities at different times.

One model of religion that has been put to use in helping to understand Christian identity is that which describes religion as a symbolic system. This model comes from the cultural anthropologist Clifford Geertz, who defined religion as:

> (1) a system of symbols which acts to (2) establish powerful, pervasive, and long-lasting moods and motivations in men by (3) formulating conceptions of a

---

[29] Bengt Holmberg, "Understanding the First Hundred Years of Christian Identity," in *Exploring Early Christian Identity* (ed. Bengt Holmberg; WUNT 226; Tübingen: Mohr Siebeck, 2008), 17.

general order of existence and (4) clothing these conceptions with such an aura of factuality that (5) the moods and motivations seem uniquely realistic.[30]

Geertz argued that the anthropological study of religion needed to understand "the system of meanings embodied in symbols which make up religion proper" and how that system related to "social-structural and psychological processes."[31] As a cultural anthropologist, Geertz formulates religion as a text that can be read by outsiders.

Gerd Theissen based his "theory of primitive Christian religion" primarily on Geertz's concept of religion as a system of signs.[32] Whereas Geertz presented religious symbols as pointing to notions, abstractions, ideas and the like, Theissen sees religious symbols as combining three forms of expression: myths, rites, and ethics. This would seem to bring us closer to Mack's more recent formulations of religion as incorporating myths, rituals, and social interests. According to Theissen, charismatic leaders create changes in religious sign systems, but these systems have a power of their own insofar as a system can "*organize itself* from its own centre," "differentiate between *reference to itself* and *reference to outsiders*," and "understand [itself] as the result of divine action."[33] This hypostasizing of symbols and symbolic structures is, as Rikard Roitto points out, "both ontologically unintelligible and methodologically misleading."[34] Symbols do not bear meaning on their own; meaning can only exist in the mind of individuals who demonstrate their understanding of

---

[30] Clifford Geertz, "Religion as a Cultural System," in *The Interpretation of Cultures* (ed. Clifford Geertz; New York: Basic Books, 1973), 90.

[31] Geertz, "Religion as a Cultural System," 125.

[32] Gerd Theissen, *The Religion of the Earliest Churches: Creating a Symbolic World* (trans. John Bowden; Minneapolis: Fortress Press, 1999).

[33] Theissen, *Religion of the Earliest Churches*, 5-6.

[34] Rikard Roitto, "Behaving like a Christ-Believer: A Cognitive Perspective on Identity and Behavior Norms in the Early Christ-Movement," in *Exploring Early Christian Identity* (WUNT 226; ed. Bengt Holmberg; Tübingen: Mohr Siebeck, 2008), 98.

that meaning through use in a community of like-minded individuals. The attribution of agency to a system of signs that has no existence outside of those individuals and their shared practices and understanding is mistaken. That symbols are important to religions is clear, but the cognitive and ontological mistakes found in Geertz and Theissen ought to be avoided in the construction of a social theory of scripturalizing.

Talal Asad also provides a critique of Geertz's definition of religion which alerts us to problems of focusing exclusively on the symbolic in the analysis of religion.[35] Asad is especially concerned with the way Geertz separates the symbolic from the social psychological realm. Asad argues that symbols do not come to have meanings on their own, but through authorizing practices that exclude other meanings, sometimes violently.[36] The focus on the symbolic separates religion from questions of power and violence and situates it in the mind. Instead of separating religious symbols from other social processes, we should instead consider them together with the authorizing discourses and practices that give symbols their possibility for existence and their authoritative status.

Rikard Roitto approaches Christian identity from a cognitive perspective, employing cognitive anthropology, self-categorization theory, attribution theory, analogical thinking, and narrative cognition. Roitto's synthesis bridges the symbolic understanding of religion, as found in Theissen, with social identity theories such as those employed by Esler. In this cognitive approach, we move from symbols to "complexes of cognitive schemata" shared within a group.[37] These schemata come to be expressed in norms through the imitation of ingroup

---

[35] Talal Asad, *Genealogies of Religion: Discipline and Reasons of Power in Christianity and Islam* (Baltimore: The Johns Hopkins University Press, 1993). For a similar critique of Geertz's separation of signs from practices and power, see also Richard Biernacki, "Language and the Shift from Signs to Practices in Cultural Inquiry," *History and Theory* 39 (October 2000): 289-310.

[36] Asad, *Genealogies of Religion*, 30-35.

[37] Roitto, "Behaving like a Christ-Believer," 101.

prototypes who embody the ideals of the group. These prototypes can be non-existent ideals, but individuals within the group can also come to be seen as embodying those ideals. These figures enjoy a higher status and have greater influence within the group. Finally, Roitto explains how narratives, such as myths, provide important resources from which individuals analogically extrapolate ideas about how to act and what to feel. Roitto's model is useful insofar as it smoothly combines social identity, narrativity, normative behaviors, and prototypes within the framework of cognitive science. On the other hand, this focus on cognition situates religion in the internal experience of individuals and ignores the practical (i.e., related to social practices) and the relations of power that Asad sees as establishing these mental concepts as authoritative.

One of the most thorough studies of early Christian identity is Judith Lieu's *Christian Identity in the Jewish and Graeco-Roman World*.[38] Lieu divides her chapters based on ways of approaching identity, which, when brought together, make for a fairly comprehensive view of early Christian identity. In her study, she includes collective memory, the role of practices, gender, the use of ethnic rhetoric, and the formation of boundaries. Lieu also points to the problematic nature of employing texts in studies of identity since these texts are more prescriptive than descriptive and since we cannot be sure how these texts were received. She doubts that we can get any further than the world the texts present to us, and to a certain extent this is most certainly the case. While there is much that is useful in Lieu's work, her primary interest in blurring the lines between Christians and non-Christians pushes her towards looking at the various ways those boundaries were constructed and not so much at the internal dynamics at play within these boundaries.

Two scholars have focused primarily on the importance of scriptural interpretation in the formation of Christian identity. In

---

[38] Judith M. Lieu, *Christian Identity in the Jewish and Graeco-Roman World* (Oxford: Oxford University Press, 2004).

Biblical Exegesis and the Formation of Christian Canon Frances Young argues that Christianity was formulated through ongoing practices of biblical interpretation.[39] It is in the reception of canonical literature that these texts were given the meanings that shaped Christian self-understanding. John David Dawson recognizes this as well, stating, "The interpretation of sacred texts is often the principal site of tension between past and future, the preservation and the refashioning of religious identity."[40] Young and Dawson both recognize the centrifugal force of sacred texts and their interpretation in the ongoing construction and contestation of identity. Neither of them, however, says much regarding the nature of identity or culture. Their importance lies primarily with shifting the focus to the reception of scripture and the creative ways in which evolving social formations were justified through scriptural interpretation.

This brief overview of select scholarship on early Christian identity is quite revealing. There is no consensus as to what identity is or how it ought to be approached in the study of early Christianity. It is also clear that the primary interest in studying early Christianity is to see how Christians were differentiated from non-Christians. Although the nature of the evidence available will prevent us from ever having a comprehensive picture of early Christian identity, much would be gained from incorporating multiple aspects of identity into the study of one particular figure or community. This project seeks to do just that by looking at the construction of Christian identity in the works of Origen of Alexandria. I look especially at the centrality of scriptural exegesis as a technique for constructing and justifying this construction. Throughout, my interest will be not on the meaning Origen reads into/out of the biblical text, but in the

---

[39] Frances M. Young, *Biblical Exegesis and the Formation of Christian Culture* (Peabody: Hendrickson Publishers, 2002).

[40] John David Dawson, *Christian Figural Reading and the Fashioning of Identity* (Berkeley: University of California Press, 2002), 207.

ways he interacts with these texts in promulgating his version of Christianity.

Scope, Aim, and Structure of This Study

As mentioned above, this project has three goals: (1) to provide a theory of scripturalizing that will be applicable in any context in which scriptures are employed, (2) to contribute to the study of early Christian identity, and (3) to provide an ideologically critical reading of Origen and his work. Scripturalizing and identity are interrelated since the use of scriptures implies the formation of a group's self-understanding in relation to a particular scripture or set of scriptures (where scriptures can be understood as anything that works as a centering symbol used for constructing and authorizing that community's identity). While this work will probably be categorized as a study of Origen, I want to stress that the study of Origen is meant to provide an example of how scripturalizing looks in practice. Although an analysis of the ideological significance of Origen's oeuvre contributes to the broader study of early Christian history, the methodological and theoretical contributions of this study are more important for the field of religious studies as a whole.

In Chapter One, I provide a multi-faceted and interdisciplinary approach to scripturalizing. If, as Smith articulated, there is no ontology of scriptures, there can still be an ontology of scripturalizing, one that is subsumed under a general social ontology. I begin with the social ontology of Theodore Schatzki, a social theorist who, like Anthony Giddens and Pierre Bourdieu, emphasizes social practices in the analysis of social structures and the perseverance and alteration of those structures. Schatzki and Bourdieu provide the map on which we can place various practices, texts, and individuals. I fill out this ontology with the concept of narrative identity, which explains how people make sense of their lives across time, both in terms of their personal, individual identity, and in terms of their membership within various communities. I then discuss the role of scriptural interpretation in this social ontology and its importance for shaping different aspects of narrative identity.

As mentioned previously, these structures and narrative identities are hierarchical in nature. Here, I rely primarily on Pierre Bourdieu's political economy of symbolic capital to focus on issues of status, power, domination, and symbolic violence in the perpetuation of social structures. I also explain how symbolic labor, the work of making these hierarchies appear natural and unquestionable, works in terms of scriptural practices. Taken together with social formation (the practices and structures of social life along with the matrices of symbolic capital that attribute status within these structures) and mythmaking (the creation of public narratives that provide a history and set of ideal figures to imitate for a community), symbolic labor rounds out the ontology of scripturalizing and provides us with the tools necessary for studying how groups are shaped in relation to scriptures.

In the following three chapters, I apply this theory of scripturalizing to Origen of Alexandria. In Chapter Two, I situate Origen within a particular field of cultural production. Specifically, I look at the forms of symbolic capital associated with philosophers, a specific class of intellectuals, in the ancient Mediterranean world. This includes a description of primary and advanced forms of education, of the status of intellectuals who produced philosophical texts, and of asceticism. I discuss the practices of philosophers, the ways in which philosophers were shown respect and deference, and the authority that they could wield because of the symbolic capital they had within their communities. This chapter establishes the hierarchies and forms of symbolic capital that were most important to Origen as a Christian scholar and cultural producer, or, put differently, this chapter explains the type of social formation that Origen seeks to maintain and support in his community.

Chapter Three then establishes a correlation between these philosophical practices, social hierarchies and symbolic capital with the narrative identity (i.e., mythology) reflected in

Origen's writings. I focus here primarily on *On First Principles* and on his homilies, since these were read before an actual congregation and thus would likely have had the greatest direct impact on shaping the views of a greater number of other members of his community. As we will see, the narrative identity Origen presents is multilayered, encompassing Israelite historiography, the life of Jesus, a complex myth about the creation of the world and the return of all created beings to their divine origin, among other things. This combination of personal, public, theological, and even metanarratives are interwoven and mutually enlightening. For reasons that will be made clear in Chapter One, all of these might be dubbed "myths" and their construction, perpetuation, and reception "mythmaking."

In the last chapter, I look at the tactics Origen employs in establishing his ideas about what it means to be Christian and the practices by which he creates and promulgates these ideas as sacred in nature, i.e., his symbolic labor. This represents the work Origen does that helps to mystify, sanctify, and protect the hierarchies he promotes. First, I look at Origen's hermeneutical method to show how he grounds his narratives in scripture, thus linking his own mythology with that of the scriptures held sacred by his community. Second, I examine the ways in which Origen denies his authority and significance and I situate this rhetoric in its appropriate context in order to underscore the ways in which such discourse is also part and parcel of the hierarchies and fields in which Origen participates. Lastly, I analyze various analogies Origen uses to reinforce his arguments for a Christian worldview in which philosophers were to be considered the best Christians in the community.

In the conclusion I draw together the three chapters on Origen to describe how these three components of scripturalizing all interacted in the context of Origen's Ceasarean community. Since this project is intended to be an in-depth analysis of this one particular figure, I suggest how this historical analysis might be extended synchronically and diachronically to give us a broader understanding of the history of early Christian identity. As I also hope to provide a theory of scripturalizing that is applicable across cultures and times, I also suggest how this theory might be further developed. After all, this project is not intended in any way to be the end of a discussion, but the development of one already in progress.

WHAT IS SCRIPTURALIZING?

As I discuss in the Introduction, W. C. Smith has been foundational in problematizing the concept of scriptures in the field of religious studies. In order to proffer a preliminary definition of scripturalizing, it will be useful to review the shift in perspective Smith called for and the ways in which other scholars have taken up this approach to scriptures. In *What is Scriptures?* Smith describes how the term "scripture," originally only designating the Bible, took on the plural form, "scriptures", as scholars came to recognize the sacred and authoritative status that other texts held in different religions. Acknowledging that other religions held non-biblical texts to be sacred meant recognizing that a scripture's sacred authority was not bestowed upon it by god, but by a community. As Smith puts it, there is a significant difference in "seeing (and feeling) something to be divine, and seeing (or feeling) it as something that people have historically (and without good cause?) thought of as divine. The former is a metaphysical judgement, the latter a sociological one."[1] Viewing scriptures sociologically and cross-culturally introduces variety, not just in terms of what texts are considered scripture, but in how those texts are interpreted, worshipped, and communicated.

Smith goes on to suggest that scripture is a bilateral term in that "it implies, in fact names, a relationship" between a community and a text, since it is only in a social context that a text comes to be scripture.[2] Smith is critical of historical criticism, which attempts to get at a text's "original" meaning. Since it is unlikely that many of the texts now considered scripture were

---

[1] Wilfred Cantwell Smith, *What Is Scripture? A Comparative Approach* (Minneapolis: Fortress Press, 1993/2005), 12.

[2] Smith, *What is Scripture?* 17.

written with the explicit intent that they would be scripture, and since, even if they were so composed, they would still require a community to receive these texts as authoritative, historical criticism does little to help us understand what scripture is or how it functions in a community. This relationship between the community and its scripture(s) is one in which the people of a community "have imposed on that text…much of their deepest concerns, aspirations, fears, hopes, outlooks, feelings," and, in the process of so doing, "have then received them back profoundly fortified and strikingly enhanced."[3] It is not authorial intent or divinely inspired content but the activities of meaning-making in relation to a text that are what make scriptures the product of human activity. Smith designates such activities "scripturalizing." This scripturalizing is not a one-time event, but an ongoing process, without which a text would cease to be scripture. It is the goal of this chapter to piece together an ontology of scripturalizing that will contextualize these textual practices within a broader context of group formation and that will introduce matters of power, domination, and resistance, which are missing from Smith's work.

Although Smith attempts to offer a purely social approach to scriptures, he still succumbs to a common propensity to attribute to scriptures some sort of inherent power or truth, and this has implications for the types of meaning-making that we would consider necessary for something to be considered "scripturalizing." Two things are especially problematic about Smith's approach for a social theory of scripturalizing. The first is that Smith sees scriptures as communicating some sort of transcendent truth. Although Smith at first would seem to want to remove the transcendent from the equation and see scriptures as simply the product of a people's interaction with a text (a bilateral relationship), he returns in the end to characterizing the relationship as trilateral between people, the transcendent, and a

---

[3] Smith, *What Is Scripture?* 16.

text.⁴ Here, Smith's applies a view of language in which words symbolically reference a signified object in scriptures with the signified object of scriptures being something transcendent. Introducing the transcendent as a category removes the study of scriptures from the purview of the social sciences and reinserts it into a theological realm of discourse which privileges matters that cannot be studied from a purely historical, naturalistic perspective.

The second issue in Smith's work that, in my reading, gets in the way of developing a social theory of scriptures is that he begins and ends with scripture, not with the ongoing activities that constitute a text as scripture. Smith seems to recognize this himself, stating that, while it is defensible to present his work as a book about scripture, "calling it that could be part of the very problem that it ostensibly is trying to solve."⁵ There are a couple of dangers in focusing on the text, one being the aforementioned tendency to view its content or referent as transcendent. In focusing instead on people and the social processes of creating shared meanings through interpreting a text, or using it as an object of reverence or ritual power, we ought to ground ourselves in a social scientific and rhetorical critical approach to religion and scriptures. This also prevents us from attributing agency to texts, as Smith does on occasion. If scriptures are merely artifacts, then we should see what they accomplish as being accomplished by human actors, not by the texts themselves. Changing the question from "What is Scriptures?" to "What is Scripturalizing?" keeps us grounded in a social scientific approach to scriptures and places the spotlight on meaning-making as a collective process in which groups, sub-groups, and individuals work together to construct meanings in relation to a text or set of texts. Our goal in defining scripturalizing is to delimit in some meaningful way the types of activities we would want to include and, in so doing, perhaps to delimit the types of

---

⁴ Smith, *What Is Scripture?* 239.
⁵ Smith, *What Is Scripture?* 237.

texts (or other non-textual objects) which we could label scripture.

In the first volume of the Signifying (on) Scriptures series, Tazim Kassam offers a definition of scriptures as textual artifacts that are "highly saturated with power and meaning. They are texts (oral and written) that are imbued with sacred authority such that they function as templates and charters of a society's cultural norms."[6] This notion of scripture as special texts is prevalent in the other contributions to the volume. Unfortunately, this does not advance us much further than Smith's pervious work. In his closing remarks, Vincent Wimbush, the series and volume editor, again pushes the discussion in a more social direction: "I want once more to try to be as clear as possible in asserting that the 'phenomenon' of focus is *not* text, but 'scriptures.' The latter is shorthand – for social textures, dynamics, behaviors, orientations, power dynamics."[7] I prefer the gerund "scripturalizing," so as not to get caught up in focusing on texts and to emphasize the dynamics of people engaging with sacred texts. And, while I appreciate Wimbush's emphasis on power dynamics, I am hesitant to allow for such an expansive definition of scripture such that any text, object, or performance could be included. Here, I side with Kassam in designating texts that have some place of primacy in shaping a community's group identity as scriptures.

At this point, I would like to propose a tentative definition of scripturalizing and of scriptures. By "scripturalizing," I mean the bundle of practices that in any way make reference to a text or set of texts that are considered sacred (i.e., scriptures) so as to shape a community's values, norms, practices, beliefs, and self-

---

[6] Tazim R. Kassam, "Signifying Revelation in Islam," in *Theorizing Scriptures: New Critical Orientations to a Cultural Phenomenon* (Signifying (on) Scriptures; ed. Vincent L. Wimbush; New Brunswick: Rutgers University Press, 2008), 29.

[7] Vincent L. Wimbush, "Talking Back," in *Theorizing Scriptures: New Critical Orientations to a Cultural Phenomenon* (Signifying (on) Scriptures 1; ed. Vincent L. Wimbush; New Brunswick: Rutgers University Press, 2008), 284.

understandings, in such a way as to make those values, norms, practices, beliefs and self-understandings seem to be divinely sanctioned. Scripturalizing can take many forms. It can include such things as making claims about the nature of the cosmos, or a group's shared history, or even the practices involved in setting those texts apart from other texts. After all, people relate to all kinds of texts, but to designate something as scripture is to recognize that it is somehow separated from other texts through practices that are peculiar to it. In fact, it is these peculiar practices and the hierarchies of symbolic power that are imbedded in these practices that give us reason to separate and study scriptures apart from other types of texts that do similar work.

In the rest of this chapter, I lay out an ontology for scripturalizing, understood as a subset of the ontology of religion, itself a subset of the ontology of the social. Stanley Stowers advocates for such an ontology of religion, one that presents religion as the product of human activity.[8] Like Stowers, I believe that ontologies that privilege social practices as the primary object of study are optimal for presenting a balanced picture of social life as consisting of individuals who are shaped by and who act within broader networks of practices, other individuals, cultural artifacts, and non-human beings. I will first describe the nature of such social ontologies, focusing primarily on the site ontology of Theodore Schatzki. This will ground scripturalizing in a set of social practices and keep us attuned to the locations in which these practices are carried out. Next, I will highlight issues of power that are internal to a community by introducing Pierre Bourdieu's political economy of symbolic capital into the ontology. Finally, contra Stowers, I will advocate for the inclusion of identity in this ontology, especially in the form of narrative identities shaped by various acts of

---

[8] Stanley K. Stowers, "The Ontology of Religion," in *Introducing Religion: Essays in Honor of Jonathan Z. Smith* (ed. Willi Braun and Russell T. McCutcheon; London: Equinox, 2008), 434-49.

scripturalizing. Taken together, we will have a way of studying scripturalizing and scriptures that, as Smith and Wimbush have called for, focuses on human activity and the power dynamics inherent in those activities.

1.1 Practices and the Nature of Social Existence

Practice theories represent an attempt to overcome one of the most significant divisions of classical social theory, that between subjectivism and objectivism, or, put differently, individualist and socialist ontologies.[9] Briefly put, individualist/subjectivist ontologies view society as consisting of individuals interacting with each other. These individuals have an agency that is singular, internal, and autonomous. Rational-choice and social network theories represent individualist ontologies, the former for having the individual autonomous human mind as the source of decision making and action, the latter for minimizing social life to a series of connections between individuals. Socialist ontologies (also referred to as objectivist or wholist), on the other hand, view society as being more than just the sum of its individual human parts. A sibling of structuralist thought, wholist ontologies view society as a structuring entity with a life of its own. Through the structuring of the human mind by society, the individual agent loses a degree of agency, becoming subject to the structuring forces swirling about him.[10]

Practice theory bridges the subjectivist/objectivist divide by viewing agency as a matter of individual will that works within a limited set of structured possibilities. As stated above,

---

[9] Pierre Bourdieu, *The Logic of Practice* (trans. Richard Nice; Stanford: Stanford University Press, 1990), 31-51.

[10] G. W. F. Hegel, Karl Marx, Emile Durkheim, Bronislaw Malinowski, Louis Althusser, Talcott Parsons, and Nicklas Luhmann are listed as scholars working with wholist ontologies in Theodore R. Schatzki, *Social Practices: A Wittgensteinian Approach to Human Activity and the Social* (Cambridge: Cambridge University Press, 1996), 2.

practice theorists situate practices as the site of social existence.[11] They are the mechanisms by which society imprints its values onto individuals who then come to respond in an appropriate manner based on what they have learned and internalized by engaging in those practices. By doing so, individuals reproduce social structures, but they can also subvert and alter them. This practical interplay between the individual and society is useful for understanding how an individual human mind develops and expresses its development in any given context.

For the first part of our analysis of social practices, we turn to Schatzki, who presents a detailed social ontology, which he calls a site ontology in order to highlight the location, understood both as a physical space and as an outlay of various relationships, in which practices take place. Schatzki suggests that social life is made up of two primary nexuses, orders and practices. Orders are "the arrangements of people, artifacts, organisms, and things through and amid which social life transpires, in which these entities relate, occupy positions, and possess meanings."[12] Orders are arrangements of actual physical space as well as a space of relationships, of which power relationships are only a subset. Orders offer a rich conception of the layout of social life as it opens up the possibility of analyzing the importance of architecture, relics, animals, nature, and much more for the make-up of social existence. This is an aspect of social existence and identity formation that is commonly left out of studies of identity or scripturalizing. The concept of orders helps us to ground our social analysis in the realm of everyday life and not just in the realm of texts and ideas; it also directs us to other aspects which affect power dynamics within a group.

---

[11] For an overview of practice theory, see Theodore R. Schatzki, "Introduction: Practice Theory" in *The Practice Turn in Contemporary Theory* (ed. Theodore R. Schatzki, Karin Knorr Cetina, and Eike Von Savigny; London: Routledge, 2001), 1-14.

[12] Theodore R. Schatzki, *The Site of the Social: A Philosophical Account of The Constitution of Social Life and Change* (University Park: Pennsylvania State University Press, 2002), 22.

Within the concept of orders, Schatzki proposes that entities relate through four principal types of relations.[13] First, there are causal relations, which are "instantiated among humans whenever a person's action(s) directly brings some state about" or when one individual reacts to the doings, sayings, or experiencing of another. Second, there are spatial relations, of which there are two kinds: (1) the locative layout of space, and (2) the layout of human activity, or what geographers call "activity space." Third, there are relations of intentionality when one entity relates to another by "performing actions toward or having thoughts, beliefs, intentions, and emotions about the other." Finally, there is prefiguration, which is how the world qualifies the paths available to people.

Social orders are also made up of meaning and identity. In Schatzki's humanist theory of social life, identity is a special subset of meaning reserved for humans.[14] Schatzki proposes that identity is multiple and labile depending on one's change in location within a social order. He also recognizes that the identity that might be attributed to an individual does not necessarily match the individual's own self-understanding. Schatzki's notion of identity is different than the more common sociological notion of roles in that roles determine social action whereas, in Schatzki's theory, actions determine meaning. Similar to Judith Butler's notion of performativity in the context of gender identity, Schatzki considers bodily performance as "instituting, that is, *establishing that there is* an individual."[15] In addition to their constitution in and amongst practices, meaning and identity are also determined by the complex of causal, spatial, intentional, and prefigurational relations.

The second half of Schatzki's site ontology is social practices, defined as organized nexuses of actions (doings and

---

[13] Schatzki, *Site of the Social*, 41-45.

[14] Schatzki, *Site of the Social*, 47.

[15] Schatzki, *Social Practices*, 86, italics in the original; Judith Butler, *Gender Trouble: Feminism and the Subversion of Identity* (New York: Routledge, 1990).

sayings) which hang together through (1) practical intelligibility, (2) practical understandings, (3) rules, and (4) teleoaffective structures.[16] Practical intelligibility is a subtle awareness of how to carry out specific actions, whereas practical understanding is what it makes sense to a person to do, or when it is best to put their practical intelligibility into action.[17] Such understanding is acquired through participation in doings and sayings.[18] For Schatzki, this type of knowledge is not expressed conceptually, as most people might conceive of knowledge. Instead it is expressed through further participation in doings and sayings, underlining the centrality of practices to the existence of individuals within a social context.

Unlike practical intelligibility, practical understanding includes rules that are "explicit formulations, principles, precepts, and instructions that enjoin, direct, or remonstrate people to perform specific actions."[19] Rules are explicit because they typically do not represent the internalized values and understandings of individuals within a community. Instead, rules are tools for controlling the actions of others and their enforcement not only admonishes the rule-breaker, but also underscores the position of power held by those who enforce the rules. This latter effect is tied closely to the fact that those who hold the most power within a social group most often define rules and have the sole ability to change or interpret the rules.

Finally, a teleoaffective structure is "a range of normativized and hierarchically ordered ends, projects, and tasks, to varying degrees allied with normativized emotions and

---

[16] Schatzki, *Site of the Social*, 77. The practices discussed here are what Schatzki calls integrative practices, as opposed to dispersed practices. Dispersed practices are those very basic actions such as greeting, examining, or walking. Integrative practices are made up of dispersed practices, but also require teleoaffective structures and directed efforts in order to be more than just an agglomeration of dispersed practices (see ibid., *Social Practices*, 91-110).

[17] Schatzki, *Site of the Social*, 77.

[18] Schatzki, *Social Practices*, 112.

[19] Schatzki, *Site of the Social*, 79.

even moods."[20] Teleoaffective structures are complex and open-ended, but still require a general agreement about their appropriateness. It is through teleoaffective structures that a social group decides which practices and arrangements (in orders) are acceptable. A given physical site can be home to multiple and competing teleoaffective structures even among participants who might all define themselves as part of the same community. This is not to say that teleoaffective structures are slippery and useless as analytical tools. In fact, it is their flexibility which makes them useful for studying the real life complexity that one finds in the world.

Now we move from the physical analysis of practices to the analysis of power dynamics within a group that shares practices. Here we turn to Pierre Bourdieu, perhaps the most prominent and influential practice theorist to date.[21] Bourdieu's theoretical framework was devised over a long career of in-depth anthropological and sociological analysis spanning topics as diverse as tribal life in Algeria to the realms of artistic production and French intellectual life. Bourdieu's theories were built up slowly as a result of his empirical studies, and Bourdieu discouraged systematizing his theories rather than seeing his work as a collection of concepts and approaches that might be used in sociological analysis.[22] Even with such warnings,

---

[20] Schatzki, *Site of the Social*, 80.

[21] For a few examples of the use of Pierre Bourdieu by scholars of religion, see: Catherine Bell, *Ritual Theory, Ritual Practice* (New York: Oxford University Press, 1992); David Swartz, "Bridging the Study of Culture and Religion: Pierre Bourdieu's Political Economy of Symbolic Power," *SociolRelig* 57 (1996): 71-85; Hugh B. Urban, "Sacred Capital: Pierre Bourdieu and the Study of Religion," *MTSR* 15 (2003): 354-89; and Bradford Verter, "Bourdieu and the Bāuls Reconsidered," *MTSR* 16 (2004): 182-92; Steven Engler, "Modern Times: Religion, Consecration and the State in Bourdieu," *CultStud* 17 (2003): 445-67; Terry Rey, "Marketing the Goods of Salvation: Bourdieu on Religion," *Religion* 34 (2004): 331-43; ibid., *Bourdieu on Religion: Imposing Faith and Legitimacy* (Key Thinkers in the Study of Religion; London: Equinox, 2007).

[22] Pierre Bourdieu and Loïc J. D. Wacquant, *An Invitation to Reflexive Sociology* (Chicago: University of Chicago Press, 1992).

however, Bourdieu himself and many of his disciples and critics have offered systematic summaries of his theory and it will be useful to provide such a summary here.[23]

Bourdieu's work has been described as a combination of the individualist sociology of Max Weber and the structuralist Marxism of Louis Althusser.[24] Bourdieu takes the Marxist stance that social life is one thoroughly saturated by conflict over scarce resources and combines it with a Weberian perspective that *"all action is interested,* including symbolic pursuits."[25] His theory is informed by economic notions of capital and personal interest, but not in a strictly economic (i.e., financial capital) sense. Instead, he posits a complicated overlay of a variety of competitive marketplaces that deal in symbolic capital instead of just financial capital. His theory consists of five central components: (1) symbolic capital, (2) fields of cultural production, (3) symbolic power, (4) symbolic violence, and (5) *habitus*. I will take each in turn.

Bourdieu developed the notion of symbolic capital primarily through his analysis of education and the production of art.[26] Symbolic capital is a type of resource which can be used to gain status in a community, attain financial capital, or exercise power over others. In their study of the French education system, Bourdieu and colleague Jean-Claude Passeron recognized that

---

[23] Pierre Bourdieu, *Outline of a Theory of Practice* (Cambridge Studies in Social and Cultural Anthropology 16; trans. Richard Nice; Cambridge: Cambridge University Press, 1977); Bourdieu, *The Logic of Practice*; *Bourdieu: Critical Perspectives* (ed. Craig Calhoun, Edward LiPuma, and Moishe Postone; Chicago: The University of Chicago Press, 1993); David Swartz, *Culture & Power: The Sociology of Pierre Bourdieu* (Chicago: University of Chicago Press, 1997).

[24] Swartz, *Culture & Power*, 38-45.

[25] Swartz, *Culture & Power*, 66.

[26] Pierre Bourdieu and Jean-Claude Passeron, *Reproduction in Education, Society and Culture* (2d ed.; trans. Richard Nice; London: SAGE Publications, 1977); Pierre Bourdieu, *Distinction: A Social Critique of the Judgement of Taste* (trans. Richard Nice; Cambridge: Harvard University Press, 1984).

academic success and advancement depends in large part on the amount of cultural capital that students had. Cultural capital, a type of symbolic capital, manifests itself in such things as knowledge of vocabulary, awareness of elite practices, and taste in art and music.[27] In *Distinction*, Bourdieu shows how subjects' taste in music is positively correlated to their economic and social status.[28] However, by an awareness of things that are highly valued in society, one can increase one's social status, even if one's actual financial status decreases in the process. Such capital is accumulated simply through an understanding and appreciation of its importance and use.[29] Unlike financial capital, spent cultural capital does not leave the hand of the one who spends it. To further extend this economic model of human action, Bourdieu argues that all actions are aimed at the maximization of capital within a field of other individuals competing over the same resources.[30] In other words, symbolic capital is as much a source of competition in the symbolic marketplace as financial capital is in the stock market or around a poker table.

The notion of symbolic capital is closely tied to the idea of fields of cultural production, even though Bourdieu's concept of fields developed years after he first wrote about symbolic capital. Late in his career, Bourdieu stressed that "*a capital does not exist and function except in relation to a field.*"[31] Fields are arrangements of individuals, hierarchically ordered, in active competition over a given type of capital, individuals who agree that the rules of the game are acceptable and the capital worthwhile. Central to the notion of a field is that individuals are positioned throughout it in positions of force.[32] In other words, individuals are positioned

---

[27] See especially Bourdieu and Passeron, *Reproduction*, 71-102 and Bourdieu, *Distinction*, 11-96.

[28] Bourdieu, *Distinction*, 13-18.

[29] Swartz, *Culture and Power*, 76.

[30] Swartz, *Culture and Power*, 66-73.

[31] Bourdieu and Wacquant, *Invitation*, 101, italics in the original.

[32] Bourdieu and Wacquant, *Invitation*, 101.

based solely on the amount of capital they have in a given field. There are, of course, as many fields as there are types of symbolic capital.[33] The field of education thus deals with cultural capital, the field of religion with religious capital, the political field with political capital, and so on. Each field has its own rules and is made up only of those individuals who buy into the value of that particular form of political capital.

The next two parts of the theory, symbolic power and symbolic violence, go hand in hand. For Bourdieu, symbolic power is simply the exercise of symbolic capital. This is a somewhat natural extension of his economic model. It is with symbolic violence that Bourdieu steps beyond the purely economic model in order to explain how it is that most people never recognize the symbolic forces at play in their lives. Bourdieu defines symbolic violence as the imposition of meanings in such a way as to legitimate said meanings while simultaneously "concealing the power relations which are the basis of its force."[34] Symbolic violence presents the political, oppressive aspects of a particular field as natural, or "taken-for-granted."[35] More importantly, symbolic violence conceals the fact that power relations are completely arbitrary and that the one imposing the values is likewise an arbitrary figure. In other words, power structures are not natural or necessary, nor are those in power naturally inherently deserving of their power. This "misrecognition" of the arbitrariness of the power forces is what keeps individuals trapped in such symbolic forms of oppression.[36] Misrecognition is not just an attribute of those dominated within fields of cultural production, but also those who benefit from the structures and dymanics in the field. Closely related to symbolic violence is symbolic labor performed

---

[33] Swartz, *Culture and Power*, 123.

[34] Bourdieu and Passeron, *Reproduction*, 4.

[35] Swartz, *Culture and Power*, 89.

[36] On misrecognition, see Pierre Bourdieu, *The Field of Cultural Production: Essays on Art and Literature* (ed. Randal Johnson; European Perspecives; New York: Columbia University Press, 1993), 75-81.

by cultural producers (i.e., intellectuals). Symbolic labor "produces symbolic power by transforming relations of interest into disinterested meanings and by legitimating arbitrary relations of power as the natural order of thing."[37] Symbolic labor contributes to shaping group identity through the production of myths, symbols, art, and other cultural artifacts that reinforce, and at times challenge, the hierarchical structure of a given field of cultural production.

Bourdieu calls the symbolic labor of cultural producers within the religious field religious labor. Religious labor generates a religious ideology, which transforms social relations into "supernatural relations," thus justifying hierarchies by appeals to culturally postulated counter-intuitive agents (e.g., gods, demons, angels, ancestral spirits, etc.).[38] As with any other field of cultural production, Bourdieu sees power and domination as inherent aspects of the religious field:

> Inasmuch as it is the result of the monopolization of the administration of the goods of salvation by a body of religious *specialists*, socially recognized as the exclusive holders of the specific competence necessary for the production or reproduction of a *deliberately organized corpus* of secret (and therefore rare) knowledge, the constitution of a religious field goes hand in hand with the objective dispossession of those who are excluded from it and who thereby find themselves constituted as the *laity* (or the *profane*, in the double meaning of the word) dispossessed of *religious capital* (as accumulated symbolic labor) and recognizing the legitimacy of that dispossession from the mere fact that they misrecognize it as such.[39]

---

[37] Swartz, *Culture and Power*, 93.

[38] Pierre Bourdieu, "Genesis and Structure of the Religious Field," *CSR* 13 (1991): 5. On counter-intuitive agents, see Pascal Boyer, *Religion Explained: The Evolutionary Origins of Religious Thought* (New York: Basic Books, 2001) and Ilkka Pyysiäinen, *How Religion Works: Towards a New Cognitive Science of Religion* (Leiden: Brill, 2003).

[39] Bourdieu, "Genesis and Structure," 9.

Within this construct, scripturalizing is a form of religious labor that necessarily shapes relations of power within the religious field. Since fields are structured so as to privilege the work of specialists, a significant component of policing a religious field and its hierarchies is to recognize only some individuals as specially authorized in the interpretation of those scriptures and to minimize or dismiss attempts to provide alternative interpretations from those who are not recognized as specialists.

Symbolic capital is created, passed on, and spent through the medium of practices. Practices represent the social and material emphasis of Bourdieu's theory. By participating in social practices, people take on a general understanding of how to act in life, a sense of know-how which Bourdieu calls *habitus*.[40] *Habitus* is not necessarily conscious knowledge that is applied in life, but is almost unconscious, automatic knowledge which people learn how to apply to various circumstances.[41] Here, Bourdieu has been accused of leaning a bit too much into the structuralist camp by stating that individuals base their actions on unconscious knowledge that is determined by their social environments.[42] In response to his critics, Bourdieu maintained that his emphasis on the unraveling of practices across time allows for a strategic use of *habitus* and not just an unmindful, robotic acting out of some program.[43] While an individual may have a set number of acceptable reactions to the actions of another, the passage of time allows for manipulation and creativity in the acting out or not acting out of expected actions.[44] It is through the introduction of strategy exercised in the passage

---

[40] See esp. Bourdieu, *Outline*, 79-87; Bourdieu, *Logic of Practice*, 52-65; Bourdieu and Wacquant, *Invitation*, 18-19 and 115-40.

[41] This is comparable to Schatzki's practical intelligibility and practical understanding.

[42] For a discussion of such critiques and Bourdieu's responses to them, see Bourdie and Wacquant, *Invitation*, 120-40.

[43] Bourdieu, *Logic of Practice*, 55.

[44] Bourdieu, *Outline*, 8-15.

of time that Bourdieu avoids the strict determinism of objectivist ontologies.

Bourdieu's work has come under attack for a number of reasons, many of which he had the opportunity to defend himself against while he was still alive.[45] One criticism has been that Bourdieu is wrong in seeing life in such a thoroughly materialist way.[46] Bourdieu's detractors have reacted strongly to his claim that everyone seeks to maximize their capital, citing altruism as a primary example that stands contrary to the very notion of profit maximization. This is understandable if altruism is seeing as being completely counter to the values of capitalism, but this critique falls on its face when one considers that altruism can actually be a mark of symbolic capital, something that earns someone higher status although it runs contrary to typical capitalistic notions. In non-individualist societies such as those in the ancient Mediterranean world, taking care of others and putting the group's interests before an individual's interests was quite common. This does not necessarily mean that a non-economic model of social action is at play, but that communal interests can also play into a communal symbolic economy.

A better understanding of social conflict and status/profit maximization can be garnered from stepping across the intellectual boundary between sociology and evolutionary psychology.[47] Lee Cronk has suggested that striving for status of

---

[45] Bourdieu and Wacquant's *An Invitation to Reflexive Sociology* can be seen as studied defense against many of Bourdieu's chief critics.

[46] Swartz, *Culture and Power*, 68.

[47] This field, although relatively young, has already produced studies that encourage a helpful rethinking of social life and human psychology in ways that many find dangerous or offensive. Still reeling from the horrendous violence unleashed on humanity in the name of biological differences, many scholars in all fields have an almost knee-jerk reaction against any claims to the importance of evolution in anything but biology. To make the leap to it influencing thought, language, or social life is one which many fear may lead down the same dangerous path as earlier forms of social evolution. I believe that this is far from the case with evolutionary psychology, however, and that

any sort is often strongly correlated to reproductive success, the typical "end" in evolutionary thought.[48] Cronk sees financial and symbolic economies as both contributing to the primary type of capital in evolutionary psychology, namely sexual reproductive capital.[49] In his introduction to the field of evolutionary psychology, Robert Wright explains how submissiveness to a dominant individual is often an advantageous decision. He cites a 1920s study on social order formation among hens (whence our term "pecking order") as one example in which animals are thrown together and, after initial violent struggle, soon fall into a hierarchical pattern which remains stable.[50] Since continued fighting for the top position would eventually result in all but one male and one female alive in any given population, it is a smart reproductive move for most hens to accept a lower spot in the hierarchy so that they get the possibility of sexual reproduction with at least some rooster instead of quickly finding their death at the hands of a stronger hen. Similarly, since symbolic violence can often be tied to actual violence, it would seem that accepting a weaker position within a field might actually be a smarter move than constantly striving to *maximize* one's capital. Positioning oneself in a field of social conflict does not necessarily take the shape of everyone climbing his or her way to the top. Instead, they might be found positioning themselves in a slightly higher position above one neighbor while still retaining a relatively low position in the field as a whole. Thus, an analysis of social life must be conscious of submission to more powerful individuals

---

social theorists continue to ignore developments in this field to their own detriment.

[48] Lee Cronk, "Behavioral Ecology and the Social Sciences," in *Missing the Revolution: Darwinism for Social Scientists* (ed. Jerome H. Barkow; Oxford: Oxford University Press, 2006), 167-86.

[49] Cronk's point, although an important insight, glosses over the extent to which some forms of symbolic capital can act in direct opposition to sexual reproductive capital as is the case with ascetic groups who renounce sexuality.

[50] Robert Wright, *The Moral Animal: Evolutionary Psychology and Everyday Life* (New York: Vintage Books, 1994), 238-50.

as much as it is of oppression and subversion.[51] What this means for Bourdieu's theory is that people are in fact constantly engaged in competitive relations within a variety of fields, but we should not expect every individual in a field to strive to maximize their capital or to achieve the highest possible position within the field.

1.2 The Place of Narrative Identity in a Practice Ontology

Most of practice theory deals with practices that are habitual in nature and with tacit knowledge. Issues of identity have not come into play since identity is generally considered to fall within the purview of psychology or social psychology. The emphasis in practice theories on rules and tacit knowledge does not seem to have a place for matters of individual identity. The performance of practices, whether out of habit or because one is following explicit rules only makes sense, however, if the actor has a notion of who he or she is, as an individual and as a member of a group or groups. Identity is not just a matter of categorization, but of having a sense of one's self in a stream of time. This narrative identity contextualizes practices of all sorts and helps to shape one's values, passions, and commitments.

In order to understand the place of narrative identity as a basic component of human existence, we turn to the philosopher Paul Ricoeur, who approaches identity through what he considers to be the fundamental challenge to notions of identity as typically conceived: permanence through time.[52] Ricoeur explores this problem through the very words used to signify the

---

[51] It may be that Bourdieu's focus on the structures of oppression caused him to play down the structures of submission that are inherent in any field. If one wants to point out the oppression of the weak, it does not make sense to highlight the submission of the oppressed to their oppressors.

[52] For a collection of articles addressing the importance of narrative for the study of religion, primarily through the lens of cognitive science, see *Religious Narrative, Cognition and Culture: Image and Word in the Mind of Narrative* (ed. Armin W. Geertz and Jeppe Sinding Jensen,; Religion, Cognition and Culture; Sheffield: Equinox, 2011).

self, relying especially on the Latin terms *idem* and *ipse*. *Idem* (which he also designates as sameness or *idem*-identity) refers specifically to the stability of identity. *Ipse* (selfhood or *ipse*-identity), on the other hand, refers to the constancy of the self over time which recognizes a continuity of development from point A to point B. Mathematically, *idem* would signify the equation $x = x$, whereas *ipse* would designate the relationship between x and y such that the two are not identical, but are points in a particular continuum. This latter concept is represented best by the ideas of "character" and "keeping a promise." Ricoeur sees "character" as "the set of distinctive marks which permit the reidentification of the human individual as being the same. By the descriptive features that will be given, the individual compounds numerical identity [*idem*] and qualitative identity [*ipse*], uninterrupted continuity and permanence in time."[53] This character consists of lasting dispositions, of habitual inclinations, which allow a person to be recognized as the same across time. Here, Ricoeur approaches Bourdieu's notion of *habitus*, which Bourdieu has variously referred to as "cultural unconscious," "habit-forming force," "set of basic, deeply interiorized master-patterns," "mental habit," "mental and corporeal schemata of perceptions, appreciations, and action," and "generative principle of regulated improvisations."[54] As Ricoeur points out, however, *habitus* is only an aspect of identity as it is expressed across time, but it alone is inadequate for understanding how individuals understand themselves or others as characters with agency.

This understanding comes about through the creation of narratives by means of emplotment, "which configures and synthesizes diverse and multiple elements into a unified

---

[53] Paul Ricoeur, *Oneself as Another* (trans. Kathleen Blamey; Chicago: The University of Chicago Press, 1992), 119.
[54] Swarz, *Culture & Power*, 101.

whole."[55] Because people exist in time, and thus experience a series of things spread out across time and space, the only way to connect these experiences and retain a sense of sameness is through connecting these experiences in some sort of developing plot. Narrative thus becomes the only means by which we can understand our lived experiences or the characters of others. Character in the attributive sense is thus understood only in characters in the nominal sense. As Holstein and Gubrium describe, "The proffered self provides an account – 'a vocabulary of motives' – for explaining and justifying conduct."[56] To understand identity, and the formation of identity, then, one must understand not just the character of a person or group, but also the narratives used to make sense of that character, the plots in which their activities and habits make sense.

Moving beyond the basic concept of narrative identity, some scholars have suggested a variety of narrative types that help us categorize aspects of identity. Somers and Gibson, for example, identify four dimensions of narrativity: ontological narratives, public narratives, conceptual narratives, and metanarratives.[57] Ontological narratives are "the stories that social actors use to make sense of – indeed, in order to act in – their lives." This would seem to be enough to cover Ricoeur's narrative identity, but Somers and Gibson take us even further. In their model, public narratives are those attached to larger

---

[55] David M. Kaplan, *Ricoeur's Critical Theory* (SUNY Series in the Philosophy of the Social Sciences; Albany: State University of New York Press, 2003), 90.

[56] James A. Holstein and Jaber F. Gubrium, *The Self We Live By: Narrative Identity in a Postmodern World* (Oxford: Oxford University Press, 2000), 12.

[57] Margaret R. Somers and Gloria D. Gibson, "Reclaiming the Epistemological 'Other': Narrative and the Social Construction of Identity," in *Social Theory and the Politics of Identity* (ed. Craig Calhoun; Cambridge: Blackwell, 1994), 60-64. Somers and Gibson point out that this final category often transcends narrativity in the sense that it offers broad categories in which to place ontological, public, and conceptual narratives, but they often lose their own narrative coherence.

interpersonal and cultural social formations, on both small and large scales. This would include narratives of group identity such as those shared by members of a particular religion or nation. Public narratives are thus especially important for the study of social identity. Conceptual narratives are the second order narratives that are constructed by scholars studying individuals and societies. Finally, metanarratives are those conceptual narratives that help us to paint history with broad strokes, such as capitalism versus communism, the battle of the sexes, or the so-called war on terror. Ontological and public narratives interpenetrate in any one individual's self-understanding and these narratives are also multiple and constantly changing in complex ways. That is to say that identity is neither stable nor singular and that some narratives, that is, some identities or aspects of an identity, become more salient at one time and less so at another.

One common way in which public narratives have been theorized is as "collective memory." Maurice Halbwachs was the first to argue that memories are socially produced.[58] Collective or social memory is shaped by individuals interacting in discursive and non-discursive practices to shape a community's understanding of its history. When this tradition is communicated to members of a community, it works to incorporate them within the group, at least to the extent that people come to see that tradition as their own. Social constructions of the past often present histories that legitimize or challenge particular ideologies in the present. Social memories are thus political in nature insofar as they participate in presenting a particular social formation as legitimate due to its place in relation to a shared history.

Duncan Bell has criticized scholars for using "collective memory" in a way that ignores the meaning and nuances of

---

[58] Maurice Halbwachs, *On Collective Memory* (Chicago: University of Chicago Press, 1992).

memory *per se*.⁵⁹ Bell suggests that we replace talk of memory with talk of mythology. Unfortunately for Bell, he does not explain what he means by "mythology," but it would seem that he takes mythology to be a public narrative of the past which people come to own as a representation of their own identity, whether it be historical "fact" or complete fabrication. Bell plays on the fictive connotation of myth in order to stress its contested, imperfect nature and to emphasize the role of the community in constructing these narratives instead of simply remembering them.

Bell is right in pointing out the problems with using "memory" as a category, and I also agree with him in suggesting "myth" as a useful alternative, although for different reasons. As already mentioned, collective memories are strategically employed in the legitimization of current social formations. This brings us back to myth and mythmaking as described by Bruce Lincoln and Russell McCutcheon. As stated in the introduction, Lincoln defines myth as "ideology in narrative form," a notion McCutcheon employs when he states that "myth is not so much a genre with relatively stable characteristics that allow us to distinguish myth from folk tale, saga, legend and fable as a class of *social argumentation*."⁶⁰ Myth is a means by which any given social organization, cultural values, and systems of control, among other things, are naturalized. They are narratives that, among other things, mask the social interests of their authors through claims of divine authority and veracity.⁶¹ In this present

---

⁵⁹ Duncan S. A. Bell, "Mythscapes: Memory, Mythology, and National Identity," *BJOS* 54 (2003): 63-81.

⁶⁰ Bruce Lincoln, *Theorizing Myth: Narrative, Ideology, and Scholarship* (Chicago: University of Chicago Press, 1999), 147; Russell T. McCutcheon, "Myth," in *Guide to the Study of Religion* (ed. Willi Braun and Russell T. McCutcheon; London: Cassell, 2000), 199-200, emphasis in the original.

⁶¹ Lincoln, in talking about the myths of the Tain, puts it thus: "It also ranks these, and misrepresents the ranking it offers as the product of nature and necessity rather than as a contingent set of human preferences advanced by interested actors, some of whom are responsible for the text. This misrepresentation of culture as nature is an ideological move characteristic of

work, the use of "myth" and "mythmaking" is intentionally meant to be provocative, the goal being to alert the reader to matters of power and domination at work in the theologies and religious histories that are too often separated from such analyses.

Scriptures, when defined as texts considered to be sacred, can be seen as providing a community with a closed set of public narratives, or myths, through which the members of that community come to identify themselves as part of that group. Scriptures can come to be a closed set of texts, but they are constantly made relevant to other communities spread out across space and time through the act of interpretation. Often, this is controlled to some extent by authoritative interpreters who engage in hermeneutical strategies that are themselves shaped by the context in which they are formulated. These interpreters mediate between the scriptures and the community, thus becoming the creators of second-order myths that are intended to help the community define itself. It is to these cultural producers that we now turn.

1.3 The Task of the Interpreter

In order to see why interpretation can be so malleable and produce a variety of interpretations of any given text, it is helpful to understand how meaning is produced by a reader and for this we turn again to Paul Ricoeur. In his hermeneutic theory, Ricoeur attempts to bridge the divide between philosophical hermeneutics (à la Hans-Georg Gadamer) and critical theory (à la Jürgen Habermas). The main point of conflict between Gadamer and Habermas, as Ricoeur reads them, is the problem of the power of tradition. Does tradition govern our understandings or do we challenge the powerful ideology presented in that tradition? Ricoeur outlines four themes at work

---

myth, as is the projection of the narrator's ideals, desires, and favored ranking of categories into a fictive prehistory that purportedly establishes how things are and must be." *Theorizing Myth*, 149.

in hermeneutics that allows for *rapprochement* between the two philosophical stances.[62] The first theme is what Ricoeur calls distanciation, meaning the space created between the author and his or her discourse the moment it becomes fixed in writing. "In short, the work *decontextualizes* itself, from the sociological as well as the psychological point of view, and is able to *recontextualize* itself differently in the act of reading."[63] By recognizing the autonomy of the written word, Ricoeur distances himself from Romantic hermeneutics that designate the text's meaning as equivalent to the message intended by the author. Once a text comes to be, it is immediately disconnected from its author psychologically, and quickly comes to be disconnected from its original context and audience sociologically since the fact of its having been written allows for the possibility of its becoming available to people in different contexts across space and time.

Moving away from notions of authorial intent, we come to Ricoeur's second and third themes, which are an analysis of the depth semantics of the text and of the world opened up in front of the text.[64] Depth semantics refers to the structural properties of the text. Ricoeur's biggest break with Romantic hermeneutics, however comes with the third theme since it here that the reader most thoroughly breaks away from uncovering the author's intent, and instead turns toward explicating "the type of being-in-the-world unfolded *in front of* the text."[65] This world of the text is a necessary correlate of distanciation. The autonomous text that has a narrative plot must be able to sustain itself on its own and refer to its own narrative, and not to the world of either the author or reader.[66]

---

[62] Paul Ricoeur, *Hermeneutics and the Human Sciences: Essays on Language, Action, and Interpretation* (ed. and trans. John B. Thompson; Cambridge: Cambridge University Press, 2006), 91-95.

[63] Ricoeur, *Hermeneutics and the Human Sciences*, 91.

[64] Ricoeur, *Hermeneutics and the Human Sciences*, 92-94.

[65] Ricoeur, *Hermeneutics and the Human Sciences*, 141.

[66] Ricoeur, *Hermeneutics and the Humans Sciences*, 140-42.

The fourth theme is that interpretation allows for a self-critical move on the part of the reader.

> The relation to the world of the text takes the place of the relation to the subjectivity of the author, and at the same time the problem of the subjectivity of the reader is displaced. To understand is not to project oneself into the text but to expose oneself to it; it is to receive a self that has been enlarged by the appropriation of the proposed worlds which interpretation unfolds.[67]

This is the flipside of the first theme of distanciation. As the text becomes automatically removed from the control of the author, it requires that the reader appropriate the text and the world it opens up at least in some degree. This appropriation takes place when the reader opens herself up to the world of the text and creatively incorporates plots, themes, vocabulary, etc., into her own narrative. It is in this act of appropriation that the meaning of a narrative is created – "at the intersection between the world of the text and the world of the readers. It is mainly in the *reception* of the text by an audience that the capacity of the plot to transfigure experience is actualized."[68] In other words, texts gain their meaning and shape identity in the reception of the text on the part of the reader and not in the creation of the text by the author. This insight helps us to understand why the all too common notion that texts make identity is so problematic. Texts and their authors do not retain an unsullied meaning that they affix to their readers, but instead they offer up possibilities which are variously appropriated and rejected as the readers see fit.

Ricoeur takes the notion of the creation of identity in the appropriation of sacred texts to an extreme that requires further comment. In *Figuring the Sacred*, Ricoeur states that:

---

[67] Ricoeur, *Hermeneutics and the Human Sciences*, 94.

[68] Paul Ricoeur, *Figuring the Sacred: Religion, Narrative, and Imagination* (ed. Mark I. Wallace; trans. David Pellauer; Minneapolis: Fortress Press, 1995), 240.

> At a second level, biblical narratives *intensify* some traits that have been overlooked in the preceding characterization of narratives in general. This *intensification* is still coherent with the usual treatment of narratives in contemporary narratology. By *intensification* I mean the following: in a sense, religious, and more specifically biblical, narratives do in their own way what all narratives do – they constitute the identity of the community that tells and retells the story, and they constitute it as a narrative identity.[69]

Here Ricoeur places the burden of meaning-making on the text itself, and the world opened up by the text. The very sense of agency attributed here to the text itself is problematic, and not in line with Ricoeur's statements in less theologically oriented works. If the creation of meaning occurs at the meeting of the horizon of the text and the horizon of the reader, then statements such as this seem to erase the horizon of the reader or equate them with the horizon of the text. While this might be an ideal that some claim to be the way in which scripture works, it is not the common experience of readers approaching texts with a vast array of preunderstandings and conflicting conceptions and narratives. It would seem that Ricoeur falls into the same trap of other Bible scholars in wanting to retain the power to shape identity within the biblical text, but this cannot be so simply maintained.

Part of the confusion reflected in this quote from *Figuring the Sacred* is indicative of the confused nature of literary theory in general. If, as Ricoeur himself explains, meaning is negotiated by a reader in the process of reading, then there is no set place where text and reader necessarily come together to produce a definitive meaning. Steven Mailloux describes this very problem in his critique of hermeneutic realism (that texts contain meanings in and of themselves independent of interpretation) and hermeneutic idealism (that interpreters construct meaning in

---

[69] Ricoeur, *Figuring the Sacred*, 241.

such a way that texts come to be almost unnecessary).[70] Both of these approaches to interpretation attempt to provide a set method for determining valid interpretations, but they both also stumble upon their own shortcomings. Realist theories suggest that meaning is discovered through shared, contextualized conventions of interpretation that allow a reader to identify the clear meanings communicated by a text. Such approaches always "suffer from incomplete coverage and lack of specificity as exhaustive accounts of interpreting" and fail to establish just how conventions of establishing meaning are embedded in texts or how those conventions would determine meaning for any particular reader.[71] In the end, realism slides into idealism which stresses the communally established practices of interpretation for establishing meaning. Idealist theories falter upon their inability to establish a context in which a "true" interpretation can be determined. In Mailloux's judgment such idealist theories "fare no better as an exhaustive account of meaning, because there is no limit in principle to the features relevant to the interpretation of specific speech acts…In other words, 'definitive' theories of interpretive context must either never begin the process of specification or never end it."[72] The shortcoming of realist and idealist approaches to texts pushes us to abandon the traditional goal of literary theories, i.e., to establish a definitive interpretation of a text, and instead to ask a new set of questions.

Mailloux proposes a rhetorical hermeneutics that rejects the very notion of establishing a unitary meaning for a text and instead analyzes the ways in which interpretations are made as contextualized rhetorical acts. Interpretations do not establish a single valid meaning but are attempts at persuading others that a particular interpretation is valid (hence their rhetorical nature). So, instead of attempting to establish the correct meaning of a

---

[70] Steven Mailloux, *Rhetorical Hermeneutics* (Ithaca: Cornell University Press, 1989), 4-14.
[71] Mailloux, *Rhetorical Hermeneutics*, 8-9.
[72] Mailloux, *Rhetorical Hermeneutics*, 11.

text, a rhetorical hermeneutics approach analyzes the cultural, institutional, and political contexts in which a particular interpretation arises in order to show how that interpretation is reflective of a particular setting. Such an approach does not require us to settle on a singular interpretive setting, and encourages us to shift our gaze to diverse settings, thus recognizing that, while meaning may be constructed by readers, the means by which different readers come to those meanings are multiple, varied, and context dependent. Put differently, Mailloux is proposing a social history of interpretation, one that rejects normative judgments about interpretations, and instead pushes us to consider the ideological context in which such interpretations are made. Rhetorical hermeneutics helps us see what is at play in the varied ways in which texts, or in our case a particular type of texts, scriptures, are made to signify within a given cultural context, as is suggested by Wimbush's call for a reorientation in scriptural study.

While it is possible to study any text and its interpretations using Mailloux's rhetorical hermeneutics as our method, we are faced with a peculiar kind of problem when it comes to scriptures.[73] If we take scriptures as textual canons, then, with Jonathan Z. Smith we can see them as a closed list, which requires a tradition and an interpreter.[74] Since the closure of the canon keeps it stable, interpretation, generally by specialists, is needed to keep it relevant to an ever-changing community and tradition. It is through interpretation that the time represented in the canon and in its formation is connected to the present through the act of interpretation. Also implicit in Smith's theory of canon is that there is a community which accepts the authority of the canon and of the interpreter. As we turn to the specifics of scriptural interpretation then, we must pay attention to the authoritative

---

[73] This would hold for any type of centering text which a community holds as central to its self-definition such as a constitution.

[74] Jonathan Z. Smith, *Imagining Religion: From Babylon to Jonestown* (Chicago: University of Chicago Press, 1982), 49.

interpreters and the rhetorical contexts in which they produce their interpretations. In focusing on the these authoritative figures, we see how their political, cultural, and institutional contexts shape their interpretations and are thus intended to shape their community's understandings of their canon and of themselves in relation to said canon.

This awareness of the importance of authoritative interpreters in a community points us away from scripture as the anchor of the community's self-understanding and to interpretive commentaries as the locus or even battleground for the production of meanings that center a community. I use commentary in a broad sense as any text, oral or written, that describes and interprets another text for a particular audience. Commentaries are presented as extensions of other texts that clarify their meanings, but, as we have seen, these meanings are, by definition, reflective of the context in which they are produced. Commentaries then proffer a meaning that necessarily supplements or even obfuscates and replaces that of the text it is meant to explain.[75] A sociological study of scriptures thus moves us even farther from the content meaning of those scriptures to the content of commentaries on those scriptures, the contexts out of which those commentaries are produced, and the forms of life that these commentaries encourage, promote, justify, and reflect.

Aaron Hughes provides a similar theoretical model for understanding the genre of textual commentary.[76] Hughes states that "commentary is the locus wherein a community confronts and, in the process, understands its past, either real or imagined."[77] Hughes sees commentary as a method of presencing this past, but, as Mailloux has made clear, it is also

---

[75] For more on this notion of commentary as a replacement for that which it comments upon, see Jacques Derrida, *Of Grammatology* (2d ed.; trans. Gayatri Chakravorty Spivak; Baltimore: Johns Hopkins University Press, 1998).

[76] Aaron Hughes, "Presenting the Past: The Genre of Commentary in Theoretical Perspective," *MTSR* 15.2 (2003): 148-68.

[77] Hughes, "Presenting the Past," 149.

just as much about making the present existent in the past, at least rhetorically.[78] In other words, through the process of interpretation both the present and the past are given meaning. As Hughes points out, this meaning-producing interaction with a shared canonical text is part and parcel of the community's self-understanding and self-maintenance. Thus, textual interpretation is always an aspect of the continual process of social formation.

Hughes' article raises an important issue in social formation which leads us to another component of our scripturalizing model: the notion of shared memory, or myth, as part of the canonical/interpretive matrix. In their introduction to a collection of articles addressing the power relations involved in the control of historical discourse, George Clement Bond and Angela Gilliam state that

> social constructions [of the past] may reflect the interrelation and interpenetration of structures of thought and human agency interacting with complex economic and political fields. On the one hand, they reflect the ways in which people are defined, apprehended and acted upon by others and, on the other, they define themselves.[79]

A belief in a shared past is a powerful force in the construction of identity and thus control over the understanding of the past through producing commentaries helps to control the construction of group and individual identity. The rhetorical situations in which commentaries are produced are thus filled with rhetorical tactics aimed at shaping the self-understanding of the members of that community.

---

[78] Hughes explicitly states that interpretation is *not* about situating the present in the past in "Presenting the Past," 163.

[79] George Clement Bond and Angela Gilliam, introduction to *Social Construction of the Past: Representation as Power* (ed. George C. Bond and Angela Gilliam; London: Routledge, 1997), 5.

1.4 What Scripturalizing Is: An Initial Response

We are now in a place where we can tentatively state what we mean when we talk about scripturalizing. By scripturalizing I mean the various practices by which a community shapes itself in relation to a set of sacred texts. This includes the practices that create a text as scripture (production, commentary, worship, etc.), as well as the practices of interpreting that text and making it relevant for the community in the present. This can include making rules, establishing norms, or shaping myths that provide a shared identity and give a narrative context for rule-governed or habitual practices. It also includes the practices which authorize these rules, norms, and myths as sacred by tying them in some way to sacred texts. Scripturalizing thus has three components: social formation, mythmaking, and symbolic labor.

SITUATING ORIGEN IN THE GREEK PHILOSOPHICAL FIELD

In Chapter One, I argued that scripturalizing consists of three components: social formation, mythmaking, and symbolic labor. In the next three chapters, I will analyze Origen's practices and writings to demonstrate how scripturalizing worked in this one particular historical instance. Although there are many people and communities from more recent history for whom we have better evidence that would make for more fruitful studies for the process of scripturalizing, as a historian of early Christianity I am focusing on Origen as our example since he is the earliest good example for scripturalizing; we know something about his life and have a considerable amount of his writings commenting directly on scripture.[1] In this chapter, I focus on Origen's social formation using Bourdieu's concept of a field of cultural production to argue that Origen is best understood as a Christian philosopher in competition with Greek philosophers and other Christian religious specialists.[2]

While Origen might be categorized in a number of different fields, in order to bring into relief the self-interested nature of his mythology, it is best to analyze Origen within the philosophical field as it existed in the Roman Empire in the third century of the Common Era.[3] The philosophical field was itself a

---

[1] We know too little about and have too few texts from Hippolytus, for example, who wrote commentaries before Origen.

[2] See p. 48 above for a brief discussion of fields of cultural production. For a similar analysis of Greek and Christian intellectuals in competition with each other see Arthur P. Urbano, *The Philosophical Life: Biography and the Crafting of Intellectual Identity in Late Antiquity* (North American Patristics Society Patristic Monograph Series 21; Washington: Catholic University of America Press, 2013).

[3] The philosophical field is not the only field in which Origen might be categorized. A more thorough study of Origen might also look at how he

subset of a larger field of intellectuals and educators. Understanding that Origen should be located in this particular field draws our attention to the importance of philosophical education, the study of texts, and the struggle for self-mastery through ascetic praxis in Origen's mythology.[4] This method of categorization thus grounds our understanding of Origen's thoughts in his lived experiences in a materialist sense, and directs us away from an abstract analysis of just his ideas and concepts. It also helps us to focus on our present concerns of understanding why the educational practices and hierarchies of elite, privileged philosophers play such a prominent role in Origen's mythology.

Not all scholars who have written on Origen agree on categorizeing him as a philosopher. Much recent scholarship has been interested in addressing the question of whether or not Origen is appropriately Christian despite his having been officially condemned in the sixth century C.E.[5] This debate is

---

was positioned vis-à-vis church officials or confessors, for example. The choice of the philosophical field as the focus for the current study was made because it is the field in which Origen seems to have been actively engaged in as a participant and thus shaped his understanding of Christianity to a large extent.

[4] I am using mythology to refer to the public narrative Origen communicates through his various writings and homilies. His mythology encapsulates his theology (what he says about the nature of god and other divine beings including human souls), ecclesiology (what he says about the church both as an aspect of his theology and in a more concrete sense in terms of how local churches should be structured), and scriptural theology (what he says about the nature of sacred texts, what they communicate, and how they should be interpreted).

[5] For critical summaries of the debate over Origen and the ways in which scholars have judged him as appropriately Christian in terms of his hermeneutics, see Karen Jo Torjesen, *Hermeneutical Procedure and Theological Method in Origen's Exegesis* (Patristische Texte und Studien 28; Berlin: Walter de Gruyter; 1986), 1-14; and Elizabeth Ann Dively Lauro, *The Soul and Spirit of Scripture within Origen's Exegesis* (Bible in Ancient Christianity 3; Atlanta: Society of Biblical Literature, 2005), 15-33. On the condemnation of Origen in the sixth century C.E. as resulting from debates having little to do with

important since at least some scholars seem to hold that Christianity and philosophy are irreconcilable categories, a position that may stem from the influential critique of Adolf Von Harnack, who considered Origen's allegorical interpretations of scripture to be overly influenced by Greek philosophy and thus not appropriately Christian.[6] That Origen's affiliation is a central concern is demonstrated by Karen Torjesen, who proposes three tasks that Origen's defenders must accomplish:

> First, they must show that Origen was faithful to the historical element of the Christian faith...Second, Origen's defenders must show that Origen has a method...Thirdly, Origen's supporters must show that Origen's exegesis is fundamentally Christian. In order to do this they must show that its principles are uniquely Christian and can be clearly distinguished from other contemporary forms of exegesis.[7]

What is implicit in this suggestion is that Origen is a figure whose legacy is still debated in regards to the extent to which he can be considered "Christian" enough and that this question is always one that must be addressed from one side of the debate or the other. If you are writing on Origen, you are either one of his critics or one of his defenders. This assumed bifurcation effectively frames modern scholarship on Origen as an extension of the debate over his legacy in the fifth and sixth centuries.

There are two interconnected ways by which Origen has been reclaimed as a Christian who can be studied with benefit by Christians today. The first is simply to state that Origen was a Christian and not a Greek philosopher. This assertion is based, in part, on Origen's stated desire to be considered "a man of the

---

Origen's actual teachings, see Elizabeth A. Clark, *The Origenist Controversy: The Cultural Construction of an Early Christian Debate* (Princeton: Princeton University Press, 1992).

[6] Adolph von Harnack, *History of Dogma*, Vol. 2 (3d ed.; trans. Neil Buchannan; New York: Russell & Russell, 1958), esp. 332-48.

[7] Torjesen, *Hermeneutical Procedure*, 4-5.

Church."⁸ Rebecca Lyman, for example, sees Origen as an intellectual who makes use of philosophy, but whose "ecclesiastical loyalty, if nuanced, is secure."⁹ In *Origen against Plato*, Mark Edwards argues that Origen's ideas are drawn primarily from Christian scripture and tradition and *not* from Platonism, the philosophical school with which Origen has most often been associated.¹⁰ The goal of such claims seems to be to show that Origen was dedicated to Christianity and should not be dismissed because of any connection he might have had with Greek philosophy.

The second technique that has often been used to make it clear that Origen was a Christian has been to label him a theologian and not a philosopher, although the relationship between these two categories is never made clear. Henri Crouzel says that "Origen cannot be considered in the strict sense a philosopher" because of his negative judgments against philosophy and so he must be considered a theologian.¹¹ According to Crouzel, though, theology *is* "a Christian philosophy," so the distinction seems to be a modern one which Crouzel reads back into the third century.¹² For Crouzel, Origen's school in Caesarea was not a school of philosophy, but "a kind of missionary school," something that could be run by a "man of God," but which would have been a foreign concept to the

---

⁸ *HomLc* 16.6 (SC 87, 244), "*Ego vero, qui opto esse ecclesiasticus et non ab haeresearchae aliquot, sed a Christi vocabulo nuncupari et habere nomen...*"

⁹ Rebecca J. Lyman, *Christology and Cosmology: Models of Divine Activity in Origen, Eusebius, and Athanasius* (Oxford Theological Monographs; Oxford: Oxford University Press, 1993), 39.

¹⁰ Mark Julian Edwards, *Origen against Plato* (Ashgate Studies in Philosophy & Theology in Late Antiquity; Burlington: Ashgate, 2002). For the connection between Origen and Platonism, see, for example, Robert M. Berchman, *From Philo to Origen: Middle Platonism in Transition* (Brown Judaic Studies 69; Chico: Scholars Press, 1984).

¹¹ Henri Crouzel, *Origen* (trans. A.S. Worrall; San Francisco: Harper & Row, 1989), 56.

¹² Crouzel, *Origen*, 161.

philosophers.[13] Antonia Tripolitis likewise calls Origen a student of philosophy, but not a philosopher, preferring instead to call him a Christian theologian.[14] And more recently, Panayiotis Tzamalikos has also acknowledged Origen's familiarity with philosophy while stating, "One point should be made clear, however: although Origen was a theologian, not a philosopher, philosophy is indispensable for studying his thought."[15] Lastly, Benjamin Blosser describes Origen "as a genuinely Christian mystic *cum* theologian, rather than as a syncretistic philosopher."[16] For each of these scholars, the unstated presupposition seems to be that philosophers were Greek (and mistaken) whereas Christians were theologians (and correct).

The distinction between philosopher and theologian, however, is anachronistic. In the third century C.E., a person could not be a theologian *or* a philosopher, but *could* be a philosopher who focused primarily on discourse about the gods, a theologian. In his study on Neoplatonic allegorical interpretations of Homer, Robert Lamberton says that *theologos* can be used to refer to the poet who writes about gods or to the allegorical interpreter of that poet, but this latter category is a subset within philosophy, not one distinct from philosophy.[17] So, even if we admit that Origen was a theologian insofar as he was interested in allegorical interpretations of texts about the Christian god, this only further supports a categorization of him as a philosopher based on his textual practices.

---

[13] Crouzel, *Origen*, 27-28.

[14] Antonia Tripolitis, *Origen: A Critical Reading* (American University Studies Series VII: Theology and Religion 8; New York: Peter Lang, 1985), 12.

[15] P. Tzamalikos, *Origen: Philosophy of History and Eschatology* (Supplements to Vigiliae Christianae 85; Leiden: Brill, 2007), xii.

[16] Benjamin P. Blosser, *Become Like the Angels: Origen's Doctrine of the Soul* (Washington: The Catholic University of America Press, 2012), 11.

[17] Robert Lamberton, *Homer the Theologian: Neoplatonist Allegorical Reading and the Growth of the Epic Tradition*, (The Transformation of the Classical Heritage 9. Berkeley, Calif.: University of California Press, 1986), 22-31.

Other scholars have not had the same compunction about categorizing Origen as a philosopher even if they still identify him as a Christian. Carl Harris suscinctly says, "Origen is a man of the Church, but he is a philosopher in the Church."[18] For Harris, there is nothing incompatible with Origen being both a Christian and a philosopher since philosophy did not bind a person to a set of beliefs or texts. Others have made the explicit connection between a shared set of practices and the categorization of Origen as a philosopher. Anthony Grafton and Megan Williams, in analyzing the techniques of book production and textual scholarship recognize that "[Origen's] best parallels in the intellectual world of the Roman Empire are the philosophers."[19] They arrive at this conclusion because their interest "is not so much with Origen's ideas as with his way of life, and the social and cultural categories through which others would have perceived it in his own day."[20] By studying Origen's textual practices, they see that he did the very same things that philosophers did and they categorize him accordingly.[21]

I adopt a similar approach to categorization here because understanding Origen's social formation based on his practices is important for exploring the material implications of the mythology he develops as a privileged member of the elite, educated class in Alexandrian society. Like Grafton and Williams, I also see Origen as a philosopher whose practices did

---

[18] Carl Vernon Harris, *Origen of Alexandria's Interpretation of the Teacher's Function in the Early Christian Hierarchy and Community* (New York: American Press, 1966), 68.

[19] Anthony Grafton and Megan Williams, *Christianity and the Transformation of the Book: Origen, Eusebius, and the Library of Caesarea* (Cambridge: Belknap Press, 2006), 23.

[20] Grafton and Williams, *Christianity and the Transformation of the Book*, 25.

[21] Ronald E. Heine comes to a similar conclusion identifying Origen as a Christian based on his ideas and a philosopher based on his exegetical method in "Articulating Identity," in *The Cambridge History of Early Christian Literature* (ed. Frances Young, Lewis Ayres, Andrew Louth, and Augustine Casiday; Cambridge: Cambridge University Press, 2007), 212-213.

not distinguish him from his non-Christian peers. He is a *Christian* philosopher because of the texts he works with (Jewish and Christian scriptures), the Christian public narrative he identified with, and the Christian community in which he worked and taught. Nevertheless, he was clearly a philosopher as I will show in greater detail throughout this chapter. First, however, we must get a better understanding of how power functions within a field of cultural production in general and then within the field of philosophy in the third century C.E. in particular.

2.1 Analyzing Fields of Cultural Production

Fields are mapped by placing individuals and institutions in relation to each other, similar to the way teams or athletes are ranked in a sport. Individual agents are positioned based on their symbolic capital and the dispositions they have toward others in the field. These dispositions and the actions they lead to are reflective of the agents' *habitus*, which is itself structured by the practices in which they engage. If an agent has a high position within a field, he is considered to be an authority and is held in esteem by other members of the field because of his expertise or virtuosity. These positions, according to Bourdieu, are objectively defined, but they are not static. The competitive aspect of fields leads to their being forever in flux. Agents are constantly competing over symbolic capital based on the unexpressed rules of the game. These rules, generally speaking, are not codified, but can be analyzed by studying the agents' *habitus*, which must be understood by looking at their discursive and non-discursive practices.

People are members of a field when they are active participants who have bought into the rules of the game. Bourdieu calls this acceptance of the game and its stakes, *doxa*.[22] Bourdieu explains that this happens through the drawn out

---

[22]Pierre Bourdieu and Loïc J. D. Wacquant, *An Invitation to Reflexive Sociology* (Chicago: University of Chicago Press, 1992), 98.

process of enculturation during which an individual comes to internalize the values of a field by unwittingly cultivating the field's *habitus*. This process creates an *illusio*, the "belief or acceptance of the worth of the game of a field."[23] Membership in the field requires some degree of active participation, again similar to a sport for which there might be millions of spectators, but only a few athletes who play professionally. One must be actively competing for symbolic capital in order to be a part of a field. That means that a field analysis is an analysis of specialists, of elite cultural producers. The field of literary production, for example, consists of different types of writers, who may be ranked in part by the size of the audiences they reach, but general readers are not members in the field. Their reading and buying patterns may help give shape to the literary field, but only those who produce texts for others to read are considered to be players in the game.

There are two types of struggle that go on within a field. As already stated, agents compete over the symbolic capital of the field. Each field has its own forms of competition that distinguish it from other fields. However, agents can also struggle to redefine the values of the field. Fields thus become arenas for the struggle over "the right to monopolize the exercise of 'symbolic violence'."[24] In other words, positions within a field can shift based on changes in the accumulation of symbolic capital, or based on a re-valuation of the capital which repositions people within the field based on new values. The first form of competition is carried out primarily through engaging in practices which are part of that field's game. The other form, however, requires discursive practices to convince others that the current values need to be reformed or replaced, while still maintaining the basic structure of the field. As we will see with

---

[23] David Swartz, *Culture & Power: The Sociology of Pierre Bourdieu* (Chicago: University of Chicago Press, 1997), 125.

[24] Swartz, *Culture & Power*, 123. For symbolic violence, see pp. 47-48 above.

Origen, he was a capable philosopher who was competitive within the field, but he was mostly active as a Christian trying to shift the values of the philosophical field so that Christian philosophers would be seen as superior to non-Christian philosophers.

When studying a field, one cannot focus on just one player, however, which is why we cannot turn immediately to Origen, but must first situate him in relation to others. According to Bourdieu, there are three inter-connected components to field analysis.

> First, one must analyze the position of the field vis-à-vis the field of power...Second, one must map out the objective structure of the relations between positions occupied by agents or institutions who compete for the legitimate form of specific authority of which this field [is] the site. And, third, one must analyze the habitus of agents, the different systems of dispositions they have acquired by internalizing a determinate type of social and economic condition, and which find in a definite trajectory within the field under consideration a more or less favorable opportunity to become actualized.[25]

Throughout the rest of this chapter, I will be carrying out this analysis on the philosophical field in the Roman Empire in the third century C.E. First, I will locate the philosophical field within a broader field of intellectuals and position these in the broader field of power in the empire. Unfortunately, due to the paucity of evidence for philosophy in Origen's time, I can only provide a sketch of the field without the fine detail we would like to have. We can at least, however, get a sense of the practices and values of the field, which is the most important component of this field analysis for understanding the connection between Origen's social formation and the pro-philosophical bias of his Christian mythology.

---

[25] Bourdieu and Wacquant, *Invitation*, 104-05.

2.2 The Philosophical Field in the Third Century C.E.

There are several scholarly treatments of the history of Greek philosophy, which trace the development of Greek thought from the Pre-Socratics through the Neo-Platonists.[26] What is lacking is a thorough treatment of the social history of Greek philosophy. What I mean by a social history is one that examines the practices that set philosophers apart from other cultural producers in Greek-speaking cities in antiquity, and that describes the nature of philosophers' particular form of symbolic capital, which we might call philosophical capital. A social history would also situate philosophers within the larger field of power and show how they came into conflict with similar figures jockeying for space in a larger field of cultural producers. By its very nature, such a work would consider individuals only within the context of this broader network of cultural producers and would focus more on networks, schools, and movements, than on ideas, which is the focus of existing histories of ancient philosophy.

Randall Collins' *The Sociology of Philosophies* gives us a glimpse of what such a project might look like. According to Collins, "intellectual life is first of all conflict and disagreement," and he describes the major disagreements that have characterized intellectual thought on a global, historical scale.[27]

---

[26] See, for example: Giovanni Reale, *A History of Ancient Philosophy*, Vol. 1-4 (trans. John R. Catan; Albany: SUNY Press, 1987-1990); ed. Keimpe Algra, Jonathan Barnes, Jaap Mansfield, and Malcolm Schofield; *The Cambridge History of Hellenistic Philosophy* (Cambridge: Cambridge University Press, 1999); or Lloyd P. Gerson, ed. *The Cambridge History of Philosophy in Late Antiquity* (Cambrdige: Cambridge University Press, 2010).

[27] Randall Collins, *The Sociology of Philosophy: A Global Theory of Intellectual Change* (Cambridge: Belknap Press, 1998), 1. Collins first frames his history with a summary of his social theory of interaction ritual chains and coalitions of the mind, which is a practice theory focusing on the everyday interactions that effect agents intellectually and emotionally. For a more in-depth presentation of this theory, see Collins, *Interaction Ritual Chains* (Princeton Studies in Cultural Sociology; Princeton: Princeton University Press, 2004).

He argues that intellectuals thrive on disagreement and problem solving, both of which lead to creativity. Creativity can take two forms: opposition or synthesis. Since creativity seemingly requires rival positions, there are generally at least three different positions at any given time. There is also, however, an upper limit of opposing positions, at least when it comes to positions being propagated through subsequent generations.[28] In his chapter on ancient Greek philosophy, Collins examines the ways in which external political, social, and economic changes influenced the development of Greek philosophy and how philosophical schools were formed, developed, and died off.

Collins is helpful in providing suggestions for what sorts of questions might be relevant to a social history of intellectuals, but his focus on intellectual change and the broad scope of his study (a global analysis of philosophy from antiquity through the 20th century) leave much to be explored concerning the social practices and symbolic capital of Greek philosophers. For something approaching this, we turn to Pierre Hadot's *What is Ancient Philosophy?* Hadot points out that Greek philosophy differs from modern philosophy primarily insofar as Greek philosophy was not just about theoretical discourse, but also about living a life that corresponded with that discourse. Today, philosophers might write and teach about ethics, but they are not necessarily expected to live up to their teachings. In antiquity, on the other hand, to become a philosopher was to join a community of like-minded scholars and students striving to live the good life however that might be defined within that particular school. As Hadot puts it,

> There can never be a philosophy or philosophers outside a group, a community – in a word, a philosophical 'school.' The philosophical school thus corresponds, above all, to the choice of a certain way of life and existential option which demands from the individual a total change of lifestyle, a conversion of

---

[28] Collins, *The Sociology of Philosophy*, 81.

one's entire being, and ultimately a certain desire to be and to live in a certain way. This existential option, in turn, implies a certain vision of the world, and the task of philosophical discourse will therefore be to reveal and rationally justify this existential option, as well as this representation of the world.[29]

Hadot goes on to show how various schools conceived of the good life and how these conceptions were made manifest in their corresponding social formations. Hadot's emphasis on living out the ideals of each particular school, however, means that he focuses on practices related to "the care of the self," but this is only one component of what it meant to be a philosopher. Living a life that reflected a school's teachings certainly contributed to one's philosophical capital, but much more was at play in the field as a whole. In order to sketch the philosophical field in full, we need to situate philosophy vis-à-vis other fields in the broader field of power and take into account a broader set of practices that contributed to philosophical capital.

Although living the philosophical life was not theoretically reserved only for members of the elite of Greek culture, this was very much the case in practice, especially by the third century C.E. Paradigmatic figures such as Socrates or Diogenes might have been admired for their ascetic renunciation of material goods, but, as Patricia Cox explains, philosophy in the third century was an elite practice:

> A more aristocratic idea had replaced their rather egalitarian thought that once apprised of the course of the truly virtuous life, all men could at least aspire toward philosophy, the one divine activity. For Porphyry's contemporaries, philosophy was a

---

[29] Pierre Hadot, *What Is Ancient Philosophy?* (trans. Michael Chase; Cambridge: Belknap Press, 2002), 3. On philosophy as a way of life, see also Bernard McGinn, "Asceticism and Mysticism in Late Antiquity and the Early Middle Ages," in *Asceticism* (ed. Vincent L. Wimbush and Richard Valantasis; Oxford: Oxford University Press, 1998).

profession limited to a select group, the teachers of the religious sects and of the philosophical circles, and dedicated to a single end, knowledge of god.[30]

Philosophy was very much an intellectual practice that required years and years of education. Only a small percentage of the population in the Roman Empire would have received any formal education at all. Of this small percentage, only a few hundred at any given time would likely have been engaged in the advanced study of philosophy or rhetoric. As Edward Watts points out, these advanced studies would likely have had the greatest impact on students and yet it was only a small minority, congregating around the few centers of higher learning in the Roman Empire, who would have been able to afford such training.[31]

Education was a marker of distinction that set off the privileged few from the uncultured masses; it also separated men from women. According to Teresa Morgan, "[Grammar] firmly separates the better from the less well educated, and it does so in radical terms, which devalue the speech as well as the reading of the less privileged."[32] Grammatical education was the second level of education within the *enkyklios paideia* which designated someone as a person of culture, i.e., a person with a considerable amount of symbolic capital.[33] Status was an important factor in determining whether or not one had access to education, but this was even more important for the few female students who were educated at the primary or secondary levels, since their social status was much more of a factor in determining whether or not

---

[30] Patricia Cox, *Biography in Late Antiquity: A Question for the Holy Man* (Berkeley: University of California Press, 1983), 7-8.

[31] Edward Watts, "The Student Self in Late Antiquity" in *Religion and the Self in Antiquity* (ed. David Brakke, Michael L. Satlow, and Steven Weitzman; Bloomington: Indiana University Press, 2005), 236.

[32] Teresa Morgan, *Literate Education in the Hellenistic and Roman Worlds* (Cambridge Classical Studies; Cambridge: Cambridge University Press, 1998/2007), 170-71.

[33] Morgan, *Literate Education*, 33.

they would be educated at all.[34] Women did not participate in rhetorical education as they were denied access to the positions of government work that required such an education.[35] Aside from very few exceptions, they were also not engaged in philosophical training. So, whether or not you were raised to value a philosophical education or had the opportunity to study philosophy was thus very much dependent on the status of the parents to whom one was born and on one's gender.

The hierarchy of symbolic capital reflected here was of significance not just for the students who were earning an education that would distinguish them as elite members of society, but also for the teachers. Cribiore notes, "In general, as today, the higher a teacher stood on the educational pyramid, the more credibility and respect he was accorded and the more secure his economic situation."[36] This was true not only based on the level at which one taught, but also where one taught. The intellectuals who could draw students at the known centers of higher education (e.g., at Rome or Alexandria) were held in higher esteem than those who taught at the same level at smaller cities or in rural villages. Citites that were renowned for their education were able to draw both the best students and the best teachers, thus acting as incubators of symbolic capital within the empire.

Philosophers seem to have understood themselves as a Greek form of a type of elite intellectual figure present in other cultures, discursively situating the philosophical field as analogous to other elite fields found in other cutlures. Diogenes Laertius begins his history of Greek philosophy by describing the parallels between these cultures:

> But the advocates of the theory that philosophy took its rise among the barbarians go on to explain the different forms it assumed in different countries. As to the

---

[34] Raffaella Cribiore, *Gymnastics of the Mind: Greek Education in Hellenistic and Roman Egypt* (Princeton: Princeton University Press, 2001), 4.

[35] Cribiore, *Gymnastics of the Mind*, 56.

[36] Cribiore, *Gymnastics of the Mind*, 59.

Gymnosophists and Druids we are told that they uttered their philosophy in riddles, bidding men to reverence the gods, to abstain from wrongdoing, and to practice courage. That the Gymnosophists at all events despise even death itself is affirmed by Clitarchus in his twelfth book; he also says that the Chaldaeans apply themselves to astronomy and forecasting the future; while the Magi spend their time in the worship of the gods, in sacrifices and in prayers, implying that none but themselves have the ear of the gods.[37]

It is unclear what these groups had in common, at least in the eyes of Diogenes Laertius, but the comparison demonstrates that philosophers were considered to be an elite class of intellectuals who best represented Greek values at least when it came to wisdom and knowledge of divine matters. Philostratus compared the method of the philosophers to that of the prophets of Egypt, Chaldea, and India.[38] In the *Contra Celsum*, Origen also compares philosophers to these groups, but points to specific practices that unite them:

> [Celsus] seems to me to have done something of this sort: he is like a man who went to stay in Egypt, where the Egyptian wise men who have studied their traditional writings give profound philosophical interpretation of what they regard as divine, while the common people hear certain myths of which they are proud, although they do not understand the meaning; and he imagined that he knew all the doctrines of the Egyptians after learning from their common people without having had conversation with any of their priests or having learnt from any of them the secret teachings of the Egyptians. What I have said about the Egyptian wise men and common people can also be seen in the case of the Persian; among them there are mysteries which are explained rationally by the learned

---

[37] Diogenes Laertius I.6 (LCL 184, 6-8).
[38] Philostratus, *Lives of the Sophists*, I.481 (LCL 134, 5).

men among them, but which are taken in their external significance by rather superficial minds and by the common people among them. The same may be said of the Syrians and Indians, and of all who have both myths and interpretative writings.[39]

For Origen, the practice that connects these figures from different cultures is their interpretation of the groups' myths, of the stories that define their culture and yet are, as Origen sees it, misunderstood by the uneducated masses. Not only are the practices shared by these groups similar, but the hierarchies in which certain educated elites are superior to the uneducated are also held in common. Diogenes Laertius and Origen both show that there was a recognition that philosophers were somehow set apart from other members of a community based on their wisdom and understanding of certain types of knowledge and also based on the types of practices in which they engaged. Compared to most people in Greek society, they were superior in respect to wisdom and the intellectual tools needed to achieve it. Diogenes, Philostratus, and Origen all saw philosophy as a uniquely Greek phenomenon with parallels in other cultures.

Despite the similarities between Greek philosophers and these comparable figures among the Egyptians, Chaldaeans, and Indians, the philosophers were not in competition with them due to differences in language, location, and culture. Within the empire, however, philosophers were not the only intellectuals who had specialized education and their own forms of symbolic capital. Lawyers, doctors, and astrologers similarly received advanced specialized training, but the group most similar to the philosophers, and thus the group in the most direct competition with them, was that of the sophists.[40] In juxtaposing these two

---

[39] *CCels* I.12 (SC 132, 108).

[40] On the competition between philosophers and sophists, see especially G. W. Bowersock, *Greek Sophists in the Roman Empire* (Oxford: Clarendon Press, 1969); Stephen Halliwell, "Philosophy and Rhetoric," in *Persuasion: Greek Rhetoric in Action* (ed. Ian Worthington; London: Routledge,

groups, we can get a better sense of philosophers' place in the larger field of power and clarify their distinctive practices and values.

While sophists, as virtuosi in the field of rhetoric, first became prominent in the Greek world in the fifth century B.C.E., there was a renaissance in rhetoric in the beginning in the secondary century C.E., which has often been referred to as the Second Sophistic.[41] As philosophy developed in the wake of Socrates, philosophers claimed to investigate the whole of the cosmos, including what it meant to be a human residing in the cosmos. Sophists were simultaneously making similar claims about what they offered students. Stephen Halliwell sums up the conflict that developed between philosophers and sophists:

> It was in the particular domains of human wisdom – the domains of psychology, ethics, and politics – that the evolution of 'philosophy' became entangled with the potentially competing claims of a 'rhetoric' which asserted its own general competence in the sphere of public discourse...At stake in the emergence and elaboration of these concepts was, in part, the status of intellectual authority and cultural influence – an authority that would give the practitioners and teachers of certain activities a pre-eminent claim to wisdom and expertise (*sophia*), and a corresponding right to present themselves as possessors of politically, socially and educationally valuable knowledge.[42]

Sophists claimed to provide knowledge on a wide range of fields since a skilled speaker ought to be able to speak extemporaneously on any topic in an intelligent manner. As

---

1994), 222-43; and Harry Sidebottom, "Philostratus and the Symbolic Roles of the Sophist and Philosopher," in *Philostratus* (ed. Ewen Bowie and Jaś Elsner; Greek Culture in the Roman World; Cambridge: Cambridge University Press, 2009), 69-99.

[41] The notion of a Second Sophistic comes from Philostratus's *Lives of the Sophists* I.481 (LCL 134, 7).

[42] Halliwell, "Philosophy and Rhetoric," 223.

Quintilian understood things, the study of rhetoric and the study of philosophy had initially been united, only splitting off into separate disciplines when people began to earn money for speaking well. At this point, according to Quintilian, sophists ceased to spend much time on ethics, and philosophers focused more on ethics, while shirking the work required for being able to deliver refined speeches.[43] But, according to Quintilian, this division was false:

> But it is surely the orator who will have the greatest mastery of all such departments of knowledge and the greatest power to express it in words. And if ever he had reached perfection, there would be no need to go to the schools of philosophy for the precepts of virtue. As things stand, it is occasionally necessary to have recourse to those authors who have, as I said above, usurped the better part of the art of oratory after its desertion by the orators and to demand back what is ours by right, not with a view to appropriating their discoveries, but to show them that they have appropriated what in truth belonged to others. Let our ideal orator then be such as to have a genuine title to the name of philosopher.[44]

According to Quintilian's clearly biased opinion, philosophers were simply a lesser form of the true sophist. However, the fact that Quintilian felt the need to recognize the eminence of philosophers within the larger intellectual community, while simultaneously asserting the preeminence of the sophists, reflects the closeness of these two fields, the philosophical and the sophistic, a closeness that bred competition.

The education of sophists and philosophers was nearly identical, though perhaps with different emphases and it was easy for the two groups of educated elites to be confused or conflated.[45] Both Philostratus and Eunapius, writing the lives of

---

[43] Quintilian I.Pr.13-15 (LCL 124, 59).
[44] Quintilian I.Pr.17-18 (LCL 124, 14).
[45] Sidebottom, "Philostratus," 69.

sophists and philosophers, respectively, included figures who were considered to be both philosophers and sophists, thus showing the overlap that existed between the two groups. Philostratus begins his *Lives of the Sophists* acknowledging this overlap:

> The men of former days applied the name 'sophist,' not only to orators whose surpassing eloquence won them a brilliant reputation, but also to philosophers who expounded their theories with ease and fluency. Of these latter, then, I must speak first, because, though they were not actually sophists, they seemed to be so, and hence came to be so called.[46]

Similarly, Aelius Aristides' scathing critique of philosophers, that they do not write lo/goi, adorn festival assemblies, honor the gods, advise cities, comfort the distressed, settle civil discord, or educate the young is all based on a catalogue of practices that were the attributes to sophists, and yet Glen Bowersock has pointed out that philosophers did in fact engage in these very practices.[47] Despite philosophers and sophists sharing several attributes and practices, they were fiercely competitive with each other and criticized each other for their perceived differences.

Sophistry and philosophy therefore represented two paths, at times divergent, at times convergent, that educated elites might take. As two groups consisting mostly of wealthy males, both sophists and philosophers occupied privileged positions within the overall field of power within the Roman Empire. Within this field of power, however, their disparate goals, one directly connected with political life, the other focused more on the cultivation of the self, meant that the fields generated different types of symbolic capital, both of which were held in esteem among cultured Greeks and Romans. Philosophers were respected, even revered, and great ones were likely to draw the attention of political leaders and wealthy patrons, but they were

---
[46] Philostratus, *Lives of the Sophists* I.484 (LCL 134, 13).
[47] Bowersock, *Greek Sophists*, 11.

mostly disconnected from political life and were sometimes criticized for the irrelevance of their work when it came to civic life. The sophists, on the other hand, trained elite males specifically to engage in the arena of civic life.[48] For anyone wanting to engage in a political or legal career, training in rhetoric was essential.[49]

While sophists trained in order to benefit their clients, their patrons, and their cities by speaking effectively in civic contexts, the goal of philosophy, its teleoaffective structure, was tied specifically to learning how to live the good life, often by disengaging from the world of politics. As Martha Nussbaum puts it, "there is in this period broad and deep agreement that the central motivation for philosophizing is the urgency of human suffering, and that the goal of philosophy is human flourishing, or *eudaimonia.*"[50] Greek philosophers recognized that luck and circumstances, and fate for those who believed things were predetermined, could greatly effect one's life. The only way to secure happiness in such circumstances is to have a particular orientation towards the world and control over one's emotions such that misfortune would be unable to cause emotional pain. Curing oneself of such emotional distress meant engaging in various ascetic practices aimed at mitigating or eliminating feelings of desire and attachment. For example, philosophers might limit their intake of food and water, or they might wear only a simple cloak and avoid financial pursuits.[51] As previously mentioned, a philosopher sought to achieve happiness not just

---

[48] See H.I. Marrou, *A History of Education in Antiquity* (trans. George Lamb; Wisconsin Studies in Classics 3; Madison: University of Wisconsin Press, 1956), 210-12.

[49] Bruce W. Winter, *Philo and Paul among the Sophists: Alexandrian and Corinthian Responses to a Julio-Claudian Movement* (2d ed.; Grand Rapids: William B. Eerdmans, 2002), 5.

[50] Martha Nussbaum, *The Therapy of Desire: Theory and Practice in Hellenistic Ethics* (Princeton: Princeton University Press, 1994), 15.

[51] Sidebottom, "Philostratus and the Symbolic Roles of the Sophist and Philosopher," 84.

by studying philosophical doctrines, but by bringing his, or occasionally her, life in line with the doctrines of a particular tradition. As Patricia Cox puts it, "The trait that complements the philosopher's wisdom is his devotion to an ascetic lifestyle."[52] This lifestyle was the practical application of philosophical teachings.

I take asceticism to include a variety of practices meant to reshape one's sense of self. Though often conceived of in terms of self-denial, asceticism is the way by which a person takes on a new type of identity by training the body and mind to conform to an alternative teleoaffective structure. This transformation can be understood as a conversion to a tradition consisting of myths, values, and practices. Richard Valantasis provides the best description of asceticism understood in these terms and deserves to be quoted at length:

> Within this definition, asceticism performs four major social functions. First, asceticism enables the person to function within the re-envisioned or re-created world. Through ritual, new social relations, different articulations of self and body, and through a variety of psychological transformations, the ascetic learns to live within another world...Second, since so much of the ascetic culture relies upon narrative, biography, demonic and angelic psychology, as well as systems of theological anthropology and soteriology, asceticism provides the method for translating these theoretical and strategic concepts into patterns of behavior...Third, the re-envisioning of the world and of human life in it requires intensive perceptual transformation... Asceticism provides the means for this retraining... Fourth, asceticism provides the means through which other domains of knowledge and understanding can be incorporated into the re-envisioned world...Because asceticism operates at the level of behavior, the behavior itself often becomes the focus of attention, yet the goal is generally not known in the specific behavior, but in

---

[52] Cox, *Biography in Late Antiquity*, 25.

the state or experience the behavior is designed to effect. The goal, however, expresses the particular culture's own peculiar systems; the ascetical practices systematize the procedure for movement into the culture; and the individual finds fulfillment and nurture in the integration into the highest aspiration expressed in the goal.[53]

As Valantasis describes it, asceticism is the bodily expression of the values of a community. Philsophers expected their teachings to be internalized and to lead to a transformation of one's way of living. The means by which this transformation was accomplished and expressed was ascetic training. Gavin Flood describes ascetisim similarly as "the internalisation of tradition, the shaping of the narrative of a life in accordance with the narrative of tradition that might be seen as the performance of the memory of tradition."[54] Asceticism shapes the individual and incorporates him into a different community.[55]

Flood also notes that such an incorporation within a tradition entails the invitation of symbolic violence in that it inculcates a novel *habitus* for the ascetic.[56] Since hierarchies are always present within human communities, asceticism aids in the expression, contestation, and appropriation of power. William Deal understands asceticism as always including a political dimension, a dimension of power: "Ascetic practice transforms a person's status within the web of complex social and political relationships and rearranges the power and authority brokered within these relationships in culturally

---

[53] Richard Valantasis, "A Theory of the Social Function of Asceticism," in *Asceticism*, 550-51.

[54] Gavin Flood, *The Ascetic Self: Subjectivity, Memory and Tradition* (Cambridge: Cambridge University Press, 2004), ix.

[55] Bruce J. Malina argues that asceticism, like philosophy, was a practice only reserved for the elites in "Pain, Power, and Personhood: Ascetic Behavior in the Ancient Mediterranean," in *Asceticism*, esp.163.

[56] Flood, *The Ascetic Self*, 6.

significant ways."⁵⁷ As individuals in the ancient Mediterranean world became involved within a philosophical school, the adoption of ascetic practice garnered symbolic capital and improved one's position within the philosophical field. These ascetic practices included not just self-mastery over one's body and desires, but also practices of textual interpretation since these were part and parcel of the process by which a tradition was internalized.⁵⁸

Whether or not an individual's life matched the teachings he or she professed to have adopted was a critical marker of philosophical capital. Plutarch reflects this expectation that the life of a philosopher should match his or her teaching when he says:

> In the first place I require that the consistency of men's doctrines be observed in their way of living, for it is even more necessary that the philosopher's life be in accord with his theory than that the orator's language, as Aeschines says, be identical with that of the law. The reason is that the philosopher's theory is a law freely chosen for his own, - at least it is if they believe philosophy to be not a game of verbal ingenuity played for the sake of glory but, as it really is, an activity worthy of the utmost earnestness.⁵⁹

Plutarch here uses the figure of the sophist as a foil to describe what makes the philosopher different and superior. The values of a philosopher were expected to be demonstrated through action, not just in the context of the classroom, but in every moment of his or her life. This ideal was represented by the idea

---

⁵⁷ William E. Deal, "Toward a Politics of Asceticism: Response to the Three Preceding Papers," in *Asceticism*, 429.

⁵⁸ On the importance of reading for Christian asceticism see: Averil Cameron, "Ascetic Closure and the End of Antiquity," in *Asceticism*, esp. 154; McGinn, "Asceticism and Mysticism," esp. 64. See also, Geoffrey Galt Harpham, *The Ascetic Imperative in Culture and Criticism* (Chicago: University of Chicago Press, 1987).

⁵⁹Plutarch, *De Stoicorum repugnantiis*1033.1A-B, (LCL 470, 413).

of the sage, who epitomized the teachings of a particular school.⁶⁰ The sage, often conceived of in the abstract, functioned as a prototypical model for how to live one's life consistently in every moment. Only through living like a sage could one find the mental stability necessary for achieving *eudaimonia*. Put differently, only through living like a sage could one lay claim to enough philosophical capital to be recognized as a virtuoso within the field.

All the practices in which philosophers and their students engaged were done with this end of *eudaimonia* in mind. It was also this goal which provided the measuring stick for philosophical capital. The closer someone was to the goal and the more actively that person was engaged in the types of practices that would most help in achieving that goal, the more philosophical capital he or she had. To be a philosopher did not just require a passive desire to be happy or united with God in some way, but an active desire expressed through performing practices that made practical sense within this teleoaffective structure. The symbolic capital did not come with mere pretence, but resulted from a philosopher's abililty to internalize his teachings thus altering his *habitus* to match the values of the philosophical field.

Since living this ascetic lifestyle was so central to the philosophical field, those philosophers who failed to live up to their teachings were harshly ridiculed as hypocrites not worthy to be called philosopher. Epictetus, for example, blames such people for contributing to a misconception among non-philosophers that philosophy brings no benefit to the student of philosophy. If someone should adopt the dress, beard, and name of a philosopher, but fail to exhibit self-mastery, that person is not actually a philosopher, according to Epictetus.⁶¹ In making such a claim, Epictetus is attempting to define membership in the philosophical field, but we cannot assume that all philosophers

---

⁶⁰Hadot, *What Is Ancient Philosophy?* 220.
⁶¹ Epictetus, *Discourses* 4.8 (LCL 218, 375-391).

would have agreed with him. Complaints about hypocritical philosophers is evidence for the existence of people who claimed to be philosophers and yet did not live up to what they studied and surely these individuals must have argued that they had a legitimate claim to the title of philosopher. What this tells us is that the goal of living a life that matched one's teachings was a topic of debate, even if it happens to be the case that the writings that have survived seem to all fall on the side of this being an important part of what it meant to be a philosopher. This debate can be seen as one way by which the philosophical field was contested by those who saw themselves as members of that field.

In the third century, the teleoaffective structure of the philosophical field was not only expressed as achieving *eudaimonia*, but as assimilation to the divine. Attempting to arrive at this philosophical *telos* was "an essentially religious endeavor."[62] Cox argues that this was not simply an invention of the biographers of these teachers of philosophy and that the philosophers themselves were aware that others saw them as superior in respect to their connection to the divine.[63] Philostratus, Eunapius, and Porphyry all describe their subjects in divine terms. According to Philostratus, for example, Apollonius of Tyana "said that it was the duty of philosophers of his school to hold converse at the earliest dawn with the gods, but as the day advanced, about the gods, and during the rest of

---

[62] Cox, *Biography in Late Antiquity*, 8. See also Glenn W. Most, "Philosophy and Religion," in *The Cambridge Companion to Greek and Roman Philosophy* (ed. David Sedley; Cambridge: Cambridge University Press, 2003), 300-22; and Philippe Hoffmann, "What Was Commentary in Late Antiquity? The Example of Neoplatonic Commentators," in *A Companion to Ancient Philosophy* (ed. Mary Louise Gill and Pierre Pellegrin; Blackwell Companions to Philosophy 31; Oxford: Blackwell, 2009), 597-622.

[63] Cox, *Biography in Late Antiquity*, 20: "There is some evidence that philosophers were not unwitting recipients of this new honor. Apollonius of Tyana, for example, was fully aware that other men considered him a god, and he himself believed that he was 'superior to most men.' Origen, the great biblical exegete, implied that he possessed the grace of the mind of Christ when he stated that accurate scriptural interpretation demanded that grace."

the day to discuss human affairs in friendly intercourse."[64] Eunapius calls Apollonius "not merely a philosopher but a demigod, half god, half man."[65] And in writing about Plotinus, Porphyry writes that the philosopher's goal was to be united with "the God who is over all things."[66] Such rhetoric elevated the work of philosophers, positioning them, at least in their shared view, above the common masses who were more concerned with material gain and bodily pleasures. From a critical perspective, we cannot take them at their word that they were indeed approaching the divine. Instead, we should see this as a strategy for elevating their ascetic practices to a higher level of value within the philosophical field. It was a discursive tactic for positioning the philosophical field at the pinnacle of the broader field of power while also elevating the philosophical elite above their less accomplished competitors within the field.

In commencing the philosophical life, the first step would have been attending the lectures of a teacher of philosophy. Which school someone chose to attend would likely have been influenced by social networks and previous familiarity with a school's basic doctrines. Porphyry, for example, describes how he was exposed to various philosophers when traveling with his parents.[67] Rarely did someone read philosophical texts alone before attending a school; most often texts would have been mediated by the teacher who could explain and comment on the text.[68] Schools were not physical buildings the way we think of them today, but were simply the collection of students around a teacher who might lecture and discourse "within the perimeter of an ancient temple, in the cell of a monastery, in a private house, or even in the open air, at a street corner or under a tree."[69] To seek out a school to learn philosophy meant seeking out a

---

[64] Philostratus, *The Life of Apollonius of Tyana* I.16 (LCL 16, 47).
[65] Eunapius, *Lives of the Philosophers* 454 (LCL 134, 347).
[66] Porphyry, *Life of Plotinus* 23 (LCL 440, 71).
[67] Porphyry, *Life of Plotinus* 20 (LCL 440, 57).
[68] Cribiore, *Gymnastics of the Mind*, 130.
[69] Cribiore, *Gymnastics of the Mind*, 21.

teacher, who, again, would most likely be teaching in a large city that had a critical mass of well educated, wealthy individuals who might support that school either as patrons or as paying students.

Although achieving the philosophical *telos* was one most clearly expressed through ascetic practices, for most philosophers intellectual practices were a central component of their life, especially the most basic practices of reading and interpreting texts. Reading is such a widespread phenomenon now that the significance of such practices in antiquity can easily escape us. Within a school, texts would have been read aloud. The ability to easily read a text written in *scripta continua* only came with years of education and practice. In fact, the word for the reading performed by a teacher was *epanagignōskein* which implied an authoritative reading.[70] There are various ways in which the simple textual performance of reading and explaining a text demonstrated accumulated symbolic capital and positioned one as an authority. Just the presence of texts, which were hard to come by, would show that the one in possession of the book had access to the material resources necessary for buying or producing texts in antiquity, which may seem ironic since philosophers were supposed to be renouncing material goods and engaging in ascetic practices. Then, the ability to read and explain the terms, especially technical philosophical terms that might differ in meaning from author to author would have positioned the teacher (or advanced student) above other students within the field, and certainly above the vast majority of other people, most of whom could not even read. Thus, "in groups where written texts were central, individuals able to serve as text-brokers accordingly occupied a position of power and prestige."[71] This prestige reflected years of study, but also

---

[70] H. Gregory Snyder, *Teachers and Texts in the Ancient World: Philosophers, Jews and Christians* (Religion in the First Christian Centuries; London: Routledge, 2000), 23.

[71] Snyder, *Teachers and Texts*, 3.

substantial material means in order to access books and sustain oneself through years of study.[72]

Gábor Betegh explains that this interest in texts, something we do not see during the birth of philosophy in fifth century Athens, was the "outcome of an interplay of complex intellectual and institutional developments." [73] According to Betegh, Sulla's destruction of Athens and the subsequent dispersion of philosophers to other cities led later philosophers to turn to the texts written by the founders of their schools as authoritative writings since they were no longer able to access the traditional knowledge maintained by the line of teachers who could trace their intellectual lineage back to Plato, Aristotle, Zeno, or other such figures. As Philippe Hoffman points out, philosophical schools had exegesis at "the heart of philosophical pedagogy," so understanding and commenting on these authoritative texts took on greater significance within schools in the Roman Empire.[74] Within a school then, there would be a canon of authoritative books and, later, respected commentaries that explained those books and interpreting these texts. The interpretation of these texts was a central practice which garnered and expressed significant philosophical capital.[75]

Even with the importance of reading and understanding these authoritative texts, however, this was not as important as the internalization of those practices in the service of the ultimate goal of self-mastery. It was not enough simply to understand texts in a disengaged fashion. Epictetus, for example chastises a student in one of his lectures for mistaking the goal of philosophical study:

---

[72] Grafton and Williams, *Christianity and the Transformation of the Book*, 55.

[73] Gábor Betegh, "The Transmission of Ancient Wisdom: Texts, Doxographies, Libraries," in *The Cambridge History of Philosophy in Late Antiquity* (ed. Lloyd P. Gerson; Cambridge: Cambridge University Press, 2010), 1:26.

[74] Hoffmann, "Commentary in Late Antiquity," 597.

[75] Hoffmann, "Commentary in Late Antiquity," 605.

> "Take the treatise *Upon Choice* and see how I have mastered it." It is not *that* I am looking into, you slave, but how you act in your choices and refusals, your desires and aversions, how you go at things, and apply yourself to them, and prepare yourself, whether you are acting in harmony with nature therein, or out of harmony with it.[76]

Epictetus could explain the foundational texts of Stoicism, but he stressed, in rather harsh terms in this instance, that book learning was useless if it did not lead one to transform his or her life accordingly. By calling the student he is addressing as a "slave", Epictetus is making it clear that mere book learning was not enough for achieving *eudaimonia*.

Teachers of philosophy not only lectured on texts, but also engaged in discussion with students and with other, sometimes rival, philosophers. Some philosophers kept their lectures closed to the public, but others, such as Plotinus, preferred to open their lectures to anyone.[77] A good example of a teacher's discourses would be the "writings" we have of Epictetus, which are not his writings at all, but are the transcriptions of lectures and debates that one of Epictetus's disciples, the historian Arrian, wrote down and preserved for posterity. Debates with rival philosophers might happen at the school's regular meeting place or in a more public arena depending on the nature of the debate.[78] Such discursive practices demonstrated a mastery of philosophical doctrines, an ability to think on one's feet, and a familiarity with the texts and teachings of other schools as well, all capabilities

---

[76] Epictetus, *Discourses*, I.4.14 (LCL 131, 31).

[77] Porphyry, *Life of Plotinus* 1 (LCL 440, 3).

[78] Sidebottom, "Philostratus," 83. Sometimes these debates turned into personal rivalries between philosophers, such as those between Apollonius of Tyana and Euphrates of Tyre or between Polemo and Favorinus, both of which are described in Philostratus's *Lives of the Sophists* 488, 490 (LCL 134, 19 and 27, respectively).

that came with years of study and were reflective of a given person's philosophical capital.[79]

The commitment to this philosophical lifestyle was usually marked in a seemingly more superficial way through the adoption of a simple cloak as one's everyday dress and, for men, with growing a beard. Sidebottom explains, "Uncoiffed hair and beard marked the philosopher as free from artificial social niceties, free to adorn the inner man not the outer, living a life according to nature."[80] The beard demonstrated one's lack of interest in physical presentation and the cultivation of one's appearance, while simultaneously being a very specific interest in physical self-presentation. As a symbol of philosophical capital, the beard and cloak represented a commitment to the philosophical way of life and functioned as a marker of identity. Thus, although the beard and cloak were a supposed reflection of a lack of concern about how one was viewed according to standard norms for the wealthy elite, they were simultaneously an important visible display within the philosophical field that was meant to earn a philosopher respect amongst his peers.

At the level of self-presentation, the sophist and the philosopher differed about as much as two groups could. As Sidebottom notes, "The symbols of the sophist and philosopher were constructed in contrast to each other."[81] Whereas the philosopher wore a simple cloak and beard, the sophist was to be meticulous in maintaining an elegant appearance, which would include wearing expensive clothing, shaving, and depilating. Through their appearance, facial expressions, tone, and gestures, sophists tried to display the most attractive, refined, and educated elements of the urban elite.[82] Sidebottom writes, "If the image of the sophist represented the ultimate insider, a member of the urban elite only more so, the philosopher evoked the

---

[79] Grafton and Williams, *Christianity and the Transformation of the Book*, 35.

[80] Sidebottom, "Philostratus," 96.

[81] Sidebottom, "Philostratus," 82.

[82] Sidebottom, "Philostratus," 77.

outsider."[83] Their opposing orientations toward culture were thus reflected in their self-presentation. These symbols, though seemingly unimportant for self-mastery, were symbolic markers of one's affiliation with the philosophical field.

In the hierarchy of philosophers, there were many students, but only a select few who would go on to be teachers in their own right. The passing on of knowledge in oral and textual forms was another important practice amongst philosophers. Teaching demonstrated a philosopher's wisdom and also his compassion for others, since the goal of such teaching was to help others achieve *eudaimonia*.[84] Another way of demonstrating this erudition, and thus further accumulating philosophical capital, was to write. Again, the ability to access the material resources necessary for writing texts was itself demonstrative of considerable symbolic capital, whether those materials were provided from one's own resources or from a patron who was willing to contribute financially to a philosopher's work. As the following quote from Porphyry reveals, though, there was a way to order hierarchically those who wrote depending on the type of writings produced:

> Of those who wrote, some produced nothing except compilations and transcriptions of what their predecessors had composed, like Eucleides and Democritus and Proclinus...One might class Heliodorus with these, for he too contributed nothing to the ordered exposition of philosophical thought beyond what his elders had said in their lectures.[85]

Porphyry seems to be expressing a level of disdain for those who were unable to produce anything innovative in their writings. Transcribing lectures, as Arrian did with the lectures of Epictetus, did not earn him the same level of philosophical capital as would

---

[83] Sidebottom, "Philostratus," 95.
[84] Cox, *Biography in Late Antiquity*, 24.
[85] Porphyry, *Life of Plotinus*, 20 (LCL 440, 59).

accrue to someone like Chryssipus or Plotinus whose writings transformed their respective schools.

Philosophical texts could come in many forms. Plato wrote dialogues, although the extent to which these dialogues were meant to reveal the official doctrines of the Academy, if such an orthodoxy even existed, is debated. The dialogue continued to be a favored philosophical genre for centuries. Philosophers also made use of epistles, both real (i.e., written by whom they purport to be written and addressed and sent to their purported recipient) and fictive (i.e., not sent to the addressee, addressed to an imagined recipient, or not written by its purported author). [86] Others composed epic poems to pass on doctrines or wrote plays in which the characters reflected those doctrines. Finally, in the imperial period, philosophers produced two other types of texts with greater frequency, the commentary and the handbook.[87] Regardless of the form it took, textual production accrued considerable philosophical capital to the author and set him apart from his peers.

It is worth noting just how important the production of commentaries had become by the third century C.E. Frans De Haas explains the factors that contributed to the popularity of commentaries at this time: (1) lacking access to an oral tradition and a successor to the founder, philosophers' self-definition came to depend on the study of canonical texts; (2) the evolution of Greek required lexical commentaries; (3) trying to establish authoritative versions amidst an awareness of diverging manuscript traditions; (4) arguing for establishing internal consistency by detecting spurious additions; (5) bringing various texts to bear on a particular single truth; (6) commentary itself

---

[86] John Dillon, "Philosophy as a Profession in Late Antiquity," in *Approaching Late Antiquity: The Transformation from Early to Late Antiquity* (ed. Simon Swain and Mark Edwards; Oxford: Oxford University Press, 2004), 409-10.

[87] Michael Trapp, "Philosophy, Scholarship, and the World of Learning in the Severan Period," in *Severan Culture* (ed. Simon Swain, Stephen Harrison, and JaśElsner; Cambridge: Cambridge University Press, 2007), 484.

was a spiritual exercise which contributed to the progress of the soul towards union with the monad.[88] Textual criticism thus became part and parcel of the teleoaffective structure of the philosophical field. The tools of analysis that had originally been developed at the library in Alexandria for studying texts became powerful tools for helping philosophers progress toward their goal of assimilating to the divine. The use of textual criticism for the purposes of interpretation made it so that "that exegesis was the province of the educator, and specifically of the philosophical educator."[89] As stated in Chapter One, however, the rhetoric of revealing the truth already held in these authoritative texts is one way for a philosopher to introduce new ideas foreign to those original texts, however much these philosophical exegetes might have denied their own practice of eisegesis.

Given this small set of practices, we can gain a sense of how we might construe the philosophical field of the third century. In the most prominent positions would be those philosophers who had earned the most symbolic capital. These would be the founders of new schools of thought or those who rejuvenated an existing school by claiming to revive its original teachings. These innovations would have been promulgated through their teachings and writings. Such a level was necessarily achieved by only a few individuals given the restrictions on how many schools might exist at any given time and given the general tendency to continue a tradition or synthesize it with others instead of being innovative. Slightly below this level would be teachers who drew many disciples through their mastery of doctrines and their ability to pass on those doctrines. The number and nature of those disciples would both play a role in determining a philosopher's status within the field. Philosophers who wrote texts of any sort would earn

---

[88] Frans A. J. de Haas, "Late Ancient Philosophy," in *The Cambridge Companion to Greek and Roman Philosophy* (ed. David Sedley; Cambridge: Cambridge University Press, 2003), 253-54.

[89] Lamberton, *Homer the Theologian*, 13.

philosophical capital through the production and dissemination of these texts. To be sure, there was greater capital accrued to those who were prolific, provided those writings were original in content.[90] Most importantly, philosophers jostling for a position of authority within the field had to live in accordance with their teachings. Philosophers who failed to do so were scathingly lambasted by others. Those who lived exemplary lives, however, would be treated almost as divine and accorded the highest honors. One thus accrued philosophical capital by dressing the part, by being in control of one's emotions, and by consistently making the choices appropriate for one's view of the world.

2.3 Origen the Philosopher

This sketch of the philosophical field in the third century C.E. has not included what might seem to be critical for any sort of history of philosophy – the ideas taught and discussed in the various schools of philosophy. As previously mentioned, scholars have often debated Origen's relationship to philosophy based on the substance of his ideas, but in order to situate Origen within a field of social practices and symbolic capital, it is his life and values that must be the criteria by which he is to be judged. I will now show why Origen should be seen as a Christian philosopher and situate him within this field of Greek philosophy based on what we know of his life and what he says about Christianity and its relationship to philosophy, especially in the *Contra Celsum*.[91] I will show that Origen embodied the

---

[90] Chrysippus, for example, was one of the most prolific writers of antiquity, producing more than 700 separate works. He was well respected for his hard work, but also heavily criticized for repeating arguments in different texts or making use of long quotes, once reportedly copying nearly all of Euripides' *Medea* in a treatise. Diogenes Laertius VII.180 (LCL 185, 289).

[91] Peter W. Martens, argues that such an analysis of Origen's view of the importance the biblical scholar within Christianity is missing in the scholarship, but he does not cite the work of Carl Vernon Harris which explores this very topic. Martens also focuses too much on textual criticism as if Origen's ultimate goal was to understand the meaning of the scriptures, in a way that might reflect a modern scholar's intellectual goal, but this does not

values of the philosophical field and sought to reshape the field in his favor by arguing that Christianity was the culmination of a philosophical tradition that he respected and hoped to transform.

Origen was critical of Greek philosophy, to be sure, but he also praised what the philosophers taught about the nature of God and about ethics, a topic which Origen claimed was almost identical as it was taught by Christians and philosophers.[92] The similarity in ethical teachings was apparently noted by Celsus as Origen writes, "Let us see also how he thinks he can criticize *ethical teaching* on the grounds that it *is commonplace and in comparison with the other philosophers contains no teaching that is impressive or new.*"[93] When discussing the overlap between philosophy and Christianity, Origen readily admits that "almost the total philosophy which is called moral and natural holds the same views we do."[94] For Origen, this similarity was proof that God would hold everyone accountable for their actions since everyone had access to teachings about what it meant to live virtuously.[95] Living virtuously, as we will see in detail in Chapter Three, is what led Christians back to their original state of being in constant contemplation of God as souls purified of their material existence and of sin, which led them away from God. Christianity and philosophy thus had identical teleoaffective structures in Origen's view, which explains their similarities.

Origen also acknowledged that philosophers could make great arguments, especially when it came to ethics and theology.

---

do justice to the role of textual scholarship in a broader teleoaffective structure in antiquity. See *Origen and Scripture: The Contours of the Exegetical Life* (Oxford Early Christian Studies; Oxford: Oxford University Press, 2012), 4.

[92] Origen was not "almost instinctively hostile to philosophy," as Alan Scott describes him, although he did not consider it complete without the wisdom provided in Christian scriptures. Alan Scott, *Origen and the Life of the Stars: A History of an Idea* (Oxford Early Christian Studies; Oxford: Clarendon Press, 1991), 113.

[93] *CCels* I.4 (SC 132, 84).
[94] *HomGn* 14.3 (SC 7, 340).
[95] *CCels* I.4 (SC 132, 84).

In his homilies on Genesis, Origen intereprets Abimelech as a symbol for philosophers:

> Abimelech means 'my father is king.' It seems to me, therefore, that this Abimelech represents the studious and wise men of the world, who by giving attention to philosophy, although they do not reach the complete and perfect rule of piety, nevertheless perceive that God is the father and king of all things. Those, therefore, so far as it pertains to ethics, that is moral philosophy, are acknowledged also to have given attention in some respects to purity of heart and to have sought the inspiration of divine virtue with all their mind and zeal.[96]

And again in a later homily on Genesis, Origen says:

> If you remember how, in what preceeds [sic], we said of Abimelech that he represents the learned and wise of the world, who have comprehended many things even of the truth through the learning of philosophy, you can understand how he can be neither always in dissension nor always at peace with Isaac who represents the Word of God in the Law. For philosophy is neither opposed to everything in the Law of God nor in harmony with everything.
>
> For many of the philosophers write that there is one God who has created all things. In this they agree with the Law of God. Some also have added this, that God both made and rules all things by his Word and it is the Word of God by which all things are directed. In this they write in harmony not only with the Law, but with the Gospels.[97]

Origen was critical of some of the teachings of philosophers and obviously disagreed about the Greek disparagement of Christian

---

[96] *HomGn* 6.2, (SC 7, 188).
[97] *HomGn* 14.3 (SC 7, 340).

scriptures, but he was not completely dismissive of Greek learning either.

With similar notions of the nature of God and what it took to be assimilated to God, it is not surprising that Origen would find much to admire about philosophy or that he would structure his schools in Alexandria and Caesarea in a manner that was common among philosophical schools. Origen even argued that teaching advanced Christians something different from what he taught catechumens was a practice he shared with philosophers, as both he and the philosophers recognized that not everyone could comprehend their deeper teachings.[98] Due to such similarities, Christianity was also prone to the same types of divisions as found among philosophical schools, a fact that Origen saw as not being fair fodder for attacking Christianity, but as proof that it was similar to philosophy which Greeks, and this case Celsus in particular, held in high esteem.[99]

Despite these positive comparisons, Origen was also critical of philosophy, at least in terms of what philosophers taught and he was wary that such teachings might lead Christians to join schools (*haereses*) that did not teach the truth (as Origen believed that he did).[100] Origen often used Egypt as a symbol of such dangers: "The waters of Egypt are the erring and slippery teachings of the philosophers."[101] Such teachings as well as the work of astrologers and prophets posed a threat to Christians in that they seemed persuasive and might draw them away from "the love of God." [102] So, while Christians might benefit from the study of philosophy, it also posed a threat, and needed to be approached cautiously.

---

[98] *CCels* I.7 (SC 132, 94).

[99] *CCels* V.61 (SC 147, 164).

[100] *EpistGreg* 2.

[101] *HomEx* 4.6 (SC 321, 132), "Aquae Aegypti erratica et lubrica philosophorum sunt dogmata…"

[102] See, for example, *HomJd* 2.3 (SC 389, 84) and *HomJr* 27.4 (SC 238, 328 [Hom 50]).

Origen taught that God sent messages to all people, but before the incarnation of the Logos in the person of Jesus, the teachings of God only came to people imperfectly. Christianity represented the complete teachings of God through the Logos and was available to all people. Origen does not seem to have thought of Christianity as an *ethnos*, but as a category that could encompass people from all *ethnē*.[103] Since each *ethnos* received the truth imperfectly, their teachers of wisdom could be only partially right. Christianity was not just comparable to philosophy, therefore, but was, according to Origen, the true path to assimilating to the divine; it was the culmination of philosophy. Philosophy could thus be used as a protreptic leading to Christianity, but Christianity was superior, not just analogous, to philosophy in Origen's eyes. Origen explains this hierarchy in the *Contra Celsum*:

> But if you were to show me teachers who give preparatory teaching in philosophy and train people in philosophical study, I would not dissuade young men from listening to these; but after they had first been trained in a general education and in philosophical thought I would try to lead them on to the exalted height, unknown to the multitude, of the profoundest doctrines of the Christians, who discourse about the greatest and most advanced truths, proving and showing that this philosophy was taught by the prophets of God and the apostles of Jesus.[104]

In Book 1 of the *Contra Celsum*, Origen even states that "no other course ought to be followed but this alone" when talking about devoting one's life to philosophy.[105] Origen even gave this advice to one of his disciples, Gregory, to whom he writes that he

---

[103] At times, Origen seems to talk about Christianity as the true Israel, and thus as part of the Jewish *ethnos* and and other times as something distinct from Israel. See for example *HomNum* 1.2.1 and *CCels* I.45, respectively, for these descriptions.

[104] *CCels* III.58 (SC 136, 136).

[105] *CCels* I.9 (SC 132, 98).

should "extract from the philosophy of the Greeks what may serve as a course of study or a preparation for Christianity, and from geometry and astronomy what will serve to explain the sacred Scriptures."[106] The debate over whether Origen's teachings were derived from his study of philosophy or from his study of scripture is not important for understanding that Origen had a positive valuation of philosophy and saw it as offering something similar to what Christianity offered. Christians and philosophers may have differed in certain teachings, but they both aimed at achieving a virtuous life and assimilation to God. By describing Christianity as the apogee of philophy, Origen was attempting to alter the philosophical field in such a way as to place Christian philosophers at the top of the philosophical hierearchy.[107]

According to Origen, Christianity's superiority to philosophy was evident not only in its teaching but also in its efficacy among the uneducated masses. Origen did not have a positive opinion of those less educated and well-off as himself, but the fact that even they could be drawn to Christianity and adopt a more virtuous lifestyle was evidence to him that Christianity was able to accomplish something that philosophy, despite the best efforts of philosophers, was unable to do.[108] Origen actually defends Christianity against the criticism of Celsus that Christians reach out to the uneducated by pointing out that Christians at least test people individually before letting them into the community, unlike, as Origen points out, certain philosophers, especially among the Cynics, who publically teach anyone that will pass by.[109] Christianity is available to the masses if they are truly interested in transforming their lives, so Christian teachers are more egalitarian than most philosophers,

---

[106] EpistGreg 1.

[107] Martens, *Origen and Scripture*, 76-77.

[108] In *CCels* VI.16 (SC 147, 218), Origen writes, "For not even a stupid person would praise the poor indiscriminately; the majority of them have very bad characters."

[109] *CCels* III.50-51 (SC 136, 120-22).

but are not indiscriminate in deciding to whom they offer their goods.[110] Of those less educated masses who do become Christians, many of them turned from their former, mistaken beliefs and wicked practices, which Origen argues is proof of Christianity's superiority.[111]

Origen's positive and yet critical remarks about philosophy make sense given his upbringing and affiliation. For this we turn to the descriptions of his life and teaching in Eusebius and Gregory Thaumaturgus. While Book 6 of Eusebius's *Historia Ecclesiastica* is primed for criticism given Eusebius's clear apologetic goals, even Patricia Cox, who has done the most to highlight the hagiographical character of Eusebius's description of Origen, agrees that "Origen was a Christian teacher with a truly philosophical approach; this seems to have been the reality behind Eusebius' confusing explanations."[112] Cox finds it ironic that Eusebius stresses the philosophical lifestyle of Origen since Origen himself clearly identified as a Christian, but in so doing she re-presents the problematic dichotomy that separates Christian practices from philosophical practices.[113] For Eusebius, as for Origen, such a dichotomy did not make sense. Cox is especially dubious about the stories of Origen's childhood and the deptictions of him as orthodox from a fourth-century perspective, but these will not concern us here.[114] For now, it is enough to focus on the descriptions of Origen as an ascetic teacher who taught philosophy and Christian doctrine as the summit of all learning.

Origen was born in Egypt, probably in Alexandria circa 185 C.E. Origen's father, Leonides, was clearly a person of some means and was a thoroughly Hellenized Christian who was able to provide for the rearing and education of his nine children, the

---

[110] *CCels* VII.60 (SC 150, 154).
[111] *CCels* I.9 (SC 132, 100).
[112] Cox, *Biography in Late Antiquity*, 99.
[113] Cox, *Biography in Late Antiquity*, 69.
[114] Cox, *Biography in Late Antiquity*, 73.

oldest being Origen.[115] According to Eusebius, Leonides saw to it that Origen learned about the Christian scriptures while pursuing a traditional Greek education.[116] As discussed above, his ability to provide Origen with such an education would mean that Leonides was wealthy and understood the benefits of a traditional education. When Origen was sixteen, his father was arrested for being a Christian, another indication of his prominence within the community. Leonides was executed and his property confiscated for the imperial treasury, leaving his wife and children destitute.

Origen was then taken into the home of a wealthy woman who supported him and other prominent Christian intellectuals including a certain Paul from Antioch who was considered a gnostic.[117] Many Christians would come to listen to Paul, including his housemate Origen who supposedly would refuse to join with him in prayer, although this is an instance in which Eusebius's desire to present Origen as orthodox should make us doubt his description. Origen's education and his having been taken in by a affluent Christian is evidence of his father's prominence within the Alexandrian community. Although it is impossible to know just how wealthy Leonides was, the fact that he had property, provided for a large family, and was able provide for Origen's education all point to him as having been financially secure. This means that from his birth and throughout his childhood, Origen was surrounded by elite figures in Alexandria who continued to provide for him after his father's death.

In order to earn money and support his siblings and mother after Leonides's death, Origen taught as a *grammatikos*, a teacher of Greek literature and literary criticism. A *grammatikos*

---

[115] Joseph Wilson Trigg, *Origen: The Bible and Philosophy in the Third-century Church* (Atlanta: John Knox Press, 1983), 10.

[116] Eusebius, *HE* VI.2 (LCL 265, 13).

[117] Eusebius, *HE* VI.2 (LCL 265, 15). Plotinus was similarly provided for in his youth by Zeuthus and Castricius, Porphyry, *Life of Plotinus* 2 (LCL 440, 7).

would explain a text in terms of its grammatical, historical, intertextual, and ethical elements.[118] Explaining the grammar would also include explaining unusual words or tracing the etymology of a word in order to bring out a particular sense that might be missed by one's students.[119] According to Heine,

> The *grammatikos* treated a text in four stages: (1) criticism to determine what the ancient author had written; (2) reading and recitation, which included memorizing the text for recitation; (3) explanation of the text, which included the meaning of unusual words, the explanation of unusual grammatical forms, etymology, and the explanation of the content or story of the text; and (4) judgment, or the moral teaching of the text."[120]

The skills that Origen needed to utilize as a successful *grammatikos* were the very ones he would employ in explicating the Christian scriptures both in his homilies and in his commentaries. They were the types of skills that were critical in gaining symbolic capital within the philosophical field which Origen would later join.

At some point, whether because, as Eusebius says, Origen no longer believed that teaching Greek literature was compatable with his life as a Christian, or for some other reason, he gave up being a *grammatikos* and sold all or most of his non-Christian library so he would not have to be dependent on others for his basic needs.[121] Around this time he was approached by certain non-Christians to teach them about Christianity, which he readily accepted since no one else was in charge of catechetical

---

[118] Cribiore, *Gymnastics of the Mind*, 206.

[119] Cribiore, *Gymnastics of the Mind*, 207-9.

[120] Ronald E. Heine, *Origen: Scholarship in the Service of the Church* (Christian Theology in Context; Oxford: Oxford University Press, 2010), 61.

[121] Seeing as how important the teaching of Greek philosophy continued to be in Origen's schools, the justification Eusebius gives for Origen leaving behind teaching as a *grammatikos* should be doubted. The fact, though, that his library was substantial enough that he could sustain himself by selling it is further proof of his father's wealth.

training at the time.¹²² The Stoic Pantaenus, as later tradition held, had instituted some sort of Christian school in Alexandria, which Clement later oversaw before leaving Alexandria during the same persecution in which Leonides was executed.¹²³ Origen's disciples seem to have been primarily converts at this time, including two brothers, Plutarch and Heraclas, the former of which would go on to be executed for his Christian affiliation, the latter going on to take over catechetical instruction from Origen and eventually becoming bishop of Alexandria.¹²⁴ Origen's students were both male and female and were numerous enough that guards had to be posted where Origen lived, apparently to protect him from mobs of non-Christians angry at his influence.¹²⁵

Eventually, Origen grew frustrated that he was spending so much time in teaching the basic aspects of Christianity and had so little time for in-depth study or teaching. He decided to divide his students into beginner and advanced students, a division common to the philosophical schools. He set his student Heraclas over the beginner students so that he could take on the more advanced instruction himself.¹²⁶ McGuckin sees this transition as evidence of Origen's growing sense of himself more of "Rhetor-Philosopher" than a "Grammarian".¹²⁷ Origen did not just focus on the advanced study of Christian scriptures. He instructed his

---

¹²² Eusebius, *HE* VI.3 (LCL 265, 19-21). Eusebius also tells us that Demetrius entrusted Origen with all catechetical instruction, but it unclear whether this was a formal recognition of a school already created or if this was the call that initiated the catechetical training.

¹²³ Eusebius, *HE* VI.6 (LCL 265, 27-29). It is unlikely that this was a formal school and it is unclear that there was a clear succession of any sort between Clement and Origen as we find in other philosophical schools.

¹²⁴ Eusebius, *HE* VI.3 (LCL 265, 17).

¹²⁵ Eusebius, *HE* VI.3-4 (LCL 265, 23-7).

¹²⁶ Eusebius, *HE* VI.15 (LCL 265, 51).

¹²⁷ John Anthony McGuckin, "The Life of Origen (ca. 186-255)," in *The Westminster Handbook to Origen* (ed. John Anthony McGuckin; The Westminster Handbook to Christian Theology; Louisville: Westminster John Knox Press, 2004), 7.

students, not all of whom were Christian, in all aspects of Greek and Christian philosophy, including geometry, mathematics, and the doctrines of the various schools of thought, earning him a reputation as a great philosopher in his own right.[128] As Watts points out, Origen "was essentially the head of a sub-group of intellectuals. These men participated in the general Alexandrian philosophical and cultural world, but they also remained sensitive to the religious implications of their participation."[129] Between Origen's Christian and non-Christian students, there would have been more things that held them together as elite educated individuals than would have separated them based on their religious differences and in Origen they found a teacher whose methods and teachings were quite similar to other philosophical schools in the city.[130] This is perhaps best exemplified by Heraclas who continued to take classes with Ammonius Saccas after joining Origen's school and who continued to dress like a philosopher even after his ordination.[131]

As Origen's reputation as a prominent Christian intellectual grew and spread, he travelled about the Empire engaging in debates, lecturing at episcopal councils, and meeting political officials. In 212 C.E. he visited Rome to meet with the bishop Zephyrinus and the teachers of Christian community there.[132] Two years later, a leader in Arabia sent letters to Demetrius requesting that Origen be sent to him.[133] McGuckin and Lyman both see these trips as evidence of Origen's desire to be a prominent Christian philosopher.[134] Between these trips

---

[128] Eusebius, *HE* VI.18 (LCL 265, 55).

[129] Edward J. Watts, *City and School in Late Antique Athens and Alexandria* (The Transformation of the Classical Heritage 41; Berkeley: University of California Press, 2006), 166-67.

[130] Watts, *City and School*, 162.

[131] Watts, *City and School*, 164.

[132] Tripolitis, *Origen*, 3.

[133] Tripolitis, *Origen*, 3.

[134] Lyman, *Christology and Cosmology*, 41; McGuckin, "The Life of Origen", 8.

abroad, in 215 C.E. persecutions broke out once again in Alexandria and Origen fled to Palestine where Theoctistus and Alexander, the bishops of Caesarea and Jerusalem, respectively, asked him to preach and lecture on the Christian scriptures.[135] Demetrius, the bishop at Alexandria, did not think it right that Origen lecture publicly in another church, especially since he was not ordained and he demanded that Origen return to Alexandria, which he did. In 222 C.E., Origen's fame was such that he visited Antioch at the request of Julia Mamaea, the mother of the new emperor Alexander Severus, an honor previously extended to Philostratus.[136] Around 229/230 C.E., Origen travelled again to Palestine and Greece to deal with certain ecclesiastical matters. It was on this trip abroad that Origen was made a presbyter in Caesarea, thus assuring a permanent rift between him and Demetrius.[137] Origen's trips abroad are evidence of the reputation he held among Christians as the preeminent Christian scholar of his generation.

There had been tension between Origen and his bishop Demetrius for some time before Origen had had enough and left Alexandria for Caesarea Maritima. This conflict was probably not just over Origen being ordained as a presbyter by the bishops of Caesarea and Jerusalem in 231. It is more likely that his ordination was the straw that broke the proverbial camel's back after years of tension between the two leading figures of the Alexandrian Christian community. This tension may be what lay behind the following comment in Origen's Homily 9 on Ezekiel:

> What sin, then, is greater than all sins? Assuredly it is that on account of which even the devil fell. What is that sin into which such a great sublimity fell, so that the Apostle says: 'having been puffed up he falls into the

---

[135] Tripolitis, *Origen*, 3; Eusebius, *HE* VI.19 (LCL 265, 63-5).

[136] Eusebius, *HE* VI.21 (LCL 265, 67-9); Laurie Guy, *Introducing Early Christianity: A Topical Survey of Its Life, Beliefs and Practices* (Downers Grove: InterVarsity Press, 2004), 89; Grafton and Williams, *Christianity and the Transformation of the Book*, 79.

[137] Eusebius, *HE* VI.23 (LCL 265, 71).

judgment of the devil'? Haughtiness, pride, arrogance - this is the sin of the devil. It is on account of these transgressions that he emigrated from heaven to earth...Pride is greater than all sins, and is the principal sin of the devil himself...The material of pride is wealth, rank, and worldly glory.

Very often the priesthood and Levitical rank are a cause of pride in men who do not realize that they have ecclesiastical positions. How many who have been raised to the priesthood have forgotten humility! As if the purpose of their ordination was for them to cease being humble![138]

Origen had a critical view of people holding church office. The office itself indicated nothing if the person holding that office did not lead a moral life and was not well versed in scripture. Rowan Williams argues that Origen's anti-clerical stance did not arise simply from his conflict with Demetrius, who most scholars assume to have been jealous of Origen's fame and popularity, but probably had its roots in the loosely structured Alexandrian church whose leaders often had to flee persecution, including during the persecution that counted Leonides among its victims.

In other words, during Origen's formative years as a teacher in Alexandria the sense of the episcopate as an unambiguous focus for the unity even of the Catholic party (using that as the least confusing term for the Christian whose position emerged as normative) must have been weak, largely, though probably not entirely because of the confused situation during sever persecution. The implied role of the influential lay patron giving protection and support even-handedly to teachers of differing theological persuasion must also reflect a certain relativising of episcopal control, very comprehensible in a context where, as we might deduce from Clement, the Christian faith is of increasing interest to the wealthy. Throughout his career, as is well-

---

[138] HomEz 9.2 (SC 352, 304-6).

known, Origen preserved a measure of scepticism about the spiritual authority, in the strictest sense, of ordained leaders, and I don't think this was entirely a symptom of his later and bitter quarrel with Demetirus. It fits well with the atmosphere of these significant early years as *grammatikos* and catechist.[139]

Origen's statements that seem critical of church officials have often been read as reflecting his struggles with Demetrius, but those struggles themselves are reflective of a broader struggle over how they viewed authority within the Christian community. There likely was a personal aspect to this fight that stemmed from Origen's resentment toward Demetrius, but that alone would not explain Origen's entire mythic system.

Upon moving to Caesarea, Origen set up a new school where he continued to attract non-Christian students, including the brothers Gregory and Athendoros. Gregory, later called Thaumaturgos, studied with Origen for years before returning to his hometown, the Caesarea in Pontus.[140] We can learn much about Origen's practices as a teacher from Gregory's speech, which itself represents a genre "paralleled many times by the addresses pagan students gave when leaving their teachers."[141] At Caesarea, Origen continued to teach all aspects of philosophical study including geometry, physics, and astrology.[142] He would lecture, but also engage his students in Socratic dialogue.[143]

Gregory's panegyric presents Origen strictly in philosophical terms.

---

[139] Rowan D. Williams, "Origen: Between Orthodoxy and Heresy," in *Origeniana Septima: Origenes in den auseinandersetzungen des 4. Jarhunderts.* (ed. W.A. Bienert and U. Kühneweg; Bibliotheca Ephemeridum Theologicarum Lovaniensium 137; Leuven: Leuven University Press, 1999), 6-7.

[140] Eusebius, *HE* VI.30 (LCL 265, 83).

[141] Watts, "The Student Self," 246.

[142] Gregory Thaumaturgus 110-13.

[143] Gregory Thaumaturgus 97.

> This man too at first used words to exhort me to philosophize, while preceding the verbal exhortation with his deeds. He did not just recite memorized formulas; on the contrary, he did not even think it worthwhile to speak if he could not do so with a pure intention and striving to put his words into action. He tried to offer himself as an example of the person trying to live a good life whom he described in words, and presented a paradigm, I would like to say, of the sage.[144]

The life that Origen was drawing them to was not the Christian life, but the philosophical life, of which Christianity was the most comprehensive and true expression. Origen heaped praise on philosophy and said that only those people who pursued philosophy truly lived life.[145] Without engaging in the philosophical life, he taught, one could not properly demonstrate true piety to god.[146] The chief aim of this life was to bring one's impulses under control, just as was the case with other Greek philosophical schools. Only through achieving this could one become "disciplined and tranquil and godlike and truly happy."[147] This life was not for everyone, however, and Origen only "deemed those worthy to philosophize who with every energy had read all the writings of the ancient philosophers and singers."[148] Origen's advanced courses were only available to those who had access to an advanced education, i.e., the wealthy urban elite. Only they could afford to pursue the years of study necessary for achieving the philosophical life and thus to be truly pious.

The flip side of Origen's preference for working with these advanced students was his frustration at the less educated masses who made up perhaps the majority of the audience for his

---

[144] Gregory Thaumaturgus 135 (SC148, 150).
[145] Gregory Thaumaturgus 76.
[146] Gregory Thaumaturgus 79.
[147] Gregory Thaumaturgus 116 (SC 148, 144).
[148] Gregory Thaumaturgus 151-152.

homilies.[149] Harris reminds us that Origen delivered his homilies to "a mixed, shifting, and not always orderly congregation. The services were daily and long, and some of the brethren attended only on feast-days, and not always then."[150] Origen would use his homilies as an opportunity to chastise his lazy, less committed congregants, especially on feast days that drew a larger crowd.[151] The following quote from *HomGn* 10 is a good example of Origen's rebuking his congregants:

> You spend most of this time, no rather almost all of it in mundane occupations; you pass some of it in the marketplace, some in business; one has time for the country, another for lawsuits, and no one or very few have time to hear the word of God.
>
> But why do I reproach you about occupations? Why do I complain about absences? Even when you are present and placed in the Church you are not attentive, but you waste your time on common everyday stories; you turn your backs to the word of God or to the divine readings. I fear that the Lord may say to you also that which is said through the prophet: 'They turned their backs to me and not their faces.'
>
> What, then, shall I do, to whom the ministry of the word is entrusted? The words which have been read are mystical. They must be explained in allegorical secrets. Can I throw 'the pearls' of the word of God to your deaf and averted ears? The Apostle did not do so.[152]

The lax attitude among them irritated the Christian philosopher, who saw them as dishonoring him and his teachings because "they do not study Scripture in their homes, they do not attend church where they can hear it publicly, or they attend church

---

[149] Harris, *Origen*, 190.
[150] Harris, *Origen*, 176.
[151] See for example *HomGn* 10.1 (SC 7, 254).
[152] *HomGn* 10.1 (SC 7, 256). See also *HomJos* 1.7 (SC 71, 112).

regularly but do not listen."[153] As Martens points out, Origen "often referred to Christians with this limited education experience or commitment as the *simpliciores*, that is, the 'simpler ones.'"[154] Origen appealed to them to study scripture with greater devotion, but his appeals fell on deaf ears it seems.

This is not just evidence of their laziness or apathy, however. From a Bourdieuian perspective, it is clear that those whom Origen called the *simpliciores* did not have the access or means by which they might devote themselves so completely to philosophy, nor did they likely have any inclination to since such inclinations are themselves the product of a *habitus* that resulted from already being a member of certain class of society.[155] Origen was thus chastising them for not completely buying into the rules of the philosophical field as he saw them.

In addition to the teaching Origen did, he also worked to establish an authoritative set of texts for his community and an authoritative interpretation of those texts, drawing on a number of established textual and exegetical methods in doing so. His training and experience as a *grammatikos* both shaped some of his goals and provided him with the tools he needed to achieve those goals. This was best evidenced by his immense *Hexapla*, a synoptic presentation of the Hebrew scriptures and the various Greek translations that were in circulation. In this massive work, "Origen applied the critical signs invented by Zenodotus to mark where the Septuagint either added to the Hebrew text or lacked things that were in that text."[156] Origen wanted an authoritative version of the Jewish scriptures and he drew on the methods used by Greek scholars engaged in similar text critical work at the

---

[153] Dively Lauro, *The Soul and Spirit of Scripture*, 101.

[154] Martens, *Origen and Scripture*, 27.

[155] Martens, *Origen and Scripture*, 28. Martens does not address the sociological implications of Origen's frustrations, although he does note the fact that it was only the elites who were drawn to Origen's philosophical teachings.

[156] Heine, *Origen*, 23.

Great Library in Alexandria.[157] As Grafton and Williams describe it:

> The Hexapla was one of the greatest single monuments of Roman scholarship, and the first serious product of the application to Christian culture of the tools of Greek philology and criticism. Its complexity and sheer costliness demonstrate the resources that Origen could draw upon, both in terms of patronage and in terms of skilled labor. In this respect, it was a typical product of the philosophical, as well as the grammatical, culture of the first half of the third century, an era that largely followed the pattern of the so-called Second Sophistic of the previous century.[158]

The project not only would have contributed to Origen's symbolic capital, but also would likely have caused others to see Jewish scriptures as an important text, worthy of the sort of attention and study that other Greek texts such as those of Homer or Plato would have had.

At Caesarea, Origen was able to establish a library, which would go on to be the greatest Christian library of the ancient world. Origen, who had once sold his own personal library to make ends meet, was now able to build a much greater one thanks to his patrons. Again, Grafton and Williams describe this interest in books as evidence of Origen's philosophical inclinations:

> Origen's bibliographic habits fit well within the philosophical culture of the book as it emerged under the Roman Empire. The contents and scope of Origen's collection, the uses to which he put his books, the ways he read and the genres in which he chose to write, and

---

[157] John Anthony McGuckin, ed., *The Westminster Handbook to Origen* (Westminster Handbooks to Christian Theology; Louisville: Westminster/John Knox Press, 2004), 27.

[158] Grafton and Williams, *Christianity and the Transformation of the Book*, 131.

the social matrix that supported his work, all find strong parallels among the philosophers...

Everywhere he lived and traveled, Origen accumulated Jewish and Christian books, which would have interested few contemporary philosophers. This part of his library set Origen apart from others who filled similar social roles. But close examination makes clear that these were differences of content, not form or function. The kinds of Jewish and Christian literature that Origen had on hand, the ways that he collected books, and the uses to which he put them closely parallel the habits of the philosophers within their own traditions.[159]

Origen's interest in texts of all sorts is indicative of his philosophical background. It also highlights the symbolic capital that went along with the collection, study, and commentary upon texts. Like other philosophers of his day, Origen's path to self-mastery was one that had textual study at its center, so he, like those philosophers, also valued education and the resources necessary to making education the center of one's life.

Origen did not just read and collect books, he also wrote them, of course. He was most prolific as a commentator on scriptures, both through having his homilies copied down by stenographers and also by writing his own commentaries aimed at a more advanced audience.[160] I will discuss Origen's use of allegory in greater depth in Chapter 4, but for now it is worth noting that his reliance on allegory as a method of interpretation placed him squarely within the philosophical tradition. As Heine notes, Origen's use of what he called "comparing spiritual things with spiritual" was comparable to what "the grammarians referred to as 'Homer interpreting Homer', and the philosophers called 'Aristotle interpreting Aristotle'."[161] Origen's textual and

---

[159] Grafton and Williams, *Christianity and the Transformation of the Book*, 56-57.

[160] Heine, *Origen*, 23.

[161] Heine, "Articulating Identity," 213. See also Heine, *Origen*, 23.

interpretive methods were methods shared with grammarians and philosophers, most notably the Stoics who had long been interpreting Homer allegorically. [162]

We should not make the mistake of seeing Origen's textual studies as an end unto themselves. Like other philosophers, Origen's goal in all of this was also assimiliation to the divine. [163] One should study scripture in order to internalize its teachings, drawing one ever closer to God. Dively Lauro argues that "Origen understands perfection in virtue and wisdom to constitute the full imitation of Christ that is necessary for salvation."[164] This imitation reflected a conquering of sin and a return toward the pre-fall state of constant contemplation of god alone, as I will describe in greater detail in Chapter Three.

As we should expect of a Christian philosopher, it was not enough that Origen teach texts; he also also lived a life that was in line with his teachings and which he believed would draw him closer to God. Eusebius depicted Origen in philosophical terms, expressly tying his categorization of philosopher to his lifestyle, not the content of his teachings. It is worth quoting him at length.

> For in his practical conduct were to be found to a truly marvelous degree the right actions of a most genuine philosophy (for – as the saying goes – 'as was his speech, so was his manner of life' that he displayed, and 'as his manner of life, so his speech'), and it was especially for this reason that, with the co-operation of the divine power, he brought so very many to share his zeal…For a great number of years he continued to live like a philosopher in this wise, putting aside everything that might lead to youthful lusts; all day long his discipline was to perform labours of no light character, and the greater part of the night he devoted himself to studying

---

[162] For a brief history of the use of allegory by Christian writers before Origen, see: R.P.C. Hanson, *Allegory & Event: A Study of the Sources and Significance of Origen's Interpretation of Scripture* (Louisville: Westminster John Knox Press, 1959/2002), 97-129.

[163] Torjesen, *Hermeneutical Procedure and Theological Method*, 121.

[164] Dively Lauro, *The Soul and Spirit of Scripture*, 4.

> the divine Scriptures; and he persevered, as far as possible, in the most philosophic manner of life, at one time disciplining himself by fasting, at another measuring out the time for sleep, which he was careful to take, never on a couch, but on the floor. And above all he considered that those sayings of the Saviour in the Gospel ought to be kept which exhort us not [to provide] two coats nor to use shoes, nor, indeed, to be worn out with thoughts about the future. Yeah, he was possessed of a zeal beyond his years, and by persevering in cold and nakedness and going to the extremest limit of poverty, he greatly astounded his followers, causing grief to numbers who besought him to share their goods, when they saw the labour that he bestowed on teaching divine things. But he was not one to slacken endurance. He is said, for example, to have walked for many years without using a shoe of any description, yeah more, to have refrained for a great many years from the use of wine and all except necessary food, so that he actually incurred the risk of upsetting and injuring his stomach.[165]

Origen's ascetic practices distinguished him as a philosopher who strove to manage his emotions and control his impulses. Living a virtuous life was, for Origen, the responsibility of the teacher who should promote virtue not just through doctrine, but through personal example.[166]

As someone who lived a life of ascetic renunciation, it is not surprising that Origen was critical of Christians who failed to live up to their teachings, especially if they were in positions of authority.[167]

> There are in the Church certain ones who believe in God, have faith in God, and acquiesce in all the divine precepts. Furthermore, they are conscientious towards

---

[165] Eusebius, *HE* VI.3 (LCL 265, 18-20).
[166] Harris, *Origen*, 169.
[167] See for example *HomEz* 2.2.

the servants of God and desire to serve them, for they also are fully ready and prepared for the furnishing of the Church or for the ministry. But, in fact, they are completely disgusting in their actions and particular habit of life, wrapped up with vices and not wholly 'putting away the old self with its actions.' Indeed they are enveloped in ancient vices and offensive faults, just as those persons were covered over with old garments and shoes. Apart from the fact that they believe in God and seem to be conscientious towards the servants of God or the worship of the Church, they make no attempt to correct or alter their habits. For those, therefore, our Lord Jesus certainly permits salvation, but their salvation itself, in a certain measure, does not escape a note of infamy.[168]

In *HomEz* 2.1, Origen calls these teachers "false prophets" because their lives do not match up with what they preach.[169] Like the philosophers, Origen was critical of such hypocrites and was content to divorce them from the name of Christian since their lives were not in accordance with Christian teaching.

This brief overview of Origen's life and practices is enough to make it clear that he is best understood as a Christian philosopher. Not only did Origen study and teach Greek philosophy, his life and values reflected them almost completely, with the important distinction being that Christian scriptures were his authoritative texts and that he understood his practices within a Christian public narrative that was at odds with the dominant Greek, Roman, and Jewish public narratives. Origen engaged in matching discursive and non-discursive practices aimed at controlling his emotions, which was the most basic definition of a philosopher. He taught literature, mathematics, geometry, physics, ethics, and interpretation. He also produced works, including commentaries on Christian scriptures, in a

---

[168] *HomJos* 10.1 (SC 71, 270-72).
[169] *HomEz* 2.1.

manner similar to his Greek philosophical contemporaries. These practices earned him symbolic capital among his peers, even his non-Christian peers, and garnered him access to the highest halls of power in the Roman Empire. Based on this approach to categorization in which practices become central, Origen was clearly a Christian philosopher.

2.4 Conclusion – Mapping the Philosophical Field

As we noted above, the philosophical field occupied a privileged position within the overarching field of power. Within this context, Christian theology did not compete with Jewish, Greek, or Roman theology, but Christian intellectuals did indeed compete with Jewish, Greek, and Roman intellectuals for position within this field. As Arthur Urbano puts it:

> In the present discussion, we can see Greek and Christian intellectuals competing to produce and acquire the same forms of cultural capital – for example, education, intellectual lineages, access to or possession of important philosophical texts, and the skills to read, interpret, and debate their content, including a linguistic capital of specialized philosophical terminology and the fora to engage in debate, rhetorical and literary.[170]

Within this field, we have to assume that Jewish and Christian philosophers would have typically been judged by their Greek peers to occupy lower levels in the philosophical field since they privileged non-traditional texts as supremely authoritative. The novelty of Christianity and its illicit status would have also caused Greek philosophers to look down on their Christian peers. This was not the way Origen would have seen the field, however. Origen employed a rhetoric of superiority in an attempt to redefine the philosophical field to privilege the Christian version of philosophy. Even with Origen's profound respect for the

---

[170] Arthur Urbano, Jr., "'Read It Also to the Gentiles': The Displacement and Recasting of the Philosopher in the *Vita Antonii*," CH 77 (December 2008), 888.

Greek philosophical tradition, he "sets up a slightly different form of disagreement between himself and the pagans ...presenting himself as offering, not a different model altogether, but rather a fuller version of the model developed by the pagans themselves."[171] Not only had Origen earned the respect of non-Greek philosophers and educated people in general despite his affiliation with an illicit superstition, he also provided the most comprehensive representation to date of Christianity as the ultimate expression of philosophy.

As a prominent Christian philosopher, Origen was among the elite of the elite. His positionality is reflected in the importance he placed on textual study, self-mastery, and assimilaiton to the divine. The values Origen held as a philosopher gave shape to a hierarchy within the church as Origen conceived of it. Origen's vision of Christianity, unsurprisingly, reflects these values, which are homologous to the values of the wealthy, educated elite within the Roman Empire. This is exactly what we should expect, since religion, as Bourdieu states, "inculcates a system of consecrated practices and representations whose structure (structured) reproduces, in a transfigured and therefore misrecognizable form, the structure of economic and social relations in force in a determinate social formation."[172] It is to the narrative form of this ideology to which we now turn.

---

[171] George R. Boys-Stones, *Post-Hellenistic Philosophy: A Study of its Development from the Stoics to Origen* (Oxford: Oxford University Press, 2001), 198.

[172] Pierre Bourdieu, "Genesis and Structure of the Religious Field," *CSR* 13 (1991): 14. As Jacques Berlinerblau reminds us, ideologues, such as Origen, are not always conscious of the ideological nature of their work. Berlinerblau explains that *doxa* generates a misrecognition on the part of the ideologue, and, with this in mind, we should not judge Origen as being consciously self-serving however much his mythology may have been self-serving. Jacques Berlinerblau, "Ideology, Pierre Bourdieu's *doxa*, and the Hebrew Bible," *Semeia* 87 (1999): 193-214.

ORIGEN THE MYTHMAKER

As previously discussed, fields of cultural production are hierarchically structured based on each field's form of symbolic capital. Since fields exist across time, they require some sort of narrative which explains the field's existence, values, and structures. Myths serve this function. As individuals come to be enculturated within a field, they come to internalize these myths as part of their own life story. This internalization goes hand in hand with one's development of a field's *habitus*, giving meaning to the practices one is inclined to engage in based on that *habitus*. Myths are necessary components of fields and help to achieve the symbolic violence that "elicits the consent of *both* the dominant and the dominated" within a field.[1]

In Chapter One, I suggested that myth is a useful designation over collective memory for the shared narratives that link a community to its past.[2] To call such a narrative "myth", as opposed to collective memory, for example, is to acknowledge (1) that our relationships to our shared past is not one of memory, but of internalizing a history that stretches beyond our personal histories, both diachronically and synchronically, and (2) that there are inherent in these narratives certain social, hierarchical structures which these myths serve to authorize. It is this latter connection between myths and power that leads Bruce Lincoln to call myth "ideology in narrative form." Lincoln links myth to ideology because a myth provides a taxonomy in narrative form and does so in a way that "naturalizes and legitimates it," which is precisely the function, he argues, of ideology.[3] Hierarchically

---

[1] David Swartz, *Culture & Power: The Sociology of Pierre Bourdieu* (Chicago: University of Chicago Press, 1997), 89.

[2] See pages 57-59 above.

[3] Bruce Lincoln, *Theorizing Myth: Narrative, Ideology, and Scholarship* (Chicago: University of Chicago Press, 1999), 147.

structured social formations are not legitimated simply by the existence of the narratives, but in the propagation, reception, and internalization of these narratives. The imposition of myths is an active, ongoing process, therefore, leading Burton Mack and Russell McCutcheon to prefer the gerund mythmaking, which emphasizes the work that goes into creating and sustaining these narrative ideologies.

Myths, like fields, are constantly in flux, sometimes through changes in their content and sometimes through their interpretation. Lincoln states:

> Myths are not snapshot representations of stable taxonomies and hierarchies, as functionalists would have it. Rather, the relation between social order and the stories told about it is much looser and - as a result - considerably more dynamic, for this loose fit creates possibilities for rival narrators, who modify aspects of the established order as depicted in prior variants, with consequences that can be far-reaching if and when audiences come to perceive those innovative representations as reality. Skilled narrators can do this subtly or bluntly, in play or dead earnest, and everything in between. In so doing, they use instruments that most often assist in the reproduction of the sociotaxonomic order to recalibrate that order by introducing new categories, eliminating old ones, or revising both categories and the hierarchic orders in which they are organized.[4]

The same description might have been used by Bourdieu to describe fields. Lincoln and Bourdieu share a post-structuralist view of social order that allows them to see the ruptures that allow for social change, both in social formation and in the myths that legitimate those formations. Perhaps the most significant locus of mythic alteration is the act of interpreting myths. The nature of interpretation allows people to introduce meanings

---

[4] Lincoln, *Theorizing Myth*, 150.

different than the ones intended by those who created the myths in the first instance, but to do so in such a way that grounds the new meaning in an already established mythic system. Interpretations can attempt to stay close to the lexical meaning of a narrative, or they can expand upon it creating new narratives in the process which supplant the original narrative.

We might also conceptualize all this as the creation of a particular form of social identity. If someone identifies as a member of a community, she internalizes the myth of this community as part of her own, thus having this mythic public narrative as part of her own narrative identity. Identities are generally not considered as hierarchical or in terms of symbolic capital, but even gender, ethnic, or religious identity is wrapped up in analogous issues of normative definitions and contestation over the contours of that identity. Even in the case of Christianity, to be a Christian is to be embedded automatically in a hierarchy based on symbolic capital. Origen's mythmaking is part and parcel of the ongoing process of Christian identity formation, since he is active in creating a narrative identity through the interpretation of scripture. This myth, as we will see, corresponds to Origen's philosophical field and supplants the original meaning of the scriptural text through the process of interpretation. For Origen, as we will see, to be a good Christian means to be a good philosopher, as his particular brand of Christian identity is wrapped up in the practices and symbolic capital of the philosophical field. To talk of Origen the mythmaker is to talk about him as a cultural producer who proffers a myth of the Christian field (and simultaneously of the Greek philosophical field) that is reflective of his own preunderstandings and dispositions.

Throughout the rest of this chapter, I will describe the contours of Origen's myth, which begins with the creation of spiritual beings and human souls and ends with the final return of all beings back to their original state of perfect assimilation to the divine. Having described this narrative of redemption, I will then show how hierarchies based on the pursuit of wisdom pervade the narrative, thus establishing a myth of Christianity as a philosophical system in which the educated elite are in the most privileged positions in the community.

3.1 *Prolegomena* to Studying Origen's Mythmaking

Scholars have long debated whether or not Origen should be considered a systematic thinker and, concomitantly, to what extent *On First Principles* (*PArch*) should be considered reliable evidence for what that system would be.[5] As David Runia interprets the debate, scholars who see Origen more in terms of Greek philosophical thought tend to categorize him as systematic and see the *PArch* as a summary of that system as evidenced by its title, which was a common one for presenting such philosophical teachings. Scholars who prefer to see Origen as first and foremost a man of the church, on the other hand, have argued that Origen was *not* systematic, but instead drew his teachings from scripture and was less than consistent in his thought when you take his full corpus into account.[6] Henri Crouzel, for one, was a staunch advocate of the latter position, seeing Origen as more of a Christian mystic than a Greek philosopher.[7] Joseph Trigg, however, writing specifically against Crouzel, suggests that the dichotomy between systematic and inconsistent is a false one. Origen, Trigg argues, is self-consciously presenting a system of thought in the *PArch*, though

---

[5] On the problems with Koetschau's edition of the *PArch*, see Ronnie J. Rombs, "A Note on the Status of Origen's *De Principiis* in English," *VC* 61 (2007): 21-29.

I have chosen to use the Greek title and abbreviation for this work, but quote authors who prefer the Latin *De principiis*, or *DP*.

[6] David T. Runia, *Philo in Early Christian Literature: A Survey* (Minneapolis, Minn.: Fortress Press, 1993) 169. See also Ulrich Berner, *Origenes* (Darmstatt: Wissenschaftliche Buchgesellschaft, 1981).

[7] Henri Crouzel, "Origène est-il un systématique?" in *Origène et la philosophie* (Paris: Aubier, 1962), 179-215; ibid., *Origen* (trans A. S. Worrall; San Francisco: Harper & Row, 1989), 167-69.

it is one that grows, changes, and develops over time.[8] Origen was indeed a man of the church in Trigg's view, but that did not stop him from expanding on basic doctrines in order to present a body of knowledge meant to enlighten.

Another way of thinking of Origen's system is, of course, as his myth, especially given the narrative dimensions of his theology and the hierarchies which define it. The *PArch* provides a grand narrative on a cosmic scale which explains the nature of the human condition, situating the individual and the Christian community within a trajectory of spiritual rebellion and redemption. Part and parcel of this myth is an explication of the nature of the divine, including teachings about God, Christ, the Holy Spirit, Satan, and a host of angels and demons populating the cosmos. The narrative begins before creation and carries through to the *eschaton*, thus providing a Christian myth that incorporates all time and all of creation. Origen may not have discussed every aspect of this myth in detail in the *PArch*, but he certainly presents the master narrative that guided his scriptural interpretations throughout the rest of his life.

In what follows, I refer to Origen's teachings both in the *PArch* and in his homilies as his myth or his mythic system. The nature of his interpretive works is such that they do not offer comprehensive overviews of his system, but they do abound in examples, modifications, and extensions of that system. On the one hand, this combination of sources should not be problematic for the present work since I am primarily concerned with broad themes in Origen's myth and the overall hierarchical structure which is consistent throughout. On the other hand, this approach to Origen's interpretive works, with the *PArch* providing the master narrative through which his homilies and commentaries are understood, does beg the question of how much Origen's audiences knew of his overall system. Surely not everyone

---

[8] Joseph W. Trigg, "Was Origen Systematic? A Reappraisal," in *Studia Patristica XLI* (ed. F. Young, M. Edwards, and P. Parvis; Leuven: Peeters, 2006), 259-64.

present at church while Origen was giving a homily would have read or even heard of the *PArch*. Given the nature of our evidence, however, we can only speculate as to how well Origen's overall system would have been understood or accepted as authoritative, but those are questions to which we will turn in the final chapter.[9]

Since I am less interested in getting at theological specificities about the nature of the trinity, to take just one example, and since I am interested more in the broad themes of Origen's myth, questions about the reliability of Origen's texts as they have come down to us primarily through the Latin translations of Rufnius and Jerome are of less consequence for this study than has been the case for other scholars. Henry Chadwick and Ronald Heine have concluded in their comparisons of Rufinus's translation with the extant Greek fragments of Origen's *Commentary on Romans* and *Homilies on Genesis*, respectively, that Rufinus generally presents Origen's thoughts faithfully, although his wording and style may often be his own.[10] Rufinus has been criticized the most, even since his own day, for changing what Origen had to say respecting the nature of the trinity and of the salvation of Satan, but neither of these issues is of enough significance to the present study for it to matter if Rufinus had indeed consistently misrepresented Origen on these matters. For our purposes, the Latin translations of both Rufinus and Jerome will suffice for analyzing the hierarchies at play in Origen's Christian myth.

As Karen Torjesen has pointed out, questions about the reliability of the translations of Origen's work are more

---

[9] The problem of reconstructing the text Origen's audience would have heard out of the extant texts is particularly well exemplified in the *Homilies on Numbers*, which, as Rufinus describes in the preface to his translation, is a combination of Origen's homilies and his scholia.

[10] For arguments about the reliability of Rufinus's Latin translations see Ronald E. Heine, "Introduction," in *Homilies on Genesis and Exodus* (Fathers of the Church; Washington: The Catholic University of America Press, 1982/2002), 27-40.

important when trying to determine the content of his theology, since this seems to have been a significant concern's of Rufinus when translating Origen. It is not as significant when examining, as Torjesen does, Origen's exegetical method or even the pedagogical structure of his hermeneutics.[11]

3.2 The Pedagogical Structure of Origen's Christian Mythology

We turn then to Origen's *Peri archon* written probably some time between 219 and 230 C.E. while Origen was still living in Alexandria, so he would have been in his late 30's or so at the time of its composition and he was already a respected Christian intellectual whose fame had earned him an audience with Julia Mammaea in Antioch. According to Eusebius, it was some time after this meeting that Origen began work on his commentaries, three of which Origen mentions in the *PArch*.[12] Its title and content situate the work within a recognized philosophical genre of texts on nature or physics, a topic which includes what we might typically call theology. The work itself is divided into four books and a preface. Origen first discusses God, Christ, and the Holy Spirit. Then he explains the nature of and relationship between rational beings who have fallen away from their primordial state of constant focus on God the Father. These include angels, daemons, and human beings. Next he explains how rational beings will be reconciled to God and return to their primordial state through a process of purification and spiritual progression. In the final book, Origen provides a theory of scripture and its interpretation, which he presents as the key to knowledge of God and thus to salvation.

---

[11] Karen Jo Torjesen, *Hermeneutical Procedure and Theological Method in Origen's Exegesis* (Patristische Texte und Studien 28; Berlin: Walter de Gruyter; 1986), 18.

[12] Origen mentions his commentaries on Genesis, the Psalms, and Lamentations, as well as his lost treatise on the resurrection. Origen had also started his commentary on John by the time he began the *PArch*. G. W. Butterworth, "Introduction," in *On First Principles* (trans. Henri De Luback; New York: Harper & Row, 1966), xiv-xv.

As Karen Torjesen has demonstrated, Origen's myth is one of pedagogical soteriology.[13] The *telos*, both temporally and ontologically, of Origen's myth comes when all rational beings have been redeemed by their savior and this process of redemption is conceived of in educational terms. Origen's metanarrative is one of God bringing his creation back to him through the work of his Son acting as a sort of teacher, whose teachings are presented in the scriptures of the Jews and Christians. The work required on the part of the individual is similarly educational in nature, with an emphasis on the study of scripture, on texts, being the primary means to achieving purification and salvation. The pedagogical nature of Origen's soteriology is neither accidental nor maliciously manipulative, but is an outgrowth of Origen's own experiences as a Christian philosopher. His myth is one that comes out of and simultaneously elevates and honors the work of intellectuals and this is not without consequences.

Origen's myth starts and ends with God the Father, an incorporeal, eternal, benevolent, omnipotent, and omniscient monad holding dominion over all things. God created everything, a position Origen articulated against the view of various Gnostics who taught that the demiurge represented in the Hebrew scriptures was not the same God worshipped by the Christians. Contra the gnostics, "Origen describes god not only as the highest source of goodness, but also as the active creator of a good world who continues to give good things to all creatures."[14] As the creator of all, God held dominion over celestial entities and over everything on earth.[15] Book I of the *PArch* begins with a refutation of the concept that God has a

---

[13] Karen Torjesen, "Pedagogical Soteriology from Clement to Origen," in *Origeniana Quarta* (ed. Emerich Coreth, Walter Kern, and Hans Rotter; Vienna: Tyrolia-Verlag, 1987), 370-78.

[14] Rebecca Lyman, *Christology and Cosmology: Models of Divine Activity in Origen, Eusebius, and Athanasius* (Oxford Theological Monographs; Oxford: Oxford University Press, 1993), 50.

[15] *PArch* I. 2.10.

corporeal nature, signaling the importance of the deity's incorporeality to Origen's theology. Because God does not have a body, God cannot be seen, heard, or touched, but can only be known intellectually. Knowledge of God then comes about through contemplation and is best achieved when the other, physical senses have been quieted.

Christ, the only-begotten Son of God, is God's Word, understood to be his wisdom. As God's wisdom, the Son has existed eternally since it cannot be conceived that God would exist without a manifestation of wisdom. As Origen explains, the Son is understood as wisdom not for being wise, but for being "a certain thing which makes men wise by revealing and imparting itself to the minds of such as are able to receive its influence and intelligence."[16] The Son is the mediating being connecting God with his creation through enlightenment and also as that aspect through which God exercises dominion.[17] "The importance of the Logos paradigm in Origen's Christology can hardly be overstressed. The accommodation of the incarnate Logos as the essential, intellectual, spiritual link between the uncreated Father and the various levels of created being was the centre of his thought and method."[18] The pedagogical nature of Origen's myth is tied directly to figure of the Logos, defining Christ as the educating aspect of God.

The relationship between God, the Holy Spirit, and other rational beings is similarly one of the Holy Spirit imparting knowledge of God to those who are worthy. The Holy Spirit is greater than all rational beings insofar as it has direct knowledge of God unmediated by Christ and is, like God and Christ, eternal, benevolent, and incorporeal. Origen does not make any clear statements about the ontological status of the Holy Spirit, but focuses instead on its activities, especially among the saints. In *PArch* I.3.5, Origen states that God and Christ are at work

---

[16] *PArch* I. 2.2.
[17] *PArch* I. 2.10.
[18] Lyman, *Christology and Cosmology*, 39.

amongst all rational beings but the Holy Spirit is only active in those who are already "walking in the ways of Jesus Christ."[19] The Holy Spirit, he says, enters Christians at baptism and thus would not have been present in non-Christians or even in catechumens.

God, Christ, and the Holy Spirit all have a role the process of redemption. Torjesen describes the process by which the person must progress:

> There are stages which they must pass through, each of which is the appropriate preparation for the next. The work of the Holy Spirit is purification. He is the principle of holiness. Through participation in the Holy Spirit the soul itself becomes holy. This is the preparatory stage which makes it possible for the soul to receive the wisdom and knowledge of Christ. As Logos, Christ is wisdom and knowledge and the soul receives the gifts of wisdom and knowledge through participation in the Logos. The final stage of this progression is participation in God the Father. Participation in the perfection of the Father means the perfection of the soul, its own complete likeness to God or divinization. Divinization in Origen is the restoration of the soul to its original state of perfect knowledge of God. It is achieved by the imitation of God, by an imitation of both his virtues and his knowledge. It is this imitation of God which reconstitutes the original 'likeness' to God and the likeness is the necessary condition for perfect knowledge of Him. The three stages in the progress of the soul, corresponding to the threefold activity of the Trinity are, therefore, purification, knowledge and perfection.[20]

---

[19] *PArch* I. 3.5. Origen makes it clear here that God is superior to the Son and that both of them are superior to the Holy Spirit, but his subordinationist views are not important for understanding the pedagogical structure of his mythology.

[20] Torjesen, *Hermeneutical Procedure and Theological Method*, 72; *PArch* I.3.8.

Origen's entire mythology is thus centered on a pedagogical soteriology in which all members of the trinity have a role. Not only do they have a role, but their very existence seems to be predicated on their roles in returning rational beings to their primordial existence of connection with God. On the flip side, to be a human being striving towards that connection was likewise to be engaged in educational activities - activities that required learning, knowledge, and reflection. As was the case among Platonists, for Origen, "doctrines are the essential element in the progress of the soul."[21]

If knowledge of God is mediated by Christ and the Holy Spirit, it is to rational beings that such knowledge is directed.[22] The souls of rational beings seem to have had an eternal existence along with God, Christ, and the Holy Spirit. As Henri Crouzel describes them, they "were absorbed in the contemplation of God and formed the Church of the pre-existence, united like the Bride to the Bridegroom with the pre-existent intelligence that was joined to the Word and had been created with them."[23] As divine entities, these *logika* were "incorporeal, immortal and perfect, participating in the life of the Logos and in perfect communion with God."[24] These *logika*, originally all equal in their relationship to God, at some point fell away from god and became the souls of human beings, angels, and demons.[25] The reason Origen gives for the fall is tied to his insistence on free will as being a defining characteristic of rational beings. Engaged in the constant contemplation of God, some became satiated and lazy and began to neglect God, thus distancing themselves from God.[26] Origen

---

[21] Torjesen, *Hermeneutical Procedure and Theological Method*, 121.

[22] Origen desctibes the fall of rational beings in *PArch* I.4.

[23] Crouzel, *Origen*, 206.

[24] Antonia Tripolitis, *Origen: A Critical Reading* (American University Studies Series VII: Theology and Religion 8; New York: Peter Lang, 1985), 20.

[25] Crouzel suggests that the equality among rational beings was a response to Valentinian beliefs that souls varied in in the degree of their awareness based on a natural difference among souls, *Origen*, 208.

[26] Crouzel, *Origen*, 210.

draws on one theory for the etymology of the word *psyche*, suggesting that the *logika* became souls by becoming cold, *psychos*, when they withdrew themselves from the warmth of the intellectual fire that is God. They did not all fall to the same degree, though, taking up various positions in the physical universe and becoming angels, daemons, and humans.

In addition to the work of the trinity, the other fallen rational beings also play an active role in the battle for embodied human souls. These beings themselves are divided into angels, who help souls move back toward God, and daemons, who try to bind souls more tightly to their fleshly existence. Each human being is attended by one angel and one daemon, both inspiring thoughts and emotions appropriate to their nature. [27] These beings engage in a constant battle over the souls of human beings as Origen states in *HomJd* 3.3: "And they are savior-angels who are represented in the outward figure either of Othniel or Ehud, because, as we often have shown, not only are we attacked by contrary powers, but also divine and good powers are sent to our aid by the Lord."[28] Not only are humans subject to these intermediary *logika*, but the Holy Spirit can even be driven out of a person should that individual give in to an evil spirit.[29] In addition to these, there are other angels and demons such as those assigned to the nations.[30] Some demons take up residence in temples and are worshipped as gods, relishing in the smoke of the sacrifices.[31]

Each person's struggle for self-control is thus part of an ongoing cosmic battle between good and evil, the result being that, as Origen puts it,

> all our mortal life is full of struggles and conflicts, since we are resisted and thwarted by those who can see no

---

[27] *PArch* III.2.4; *HomLc* XIII.4.

[28] *HomJd* 3.3 (SC 389, 102).

[29] *HomNum* 6.3 (SC 415, 148).

[30] Alan Scott, *Origen and the Life of the Stars: A History of an Idea* (Oxford Early Christian Studies; Oxford: Clarendon Press, 1991), 136.

[31] *ExhMart*, XXXII, XLV.

way back to the better state from which they fell, those, namely, who are called 'the devil and his angels', and other orders of wicked beings whom the apostle enumerates among the opposing powers.[32]

Being apart from God and being embroiled in sin, understood as that which continues to keep one from God is the defining characteristic of being human. Since an embodied existence is only necessary for those beings that have turned from God of their own accord, anything that draws one toward corporeal existence is considered to be sinful. For Origen, sin is an issue of the mind, of intention and of love. If someone loves wealth, that person is sinful, not because they have wealth, but because their love of wealth draws them away from God. Love should only be directed to God and to other people.

The embodied person is made up of three parts: flesh, the soul, and the spirit, with the soul being intermediate between the other two and able to be drawn in either direction. "If [the spirit] gives itself up to the delights of the flesh, it makes men fleshly; if, however, it joins itself to the spirit, it causes a man to be 'in the spirit' and on this account to be called spiritual."[33] The soul is not divided into two parts, a higher and a lower one, but it has these two tendencies, one towards the flesh and one towards the spirit.[34] The flesh represents all that is sinful and apart from God and so, the spiritual person wars against the flesh.[35] In this battle for control of the the individual soul, the soul can become assimilated either entirely to the flesh or to the spirit.[36] This tripartite division within the individual is mirrored in a tripartite anthropology in which Origen characterizes people as fleshly, soulish, and spiritual. These divisions exist based on the extent to which Christ is present in each individual based on

---

[32] *PArch* I.6.3.
[33] *PArch* III.4.2.
[34] Crouzel, *Origen*, 88.
[35] *PArch* III.4.4.
[36] Crouzel, *Origen*, 89.

his own merits.[37] One cannot become spiritual or even soulish without the aid of the Holy Spirit, which means, since only Christians who have been baptized have the Holy Spirit in them, that these people can only be found in the church. Jews and Gentiles are all fleshly or earthly, though not all in the same way since even among these three divisions of rational creatures there are still gradations within each.[38] The entire world, according to Origen, can be mapped out on a hierarchy moving from those who are farthest from God to those who are closest to perfection, with Christian philosophers being at the pinnacle of the hierarchy.

This mythology of the fall and redemption of all rational beings makes up the cosmic aspect of Origen's Christian narrative identity. The cosmic nature of this myth is not detached from history, however. Knowledge of God is tied to the scriptures of the Jewish people and these writings testify to the relationship between God and the Israelites with whom God communicated through his Son and the Holy Spirit. As Origen affirms, against the teachings of Marcion, Valentinus, and other so-called gnostics, the God whose Son came in the person of Jesus was the same God of Adam, Noah, Abraham, Moses, and the Israelite prophets.[39] Similarly, it was the Holy Spirit that inspired the writers of both the Old and the New Testaments.[40] The Jewish people were thus set apart from the Gentiles as God's chosen nation and their history was part of the story of God's ongoing relationship with humans.

What happened to the Jewish people was all a run-up to the most significant historical moment when the Son took human form in the person of Jesus. It was at this time the teachings hidden in the law of Moses were finally revealed in their true form for those who could receive them.[41] Through his lived

---

[37] *PArch* IV.4.2.
[38] *PArch* II.9.3.
[39] *PArch* I.1.4.
[40] *PArch* I.1.4.
[41] *PArch.* IV.1.6.

experiences and his teachings, Jesus exhibited the true meaning hidden in the Jewish scriptures. Anyone who accepted these teachings, i.e. Christians, thus came to supplant the Jews as God's chosen people. The very real sufferings of the Jews that resulted in the destruction of the temple and termination of their sacrificial system was, for Origen, proof of the fact that they failed to understand the true meaning of God's teachings, even as found in their own scriptures since the teachings of the Jewish scriptures, when read literally, could not possibly still be relevant after the destruction of the temple in 70 C.E. For Origen, nothing so signified the death of the Jewish Law as the destruction of the temple and the fact that sacrifices were no longer carried out according to the law. [42] This was proof that the writings of the Old Testament were meant to be understood allegorically - that the literal prescriptions for how to worship God were not to be followed.

In order to be saved, one had to be part of the Christian church, meaning the full community of all Christians, which Origen considered to be, ideally, "a group of individuals who following reason have been able to detach themselves from all material things and to live in agreement with God's laws."[43] It is only within the Church that one can achieve salvation.[44] A person must be baptized and trust in Christ, which was the minimum that was required for salvation.

In analyzing social identity, it is common to focus on the hierarchies between differnt communities, but we must also keep in mind the hierarchies within each social identity. The hierarchies that marked Origen's anthropology and ethnography were also carried over into his ecclesiology.[45] Here again, "every

---

[42] See *HomGn* 6.3, *HomJos* 2.1, *HomJos* 17.1 and *HomJr* 4.2.

[43] Tripolitis, *Origen*, 8.

[44] *HomJos* 3.5 (SC 71, 142).

[45] The extraordinary example of martyrs and confessors would likely be at the apex of Origen's ecclesiological hierarchy, but I pass over discussing them since doing so would distract us from the class hierarchies that structured Origen's communities in a more direct, day-to-day manner.

Christian had a place according to his degree of spiritual development."[46] As Adele Castagno describes it:

> [Origen] thought of the church as consisting of a very small number of *bellatores*, whose weapons were rigorous mystical exaltation and total dedication to the Word of God, and a mass of *infirmiores*, 'whether through age, whether through their sex, whether through decision' (sive per aetatem, sive per sexum, sive per propositum). Among the polloi, the *simpliciores*, they were people whose minds were not able to conceive anything lofty or deep, no spiritual thought, but in whom, nevertheless, the passions of the flesh were dead. These people were not able to raise themselves to spiritual awareness, but could carry out works of justice and respect God's commandments, 'which serve the simpler life' (quae sunt simplicioris vitae ministeria). Nevertheless, most of the *simpliciores* were not only 'beasts', but 'carcasses of beasts' (Lev 5:2-3); to touch them made one unclean, since they 'roll in the dirt of sin'. They went to church, they knelt in front of priests, they respected them, they contributed to church upkeep, but they were not committed to repressing their sins.[47]

Christians differed in the degree to which they were enlightened by Christ, which was dependent on their own capabilities and choices, but these were shaped by their social location.[48] All Christians partook of the Holy Spirit at the moment of baptism and exhibited faith in Christ, but knowledge was the perfection of faith and this came only to those who could devote themselves fully to the contemplation of the teachings of Christ.

---

[46] Tripolitis, *Origen*, 8. See *CCels*. VI.48; IV.26; III.30.

[47] Adele Monaci Castagno, "Origen the Scholar and Pastor," trans. Frances Cooper, in *Preacher and Audience: Studies in Early Christian and Byzantine Homiletics* (ed. Mary B. Cunningham and Paul Allen; A New History of the Sermon 1; Boston: Brill, 1998), 72-73.

[48] *HomGn.* 1.

Some scholars have defended Origen against the charges of elitism. Crouzel, for example, denies that Origen was a "spiritual aristocrat" based on the fact that Origen delivered homilies to a diverse congregation and that included in his homilies, time and again, are exhortations to moral improvement that reflect an optimism on Origen's part for the capacity of every individual to progress as he himself had.[49] Torjesen likewise argues "Origen's polemic against the 'simple' Christians is intended only to provoke their own advance."[50] In granting that all Christians had the ability to progress towards God, Origen differed from the gnostics who claimed that a person's nature was inherent in their very being and could not be altered. On this reading, Origen describes Christianity as a meritocracy in which anyone can achieve perfection through their own hard work. This makes Origen's vision of Christianity seem to be more egalitarian than that of the gnostics, but we must keep in mind that the notion of a meritocracy ignores the power of habitus in maintaining class dicstinctions.[51] Origen's anthropological distinctions, while allowing for the possibility of improvement, mapped closely to classes within Greco-Roman society and it is difficult to imagine that any of the *simpliciores* would have found Origen's philosophical path to salvation as a plausible choice. Given the privileged social location of educated individuals such as Origen, and given his own frustration with the uneducated masses, it would not be surprising if Origen was considered to be an elitist by many in his congregation.

To achieve salvation, one had to learn about God, which required studying scripture, the teachings of Christ. Origen says in the *PArch*:

> We, however, in conformity with our faith in that doctrine which we hold for certain to be divinely inspired, believe that there is no possible way of

---

[49] Crouzel, *Origen*, 114-15.

[50] Torjesen, *Hermeneutical Procedure and Theological Method*, 43.

[51] Craig Martin, *A Critical Introduction to the Study of Religion* (Bristol: Equinox, 2012), 71-91.

explaining and bringing to man's knowledge the higher and diviner teaching about the Son of God, except by means of those scriptures which were inspired by the Holy Spirit, namely the gospels and the writing of the apostles, to which we add, according to the declaration of Christ himself, the law and the prophets.[52]

Scripture is not easily understood, however. In fact many things in scripture are not to be understood literally, but symbolically, and uncovering this hidden meaning is the work of all Christians striving to achieve perfection. Those Christian intellectuals who advance in their understanding of scriptures can aid others in their own progression through exegesis.[53] As Torjesen describes it, it is "the ministerial task of exegesis in the church to discover the presence of Christ the Logos in Scripture, who through his teachings (the progression of spiritual doctrines) completes the work of redemption in each individual soul (divinization through knowledge)."[54] The Christian teacher "is not an optional extra whose needs or interest are, so to speak, indulged by the church at large, but someone who can make plain the hidden harmonies that make sense of the whole doctrinal system."[55] In Origen's mythology, the salvation of most people was dependent on the education they received from their Christian teachers. Teachers were the lynchpin holding together the historical and cosmological components of Origen's myth and they did so through their interpretations of scripture. Such an understanding makes Christian philosophers, such as Origen, the mediating figures between people and divine truth in a manner similar to

---

[52] *PArch* I.3.1 (SC 252, 144).

[53] Torjesen, *Hermeneutical Procedure*, 43.

[54] Torjesen, *Hermeneutical Procedure*, 147.

[55] Rowan D. Williams, "Origen: Between Orthodoxy and Heresy," in *Origeniana Septima: Origenes in den auseinandersetzungen des 4. Jarhunderts.* (ed. W. A. Bienert and U. Kühneweg; Bibliotheca Ephemeridum Theologicarum Lovaniensium 137; Leuven: Leuven University Press, 1999), 7.

how Christ the Logos acts as a mediating figure between God and creation.

Origen could not take it for granted that his audience would deem scripture to be as authoritative as he considered it to be. Even though there was an established tradition among Christians of reading Jewish scriptures, which they called the Old Testament, and of reading certain Christian texts making up their New Testament, there was much debate as to what texts should be considered as authoritative and appropriate for use in the worship of the church, i.e. as scripture. Origen defended the canonicity of the Old Testament against the Marcionites, who rejected the use of Jewish scripture. Even among those who accepted the Old Testament, there were still debates about which texts were to be considered canonical, as is evidenced by Origen's letter to Julius Africanus defending certain additions to the books of Daniel.[56] Other texts, such as the Shepherd of Hermas, Apocalypse of Peter, Acts of Paul, and the Epistle of Barnabas could be read and considered acceptable for study and reflection, but probably did not have the same canonical status in Origen's eyes as the texts that still make up the Christian New Testament. The fact that the texts Origen considered canonical had traditionally been used in the worship of the church was not enough to establish them as authoritative, especially in the eyes of Christianity's new converts and ever-present critics. One tactic Origen employed in defending scripture was to point out its widespread use and efficacy. In his fourth book of the *PArch* on scripture and its interpretation, he argues that the proof the divine inspiration of the teachings of Jesus is provided in the fact that Jesus's teachings have drawn disciples not just from among the Jews, but from peoples of all nations.[57] That Chrsitian scriptures, he says, teach the truth is also evidenced in the accuracies of the prophecies contained in them. Scripture's ability

---

[56] *EpistAfr.*
[57] *PArch* IV.1.

to communicate such truths is, according to Origen, due to its divine nature.

Origen considered scripture to be the teachings of the divine Logos, delivered through the authors of the texts who were themselves inspired by the Holy Spirit.[58] Origen stresses time and again in the *PArch* that the same spirit inspired both the writers of the Old Testament and of the New. These inspired writings present the direct teachings of Christ, the Logos of God. As Torjesen puts it, "The content of Scripture is nothing other than the Logos incarnate in language, for the doctrines in Scripture disclose each in a partial and progressive or sequential way the nature of the Logos who is fully disclosed in his incarnation." [59] To read scripture is thus to engage directly with the divine. David Shin describes this notion of scripture as sacramental in that it indicates "a dynamic and relational liturgical action through which the divine and human encounters occur, resulting in personal transformation."[60] Scripture is the divine, authoritative teaching of God, presented by the Logos, and mediated by writers inspired by the Holy Spirit, and this authority is proven by its oracular nature and wide ranging efficacy.

The nature of scripture, however, was such that the teachings of the Logos were not presented in a straightforward, literal manner.[61] The teachings of the Logos were communicated through the *nous* of the scriptural text, its inner, hidden

---

[58] For more on the divine inspiration of the writers of the biblical texts, see: Enrique Nardoni, "Origen's Concept of Biblical Inspiration," *SecCen* 4 (1984): 9-23.

[59] Torjesen, *Hermeneutical Procedure and Theological Method*, 120.

[60] Daniel Shin, "Some Light from Origen: Scripture as Sacrament," *Worship* 73 (1999): 399.

[61] Mark Julian Edwards, "Precursor's of Origen's Hermeneutic Theory," in *Studia Patristica XXIX: Historica, Theologica et Philosophica, Critica et Philologica* (Leuven: Peeters, 1997), 232-37. The unity of scripture's meaning, despite its apparent mediocrity, and the progressive nature of scriptural understanding and interpretation, Edwards argues, comes from the Pythagoreans as evidenced in Thrasyllus's understanding of Plato's texts.

meaning.⁶² In Book IV of the *PArch*, Origen describes three different levels of meaning in the scritpure:

> One must therefore pourtray the meaning of the sacred writings in a threefold way upon one's soul, so that the simple man may be edified by what we may call the flesh of the scripture, this name being given to the obvious interpretation; while the man who has made some progress may be edified by its soul, as it were; and the man who is perfect like those mentioned by the apostle: 'We speak wisdom among the perfect; yet a wisdom not of this world, nor of the rulers of this world, which are coming to nought; but we speak God's wisdom in a mystery, even the wisdom that hath been hidden, which God foreordained before the worlds unto our glory' – this man may be edified by the spiritual law, which has 'a shadow of the good things to come'. For just as man consists of body, soul and spirit, so in the same way does the scripture, which has been prepared by god to be given for man's salvation.⁶³

As Dively Lauro has shown, Origen categorizes scripture into two types of meaning: literal (the somatic, or bodily, meaning) and non-litereal, with there being two sub-categories of non-literal meanings, the psychic (soulish) and pneumatic (spiritual). Dively Lauro argues that this treefold division of scripture is not just theoretical, as presented here in the *PArch*, but is something he employs in his interpretive works as well. Each level of meaning has a different function:

> The somatic sense is the literal, straightforward reading of the text that renders either historical information about God's interaction with humankind of morally relevant instruction through precepts or examples that

---

⁶² Karen Jo Torjesen, "'Body,' 'Soul,' and 'Spirit' in Origen's Theory of Exegesis," *ATR* 77 (1985): 18; Shin, "Some Light from Origen," 406.

⁶³ *PArch* IV.2.4; *HomLev* 5.5 (SC 286, 230), "For often we have said that a triple mode of understanding is to be found in divine Scriptures: the historical, the moral, they mystical. From this we understood the body, the soul, and the spirit."

> direct growth in specific virtues. The psychic sense is a nonliteral, figurative reading of the text that more generally calls the hearer to shun vice and grow in virtue so that he will become like God. The pneumatic sense is a separate nonliteral sense that enlightens the reader concerning God's plan of salvation through Christ and, more specifically, his Incarnation, the church's emerging role from it, and his culminating power at the Eschaton.[64]

As Torjesen has shown, Origen does not interpret every passage of scripture in this threefold manner. No passage has only a literal meaning, since all of scripture communicates divine teaching, but Origen does not read all three levels of meaning into each passage. Scripture had the potential of communicating at either the psychic or pneumatic level (or both), however, in order to draw people closer to God. Within Origen's salvific economy, scriptural understanding was the primary form of what we might label salvific capital, although such a label would mask its fundamentally philosophical nature. Like the philosophers, Origen understood a closed set of texts as bearing a hidden meaning that led one toward assimilation with the divine.

That the different meanings in scripture matched the different types of people within Origen's anthropology is not coincidental. Each division of human being was marked, in part, by its ability to understand scripture at these analagous levels.[65] Contra the gnostics, Origen did not see these levels of understanding as inherent, but as the effect of a choice one made either to study scripture more diligently or not.[66] For Origen,

---

[64] Elizabeth Ann Dively Lauro, *The Soul and Spirit of Scripture within Origen's Exegesis* (Bible in Ancient Antiquity 3; Atlanta: Society of Biblical Literature, 2005), 2. See also, Crouzel, *Origen*, 88.

[65] Torjesen, "'Body,' 'Soul,' and 'Spirit,'" 20.

[66] *HomEz* 1.11 (SC 352, 86), "For just as each threshing floor is circumscribed and is full of grain or chaff, it is neither all grain nor all chaff, so in the churches on earth there is some grain, some chaff. But in the former

what distinguished Christians from non-Christians was the acceptance of the authority of scripture, including the New Testament, and a willingness to know god through the teachings of the Logos. What distinguished different types of Christians from each other, however, was the ability to properly understand these texts, which could only come about through years or study.

A true understanding of scripture could not come without the guidance of a teacher who had already completed those years of study and could lead the uninitiated through the mysteries of the sacred writings. A teacher could properly interpret scripture and bring a disciple into communion with the divine. Only within this pedagogical context within the church could one come to know God.[67] For Origen, both the biblical author and the biblical exegete were inspired by the Holy Spirit and only those so inspired could be trusted to communicate the hidden meanings of scripture.[68] The divine teachings of scripture could not be understood by just anyone, but only by those who had earned their wisdom through hard work and the gifts of the Holy Spirit. In *HomJos* 17, Origen poses the question: "What else can we understand by this, except that in the Church of the Lord there are certain persons who precede all the rest by the strength of their spirit and on account of their merits?"[69] Such spiritual

---

case, the chaff is chaff, not because of itself, nor through its own will; nor does the grain choose to be grain; but in the latter case, whether you are chaff or grain has been put under your own control."

[67] Karen Jo Torjesen, *Hermeneutical Procedure and Theological Method in Origen's Exegesis* (Patristische Texte und Studien 28; Berlin: Walter de Gruyter; 1986), 122.

[68] *PArch* IV.2.2; Karen Jo Torjesen, "The Rhetoric of the Literal Sense: Changing Strategies of Persuasion from Origen to Jerome" in *Origeniana Septima: Origenes in den auseinandersetzungen des 4. Jarhunderts* (ed. W. A. Bienert and U. Kühneweg; Leuven: Peeters, 1999), 639.

[69] *HomJos* 17.2 (SC 71, 274).

In *HomGn* 2.3, Origen compares the hierarchies of understanding among Christians with the different layers of the ark: "But since neither the merit of all nor the progress in faith is one, therefore, also that ark does not

excellence was beneficial for the individual who attained it, but this excellence was only significant in the context of educating others and leading them towards salvation. This emphasis on communicating one's wisdom is yet another way in which Origen matched his Greek philosophical peers.

This need for a learned guide through the process of interpretation highlights an important aspect of Origen's theory of scriptural interpretation, namely that the focus of the interpretive act is not so much an understanding of the text as it is a transformation of the soul of the disciple by means of understanding the text. As Torjesen describes it, "Instead of offering us an exegetical hermeneutic of the text, he offers us a pedagogical hermeneutic of the soul."[70] For Origen, the relationship between his audience and the Logos, as mediated by Origen himself, is at the center of his interpretive activity. Just as Epictetus, quoted above, disparaged textual understanding that did not reflect a transformation of the soul, so too did Origen see this as the primary goal of scriptural study.[71] Seen in this light, scriptural interpretation is the means by which social hierarchies are created and maintained, since it is only within the context of pedagogical activity that scriptural exegesis becomes worthwhile.

Reading Origen's scriptural theology through the lens of a hermeneutics of suspicion, his assertions that the Logos is at work in scripture and in the scriptural exegete can be understood as strategies for authorizing the hierarchies that shape his

---

offer one abode for all, but there are two lower decks and three upper decks and compartments are separated in it to show that also in the Church, although all are contained within the one faith and are washed in the one baptism, progress, however, is not one and the same for all, 'but each one in his own order.'"

HomGn 2.3 (SC 7, 90).

[70] Torjesen, "'Body,' 'Soul,' and 'Spirit'," 22.

[71] Martens sees Origen primarily as a philologist with textual understanding as being his ultimate goal, but this reflects a modern, academic understanding of the role of the scholar and misses the pastoral aspect of Origen's work.

mythology. Torjesen points out that, for Origen, the true teacher is the Logos itself and that when someone, such as Origen, unlocks the meaning of scripture and communicates that to someone else, it is not the teacher who speaks, but the Logos. For example, in *HomEz* 2, Origen states:

> For if someone has this passage refer to those things that Jesus Christ the Lord has spoken, and if he interprets them in such a way that, when he teaches, it is clear that he is speaking not out of his own heart, but from the Holy Spirit, then he is speaking the words of Jesus the Son of God. If he agrees with the intention of the Holy Spirit, of him who has spoken in the apostles, he speaks not out of his own heart, but from the heart of the Holy Spirit who spoke in Paul, who spoke in Peter, who spoke in the other apostles as well.[72]

Here, Origen is speaking against those who teach a message that is not in accordance with what Origen would consider orthodoxy. Only those teachers who teach the truth about scripture's meaning (such as Origen himself), have the Holy Spirit inspiring their words. They become the mouth of God, in a sense, acting as the trustworthy bearers of divine truth. As Torjesen explains, Origen rhetorical establishes the Logos as the true speaker in his interpretive works.[73] In the actual context of Origen's church or philosophical classroom, however, it Origen who is doing the interpretive work and presenting a mythology of pedagogical soteriology, not the Holy Spirit or the Logos.

We must take care that we not re-present Origen's rhetoric of interpretation as the reality of interpretation. In other words, instead of seeing exegesis as "the mediation of Christ's redemptive teaching activity to the hearer," we should look at it as a way for substituting a mythology not directly found in

---

[72] *HomEz* 2.2 (SC 352, 102-4).
[73] Torjesen, "The Rhetoric of the Literal Sense," 17. See also: Castagno, "Origen the Scholar and Pastor," 68.

scripture by claiming that it arises out of a sacred text and that it is the true teaching of God's Logos.[74]

3.3 Conclusion – A Christian Ideology in Narrative Form

Following the suggestion of Bruce Lincoln in seeing myth as "ideology in narrative form," once we have situated Origen in his philosophical context, it becomes much easier to see the interested nature of his Christian mythology. For Origen, all of existence is predicated upon the need for philosophical education. From the initial moment of an intentional fall from constant contemplation of God to the final moment of universal restoration, all of existence is dependent on the role of the Logos as a teacher whose work is mostly accomplished through scholars who have devoted themselves to scriptural study and self-mastery. Origen the mythmaker was thus constantly engaged in legitimating his position and in the next chapter we will turn to examples of how he did this by reading his mythology into the sacred texts he interpreted.

---

[74] Torjesen, *Hermeneutical Exegesis and Theological Method*, 14.

ORIGEN'S SYMBOLIC LABOR

In the previous chapter, we saw how myth can act as ideology in narrative form by providing a narrative group identity that is hierarchically structured and how it perpetuates those hierarchies by shaping the self-understanding of the members of the community that shares that narrative identity. The blatant congruities between these narratives and the hierarchies they legitimate may lead one to accuse cultural producers such as Origen of disingenuous manipulation for their personal benefit. One also might wonder how such myths ever come to be accepted, especially by those who are among the dominated in a community. Bourdieu proposes that both the dominant and the dominated within a field misrecognize the interested nature of the symbolic capital that defines their field and its particular hierarchies. This misrecognition is the product of symbolic labor and its necessary companion, symbolic violence.

Symbolic labor is the work that cultural producers, in this instance Christian philosophers, perform that masks the interested and oppressive relationships between members of a field and presents them as disinterested and legitimate. The result of symbolic labor is symbolic capital, "a form of power that is not perceived as power but as legitimate demands for recognition, deference, obedience, or the services of others."[1] The exact form of symbolic labor will of course vary from field to field, but its effects are the same in presenting arbitrary hierarchies of status as somehow natural and unquestionable resulting in that misrecognition that is so crucial to the perpetuation of these hierarchies.

---

[1] David Swartz, *Culture & Power: The Sociology of Pierre Bourdieu* (Chicago: University of Chicago, 1997), 43.

Bourdieu also describes symbolic labor as the exercise of symbolic power or in terms of symbolic violence, which he describes as "the *violence which is exercised upon a social agent with his or her complicity.*"[2] Symbolic violence allows for the "peaceful" enforcement of systems of oppression by shaping the dispositions and self-understandings of the dominated (and dominant) without their recognizing that the wool is being pulled over their eyes. As Bourdieu points out, the exercise of symbolic power requires us to "[forsake] entirely the scholastic opposition between coercion and consent, external imposition and internal impulse,"[3] since it is a form of violence that makes the use of force unnecessary, but is still dependent on a form of cultural coercion through the shaping of habitus and identity. It is through this type of socialization process that the dominated become complicit in the violence done to them.

Ironically, cultural producers are, Bourdieu asserts, the least likely to discover the violent nature of their work "given that they have been subjected to it more intensively than the average person and that they continue to contribute to its exercise."[4] We should thus expect that cultural producers will be the most invested in their field, which is evident in their commitment of time and energy to preserving it and to achieving a dominant position within the field. Others who may not be cultural producers within that field, but who accept the rules of the game will be similarly invested, though to a lesser degree. Finally, there are those who accept the rules of the game, or have the rules thrust upon them, who may seem less interested in that form of symbolic capital, but may still recognize its legitimacy.

When we talk about the symbolic labor of the act of mythmaking, it is important to keep in mind that power comes into play even in the exchange of words between people, whether

---

[2] Pierre Bourdieu and Loïc J. D. Wacquant, *An Invitation to Reflexive Sociology* (Chicago: University of Chicago Press, 1992), 167, italics in the original.

[3] Bourdieu and Wacquant, *Invitation*, 172.

[4] Bourdieu and Wacquant, *Invitation*, 170.

in spoken or written form. Bourdieu criticizes J. L. Austin for missing just this in his influential speech act theory.[5] Austin, Bourdieu asserts, fails to recognize the social conditions that allow a person to speak authoritatively, focusing attention on the words and their meanings but not on the social dynamics at play in any given exchange.[6] The power of words comes not from the words themselves, but from the location of a speaker within a field of cultural production and the practices, dispositions, and symbolic capital at play in the discursive moment. The power to engage in mythmaking thus comes not just from the forms of discourse employed but from the authoritative position of the speaker or author. Not only must the appropriate cultural producer be producing, or reproducing, the myth, it must also be accepted and internalized by other members of the field. The dominant and the dominated must both recognize the authority of the intellectual and his or her productions as legitimate.

In this final chapter, I will look at aspects of Origen's symbolic labor to round out our analysis of his scripturalizing. First, I describe the social conditions that lend his voice authority within his community. Next, I present Origen's claims about the nature of scripture as a strategy for establishing his authority and the authority of his myth. Lastly, I will look at the ways in which Origen asserts his role as teacher as the most important within the Christian community through various typologies and analogies which he presents in his interpretive works.[7] Taken

---

[5] John L. Austin, *How to Do Things with Words* (Cambridge: Harvard University Press, 1975).

[6] See Pierre Bourdieu, *Language and Symbolic Power* (ed. and intr. John B. Thompson; trans. Gino Raymond and Matthew Adamson; Cambridge: Harvard University Press, 1991), esp. pp. 107-16; and Bourdieu and Wacquant, *Invitation*, 147-49.

[7] In order to keep the scope of this project manageable, I am only able to discuss a representative sample of how Origen reads his myth out of/into the scriptures. I have decided to focus on examples in his homilies in which he makes assertions about the educational hierarchies of his mythology, but a there are many other topics which might similarly be explored in his extensive corpus.

together, these three strategies of (1) using the tools of a respected philosophical and text-critical tradition to (2) interpret a venerated text in such a way as to (3) textualize a myth of Christianity that situates teachers as the prototypical Christian constitute Origen's symbolic labor, at least to the extent that we can recover it all these many centuries later.

4.1 Origen the Scholar and Presbyter

As mentioned above, Bourdieu asserts in *Language and Symbolic Power* that the efficacy of speech acts relies not just on the pronouncement of certain words or combinations of words, but on the social conditions at play which establish a speaker as having a particular type of authority, an authority recognized and respected by at least some others. Bruce Lincoln makes a similar argument about the nature of authority being context specific. He argues that the effect of particular speech act is:

> the result of the conjuncture of the right speaker, the right speech and delivery, the right staging and props, the right time and place, and an audience whose historically and culturally conditioned expectations establish the parameters of what is judged 'right' in all these instances.[8]

In order to understand how Origen could present his myth of Christianity in a way that would be at all accepted by his fellow Christians, we need to consider his social location, which established him as an authoritative figure in the Christian community. It is insufficient to resort to claims of charismatic authority. Instead we need to look at the established forms of philosophical capital he wielded and the official positions he held within the church. Through his social location as a scholar, catechetical instructor, and presbyter, Origen engaged in practices that lent weight to his words and made it more likely that he would be positively received by others.

---

[8] Bruce Lincoln, *Authority: Construction and Corrosion* (Chicago: University of Chicago Press, 1994), 10-11.

Part of Origen's symbolic labor, then, was simply acting out the roles of teacher and presbyter, roles that were already established as figures who were meant to be listened to and respected. To participate in already accepted forms of symbolic labor allows one to draw on those forms of symbolic capital, thus making Origen's interpretive method part and parcel of his symbolic labor. When Origen would expound upon scripture, his interpretation would have been understood to be an authoritative one. When Origen wrote a commentary at the request of his patron Ambrose, it would have been received as an authoritative statement by a respected philosopher whom Ambrose was supporting with actual capital in order to have access to his teachings. As a mythmaker, Origen's social location would have guaranteed that at least some people would have taken his teachings as authoritative, although just how many people would have done so and to what extent is something to which we will have to return. For now, we turn to that object which anchored Origen's authority and his practices: scripture.

The respect Origen was shown as a Christian philosopher was great, but his official position as a teacher, and later as a presbyter, would indeed have enhanced his authority with the church's seal of approval. In Alexandria, Origen first began taking students of his own accord as there was a vacuum in leadership during the Severan persecutions.[9] Demetrius sanctioned this work officially, perhaps in an effort to assert episcopal control over the influential, independent teacher. Demetrius may have been recognizing a *fait accompli*, but the official recognition of his bishop would likely have further elevated Origen in the eyes of his disciples. The symbolic capital associated with this would only have increased when the school was separated into catechists, now taught by Heraclas, and advanced students whom Origen taught.

Origen's position as an authoritative figure would have been enhanced when he was made a presbyter in Caesarea in 231.

---

[9] Eusebius, *HE* VI.2.

The precise role of the presbyter, like that of the teacher, varied from church to church, but it was a recognized position of authority only slightly below that of the bishop. As presbyter, Origen delivered homilies before his congregation. The designation of presbyter would have signaled to others that he ought to be listened to and Christians were certainly already accustomed to viewing the person delivering the homily as authoritative figure. Just the very acts of standing before the congregation and explaining the meaning of a scriptural passage to a congregation would have added to Origen's authority. Origen's roles within the church, in combination with his asceitc lifestlye, located him in such a way that his message would be taken seriously, especially by those who shared his values and vision of the church.

Although Origen moved to Caesarea and became a presbyter, it is in his role as a teacher that Origen seems to place more value on. The office of bishop or of presbyter does not make someone good in the way that people who have progressed through study to the level that Origen has have demonstrated their goodness through their understanding and through the application of that understanding to their own lives. Attaining an official position within the church did not guarantee that someone was not a hypocrite and Origen warned his congregation against giving undue honors to deacons, presbyters, and bishops who did not live up to the Christian teachings. Not only did Origen argue that people in office can sin, but he expected them to receive an especially harsh punishment should they do so:

> For all who are sinners in the church, who have tasted the word of God and transgress it, deserve penalties, to be sure; but each one will be tormented according to the rank they occupy. The one who presides in the church and commits sins will have a greater punishment. Or does not a catechumen deserve more mercy in comparison with one of the faithful? Is not a layman worthy of more pardon if he is compared to a deacon?

> And again, in comparison with a priest, does not a deacon have a better right to pardon?[10]

The integrity that came with being a Christian philsopher devoted to the rightful teaching of the universal church was something that had to be earned. This work could not be assumed of someone who was a church official. Even though Origen may have garnered more symbolic capital with his ordination, he seems to have wanted to be judged only in terms of the philosophical values he considered to be at the heart of Christianity.

Origen's interpretive methods, drawn as they were from a long history of textual criticism in the Greek world, were also components of his symbolic labor in so far as they demonstrated Origen's symbolic capital and grounded his work in a respected tradition. One method Origen employed, for example, was to interpret scriptural passages in light of other scriptural passages.[11] For Origen, such a practice would have made sense, since the Logos was the ultimate author of all scripture. What are now considered distinct writings written and redacted in different times by different people with a variety of theological and political agendas Origen considered to be one unified canon, all communicating God's saving message, thus allowing him to draw on this tradition of reading disparate passages together. Because scripture was aleay considered authoritative within the Christian community, the use of an authoritative text in order to justify the interpretation of another text is also part and parcel of Origen's symbolic lablor.

The other method, which will be the focus of the remainder of this chapter, is that of interpreting scripture allegorically. The Stoics had utilized allegorical interpretation as a method for reading revered texts in a manner that sustained

---

[10] *HomEz* 5.4 (SC 352, 200-2).

[11] Ronald E. Heine. "Articulating Identity," in *The Cambridge History of Early Christian Literature*, (ed. Frances Young, Lewis Ayres, and Andrew Louth; Cambridge: Cambridge University Press, 2004), 213.

their relevance for a reading community that no longer shared the worldview and values which the text reflected.[12] This was most definitively the case with the Homeric texts, which were the cornerstone of Greek education, but which expressed a concept of the divine that Stoics could not get behind. In order to maintain the cultural relevance of the Homeric texts, the Stoics taught that Homer was communicating (Stoic) truths in an obscure fashion, but that these truths could not be arrived at from a literal reading of his poetry. Origen was faced with a similar problem in reading the Jewish scriptures. Since these texts could clearly not be taken literally in an era in which the temple cult no longer existed, and since they conveyed the teaching of the Logos itself, there must have been another meaning that had to be read from the text allegorically. Again, Origen would Christianize this method of reading, drawing not on Stoic precedence, but on Pauline, citing his allegorical readings of Jewish scriptures.[13] By grafting his interpretation into an authoritative text Origen engages in symbolic violence by making his reading seem equally authoritative as the scriptures from which he was deriving them.

Following Steven Mailloux, Karen Torjesen argues that we should understand Origen's interpretations as rhetorical tools meant to persuade his audience of the truth of his message and not just as clarification of the scriptural text.[14] Read in this light,

---

[12] On the development of allegorical interpretation among the Greeks see Glenn W. Most, "Hellenistic Allegory and Early Imperial Rhetoric," in *The Cambridge Companion to Allegory* (ed. Rita Copeland and Peter T. Struck; Cambridge: Cambridge University Press, 2010), 26-38; and Dan G. McCartney, "Literal and Allegorical Interpretation in Origen's *Contra Celsum*" *WTJ* 48 (1986): 282.

[13] Heine, "Reading the Bible with Origen," 135.

[14] Karen Jo Torjesen, "The Rhetoric of the Literal Sense: Changing Strategies of Persuasion from Origen to Jerome" in *Origeniana Septima: Origenes in den auseinandersetzungen des 4. Jarhunderts* (ed. W. A. Bienert and U. Kühneweg; Leuven: Peeters, 1999), 635.

Even Origen seems to have understood his homilies in this light: *HomLev* 7.1 (SC 286, 298), "For now we are engaged not in the ministry of expounding the Scriptures but in that of edifying the Church."

Origen's allergorical exegesis can be seen as the way by which Origen sought to assert his vision of Christian social formations as divinely sanctioned. Torjesen sees Origen's rhetoric of literal and symoblic meanings of scriptures as a way to appropriate Jewish scriptures for a Christian community and thereby place the Jews in a subordinate position vis-à-vis Christians.[15] Delman Coates similarly sees Origen's allegorical interpretation as "a rhetorical-discursive weapon used by socially marginalized individuals to resist dominant cultural worldviews and orientations."[16] As is often the case when analyzing the formation of identity, Coates focuses on boundaries between communities and situates Origen among the marginalized in relation to Greek philosohpers, Jews, and apparently even gnostic Christians and the *simpliciores*.[17] While it is certainly the case that Origen was attempting to clarify the lines between "orthodox" Christians and these other communities, we should not ignore the ideological implications of his rhetorical hermeneutics for those within his own community.

4.2 The Use of Analogy in Origen's Symbolic Labor

In this final section, we will look at a number of examples drawn from Origen's homilies in which the Christian philosopher connected his pedagogical mythology with the narratives found in scripture. As acts of commentary, Origen's homilies substitute his own meanings for those of the text while depending on the authority of the text to make them seem equally authoritative. I focus on his homilies since his audience for them would have been more diverse than the intended audience of his commentaries and treatises. Only with his homilies can we expect that Origen was communicating directly with the less educated members of his community. Their

---

"Non enim nunc exponendi Scripturas, sed aedificandi Ecclesiam ministerium gerimus…"

[15] Karen Jo Torjesen, "The Rhetoric of the Literal Sense," 639-41.
[16] Delman L. Coates, "Origen of Alexandria," *USQR* 59 (1999), 109.
[17] Coates, "Origen of Alexandria," 107-08.

presence makes the ideological aspects of his mythology all the more poignant since he would have been speaking to those whose social location would pretty much guarantee their domination within Origen's vision of Christianity.

Throughout his homilies, one of the primary ways Origen connected the hierarchies he shared with other philosophers was to compare groups of people, especially within the church, to characters in the narratives he was interpreting. These analogies gave sanction to these hierarchies by connecting them with texts already considered to be uniquely inspired. Egypt, as source of oppression and persecution against the Israelites, made for an easy analogy for those who might draw Christians away from God, especially Greek cultural producers:

> The waters of Egypt are the erring and slippery teachings of the philosophers. Since those teachings deceived some who were deficient in understanding the children in knowledge, when the cross of Christ shows the light of truth to this world, those teaching have to pay the penalty for the death of the children of the guilt of blood...I think the songs of the poets are indicated figuratively by the second plague in which frogs are produced. The poets with a certain empty and puffed up melody introduced deceptive stories to this world as if by the sounds and songs of frogs...After this the mosquitoes are produced...This kind of animal, therefore, I think most fittingly to be compared to the art of dialectic, which bores souls with minute and subtle stinging words and circumvents so shrewdly that the one who has been deceived neither sees nor understands the deception. In the fourth place, I would compare the fly to the sect of Cynics who, in addition to the other depravities of their deception, proclaim pleasure and lust as the highest good...But Egypt is struck in the fifth place by the death of animals or cattle. In this the madness and foolishness of mortals are reproved who, for example, gave worship to irrational cattle and the designation of god to figures not only of men, but also of cattle, impressed in wood and

stone...After this sores and feverish boils are produced in the sixth plague. It seems to me that in the sores deceitful and festering malice is reproved; in the boils, swelling and inflated pride; in the fevers, the insanity of anger and madness, etc.[18]

Here, Origen targets poets, sophists, and Cynics, suggesting that such individuals lead Gentiles to idolatry and immorality. Here, Origen seems to be associating the Cynics with slanders more commonly applied, even by Origen himself, to Epicureans, so this may be a mistake on the part of Rufinus or a later scribe. If Origen had originally spoken about Epicureans, then these three groups of cultural producers were those often mocked by other philosophers. Origen likewise associated astrologers with Egypt:

> And moreover, even after the crossing of the Jordan and after the second circumcision of baptism, there is that reproach of Egypt that, if you neglect it, is prompted by the blight of an old habit to pay attention to auguries, to inquire of the course of the stars and to pry into future events through them, to heed omens, and to be entangled by other superstitions of the same kind.[19]

By making this connection, Origen reminds his audience, which most likely consisted of a number of converts and even non-Christians, that turning back to their traditional religious practices meant aligning themselves with the enemies of God's people. A person is distanced from this past through Christian learning:

> By this diversity, as my insignificant perception comprehends, I think it is indicated that the first food that we carry with us when leaving Egypt is this little school learning (or even more advanced learning if, by chance, anyone has acquired it) that is able to help us only a little. But, placed in the desert, that is, in the condition of life in which we now are, we enjoy the

---

[18] *HomEx* 4.6 (SC 321, 132-36).
[19] *HomJos* 5.6 (SC 71, 174).

manna only through what we learn by the instructions of the divine law. But the one who will deserve to enter the land of promise, that is, to obtain that which has been promised by the Savior, that one will eat fruits from the region of the palms.[20]

For Origen, to be a Gentile meant being ignorant, even if one was well educated. The solution to this problem was to be educated by a Christian teacher who could lead them to God's true teaching through a study of scripture and, through that, to wisdom and salvation. While this connection between Egypt and all Gentile Christians may have been useful for defining and maintaining boundaries between Christians and non-Christians, it would have been most effective in making Christians feel good about their choice to stay in the church and to avoid Greek literary culture. Since it was education which differentiated Christians from non-Christians in Origen's mythmaking, this analogy keeps Origen's educational hierarchy at the forefront of Christian identity formation by encouraging them to think of themselves as better educated than their non-Christian neighbors.

In *HomJos* 7, Origen uses Jericho as an analogy for non-Christian religious practices, including philosophical study.

> We had said before that Jericho may possess the sign of the present age, whose forces and defenses we see to have been destroyed. For indeed the strength and defenses that that world used as walls was the worship of idols, the deceit of divinations directed by the skill of demons and devised by soothsayers, and magicians. By all these most powerful walls, as it were, this world was encircled. Moreover, as though with certain tall and strong towers, it was also fortified with diverse dogmas of philosophers and the most eminent assertions of contentions.[21]

---

[20] *HomJos* 6.1 (SC 71, 182).
[21] *HomJos* 7.1 (SC 71, 194).

In *Josh* 6, Jericho is the first city in the promised land to be destroyed by the Israelites. For Origen, the city epitomizes non-Christian opposition and a threat that must be avoided, if not destroyed. Origen then suggests that Rahab, the prostitute who helped the Israelites defeat Jericho, represents those who convert to Christianity and thus gain life. Again, in connecting an enemy of Isreal with the Gentiles, Origen is able to assert the superiority of Christianity over non-Christian culture and thus encourage his auditors to remain within the church.

If bad people, i.e., miseducated people, are represented by Israel's enemies throughout the Old Testament, then good people from Israel's history and even good objects can be used as analogies for Christians.[22] The whole of Origen's symbolic labor was part and parcel of this attempt to shape Christianity in such a way that teachers were seen as the prototypical Christians, i.e., as those Christians with the most symbolic capital. Through his typological and allegorical interpretations of scripture, Origen was able to further push this view by drawing analogies between teachers and important figures and spaces found in scripture. For example, in *HomGn* 2, Origen uses the contents and structure of the ark of Noah to explain hierarchies within the church.

> These, indeed, who live by rational knowledge and are capable not only of ruling themselves but also of teaching others, since very few are found, represent the few who are saved with Noah himself and are united with him in the closest relationship, just as also our Lord, the true Noah, Christ Jesus, has few intimates, few sons and relatives, who are participants in his word and capable of his wisdom. And these are the ones who are

---

[22] While it is more common now to refer to the Old Testament as the Hebrew Scriptures, I use the former term since it better reflects Origen's own understanding of them and since it highlights the hierarchical distinction between the Old and New Testaments.

placed in the highest position and are gathered in the uppermost part of the ark.[23]

It is hard to imagine that the analogy would be lost on anyone in Origen's audience as he delivered this homily. Only a select few of the Christians in Caesarea would have been able to be educated well enough to merit participation within Origen's inner circle of advanced students. Not even all of these students, since some of them were apparently not yet converted to Christianity, would be included in this small number of wise devotees who shared this close connection to Christ. Origen then follows up this analogy with another, this time reading the design of the ark as indicative of the hierarchies within the church:

> Let us see, therefore, what the squared planks are. That is squared which in no way sways to and fro, but in whatever way you turn it, it stands firm with trustworthy and solid stability. Those are the planks which bear all the weight either of the animals within or the floods without. I think these are the teachers in the Church, the leaders, and zealots of the faith who both encourage the people who have been placed within the Church by a word of admonition and the grace of the teaching, and who resist, by the power of the word and the wisdom of reason, those without, whether heathens or heretics, who assail the Church and stir up floods of questions and storms of strife.[24]

Christian teachers help save those who are less advanced in their studies and protect them from the dangers associated with Gentiles and non-orthodox Christians. Through this reading, God's saving instruments are not the ark and his favored individuals are not Noah and his family. Instead, Christian philosophers are depicted as the most important and devout

---

[23] *HomGn* 2.3 (SC 7, 90).
[24] *HomGn* 2.4 (SC 7, 94).

individuals who are closest to Christ and who do his work in protecting the less educated masses.

Origen also links the role of teacher with a number of other important figures in Israelite mythology. One of the most significant figures Origen compared to teachers was that of the priest. Joseph Trigg has nicely summarized Origen's use of this analogy:

> The Old Testament priesthood was appealing to Origen, in the first place, because priests were a tribe apart, entirely consecrated to God's service. On his return to Alexandria after his first sojourn in Caesarea, Origen wrote about this at the beginning of his *Commentary on John*. Priests, he explains, are persons consecrated to the study of the word of God, and high priests are those who excel at such study...Thus Origen follows Clement of Alexandria in interpreting the priest as a spiritual man. But if the priest has a privileged access to divine secrets, this is only so that, as a teacher, he might mediate God's word to others. Origen transforms the Jewish ritual legislation into an exposition of the priest's vocation as a teacher.[25]

Trigg likewise suggests that Origen drew on the symbolism of the priesthood in order to "oppose the pretensions of official authority, which was rapidly appropriating these very symbols to legitimate episcopal authority."[26] The actual Jewish priesthood was something that disappeared with the destruction of the temple, making these favored figures of Jewish scripture potent symbols in Origen's allegorical exegesis. Even in world without priests, however, Christians would have been familiar with the power and authority of gentile priests who were still engaged in similar sacrificial systems.

---

[25] Joseph W. Trigg, "The Charismatic Intellectual: Origen's Understanding of Religious Leadership," *CH* 50 (March 1981): 9-10.

[26] Trigg, "The Charismatic Intellectual," 12.

As Origen was making these comparisons, Christians themselves did not yet have priests. This is an important point that is often forgotten since we are so accustomed to thinking of bishops and presbyters as priests.[27] For example, Heidi Marx-Wolf compares Origen's comments on the priesthood with those of Porphyry and Iamblichus. Marx-Wolf states that "it is difficult to miss certain connections he drew in this corpus of sermons between the high priests he interpreted in figural terms and the real priests of the Christian church, an order to which he himself belonged."[28] Origen was indeed a presbyter, but we have no evidence that presbyters were considered priests at this time. Cyprian is widely recognized as having been influential in the Christian appropriation of this label for Christian bishops and presbyters, but this process took time to develop and Origen never calls himself a priest in light of his role as presbyter.[29] Instead, Origen appropriates hieratic language and symbolic capital primarily for the Christian philosopher, the one who studies scripture and engages with the divine through study and reflection, not through ritual. That this is just one possible analogy out of many and that the priesthood does not just refer

---

[27] Scholarship on the development of the priesthood in early Christianity reads back into the earliest sources a much later connection between these offices and the notion of a priesthood. See, for example, James A. Mohler, *The Origin and Evolution of the Priesthood: A Return to the Sources* (Staten Island: Alba House, 1970).

[28] Heidi Marx-Wolf, "High Priests of the Highest God: Third-Century Platonists as Ritual Experts," *JECS* 18 (Winter 2010): 489. Marx-Wolf is in good company in seeing Origen as a priest - see also, for example: Thomas P. Scheck, Intoduction to *Origen: Homilies 1-14 on Ezekiel* (Ancient Christian Writers 62; New York: Newman Press, 2010), 1-2; Adele Monaci Castagno, "Origen the Scholar and Pastor," trans. Frances Cooper, in *Preacher and Audience: Studies in Early Christian and Byzantine Homiletics* (ed. Mary B. Cunningham and Paul Allen; A New History of the Sermon 1; Boston: Brill, 1998), 65.

[29] See especially John D. Laurance, *'Priest' as Type of Christ: The Leader of the Eucharist in Salvation History according to Cyprian of Carthage* (American University Studies: Theology and Religion, 5; New York: Peter Lang, 1984).

to bishops and presbyters is clear by the number of analogies Origen draws from the Israelite priesthood.[30]

Following the *Letter to the Hebrews*, Origen uses the priesthood to refer to Christ. In *HomGn* 8, Origen compares Christ to Isaac since both of them participate in their own sacrifices.[31]

> For this reason he himself is both victim and priest. For truly according to the spirit he offers the victim to the Father, but according to the flesh he himself is offered on the altar of the cross, because, as it is said of him, 'Behold the Lamb of God, behold him who takes away the sin of the world,' so it is said of him: 'You are a priest forever according to the order of Melchisedech.'[32]

Neither Christian bishops nor presbyters presided over something they considered a sacrifice at this time, so the appellation of 'priest' would not have made sense in a literal fashion except for Christ, whose death Origen understood in terms of sacrifice.[33]

---

[30] There are a number of times that Origen seems to be referring to church offices in terms of the priesthood, but because Rufinus often translates *presbyteros* and *episkopos* as *sacerdos* in his translation of Eusebius's *Ecclesiastical History*, we cannot be sure that Origen was originally using words having to do with the priesthood in these passages. At other times, it is not clear if Origen is referring to church officials or to teachers. For these passages, see *HomLev* 5.3, 6.3; *HomNum* 10.1; *HomJos* 4.1, 7.6; *HomJd* 2.5. In *HomJr* 12.3, Origen uses the priest analogy to refer to both presbyters and deacons, but this is clearly allegorical – he does not seem to literally see either of these offices as priestly.

[31] *HomGn* 8.6 (SC 7, 222), "That Isaac himself carries on himself 'the wood for the holocaust' is a figure, because Christ also 'himself carried his own cross,' and yet to carry 'the wood for the holocaust' is the duty of a priest. He himself, therefore, becomes both victim and priest. But what is added also is related to this: 'And they both went off together.' For when Abraham carries the fire and knife as if to sacrifice, Isaac does not go behind him, but with him, that he might be shown to contribute equally with the priesthood itself."

[32] *HomGn* 8.9 (SC 7, 230).

[33] On the abstention from sacrifice by Christians, see Daniel C. Ullucci, *The Christian Rejection of Animal Sacrifice* (Oxford: Oxford University Press, 2012).

Origen also uses priesthood language to refer to the apostles since they were a special set of disciples while Christ was incarnate. At times, the connection seems to be so obvious to Origen that it requires no explication, as in *HomLev* 6 when Origen says, "Jesus prohibitied his priests, our apostles…"[34] and again in *HomLev* 7 when he describes them as priests in the company of their high priest, Christ.[35] Among the apostles, Origen described Paul, his favorite apostle and intellectual forefather, as not just a priest, but as a high preist: "Paul, the wisest of the high priests and the most knowledgeable of the priests, used to do this."[36] Origen saw Paul as the most advanced of all Christians and called him "a fellow priest of Christ."[37] Lastly, Origen extended the titles of priest and apostle to all the authors of Christian scriptures:

> But when our Lord Jesus Christ comes, whose arrival that prior son of Nun designated, he sends priests, his apostles, bearing 'trumpets hammered thin,' the magnificent and heavenly instruction of proclamation. Matthew first sounded the priestly trumpet in his Gospel; Mark also; Luke and John each played their own priestly trumpets. Even Peter cries out with trumpets in two of his epistles; also James and Jude. In addition, John also sounds the trumpet through his epistles, and Luke, as he describes the Acts of the Apostles. And now that last one comes, the one who said, 'I think God displays us apostles last,' and in fourteen of his epistles, thundering with trumpets, he casts down the walls of Jericho and all the devices of idolatry and dogmas of philosophers, all the way to the foundations.[38]

---

[34] *HomLev* 6.3 (SC 286, 280).
[35] *HomLev* 7.1 (SC 281, 306), "…to the true high priest, Jesus Christ our Lord, and to his priests and sons, our apostles."
[36] *HomLev* 4.6 (SC 286, 182).
[37] *HomJos* 7.3 (SC 71, 202).
[38] *HomJos* 7.1 (SC 71, 194-96).

Here, Origen combines imagery of the priesthood with imagery of the destruction of Jericho, here, again, representing gentile culture. Never once does Origen suggest that the apostles are priests in fact, but he uses the label as a way to distinguish them as special individuals who have an access to the divine that is not to be found among all Christians.

That, said, following 1 Peter, Origen also uses the title of priest to refer to all Christians.[39] In *HomLev* 4, Origen links the fire of the altar with education, thus using the priesthood analogy again to emphasize the importance of education:

> Observe that there always ought to be 'fire on the altar.' And you, if you want to be a priest of God, as it is written, 'For every one of you will be priests of the Lord.' For it is said that you are 'an elect race, a royal priesthood, an acquired people.' If, therefore, you want to exercise the priesthood of your soul, let the fire never depart from your altar. This is what the Lord also taught in the Gospels that 'your loins be girded and your lamps burning.' Thus, let the 'fire' of faith and the 'lamp of knowledge always be lit for you.[40]

The application of the priesthood in this analogical sense would help Origen to legitimize his pedagogical soteriology, but this was not *just* an analogy for Origen. It was also meant to have practical implications as he argues in *CCels* VIII that Christians should be exempt from military service like other priests in the empire.[41] Origen does not use the priesthood in a strict, legal sense, but in a rhetorical sense; he uses it to try to convince others of how to view themselves and other Christians.

The priesthood was not without its hierarchies, of course, and Origen uses those as a way to scripturalize the educational hierarchies he sees within the church. As we have seen, though, Origen does not refer to Christian teachers as priests in a literal

---

[39] *HomLev* 9.9 (SC 287, 116).
[40] HomLev 4.6 (SC 286, 180). See also, *HomJos* 7.2 (SC 71, 200).
[41] *CCels* VIII.73 (SC 150, 346).

sense. Instead, he uses it allegorically to read his views of education into the scriptural text. Since Origen saw the philosophical ideal as one that could theoretically be reached by anyone, he extends the possibility of achieving the high priesthood to anyone who lived a properly philosophical life:

> As we have already said often, you too can function as a high priest before God within the temple of your spirit if you would prepare your garments with zeal and vigilance; if the word of the Law has washed you and made you clean, and the anointing and grace of your baptism remained uncontaminated; if you were to be clothed with two garments, of the letter and of the spirit; if you were also girded twice so that you may be pure in flesh and spirit; if you would adorn yourselves 'with a cape' of words and 'a breastplate' of wisdom; if also he would crown your head 'with a turban' and 'a golden plate,' the fullness of the knowledge of God; although, I would have you know, you may be hidden and unknown before men.[42]

Origen uses the clothing of the Israelite priests as a way to advocate the ascetic lifestyle he himself had adopted. While baptism is a necessary component of this lifestyle since it allows the individual to be filled with Holy Spirit, the rest of Origen's analogy is derived from his philosophical values. If all Christians are priests, then teachers like Origen are the high priests who pursue knowledge and understanding. And again in *HomJos* 9, Origen distinguishes between all Christians as priests and the true priests who are those who live virtuously.

---

[42] *HomLev* 6.5 (SC 286, 288-90). See also *HomJos* 9.5 (SC 71, 254). "For indeed whoever lives by a priestly religion and by holiness are themselves truly the priests and Levites of the Lord. It is not just those who seem to sit in the priestly assembly, but even more those who behave in a priestly manner. Their portion is the Lord, and they do not possess any portion on the earth. They carry the Law of God on their shoulders, namely, by doing and accomplishing through their work those things that are written in the Law."

Origen also uses the priesthood as an analogy specifically for buttressing the authority of the Christian philosopher as the interpreter of scripture.

> I myself think that the priest who removes the hide 'of the calf' offered as 'as a whole burnt offering' and pulls away the skin with which its limbs are covered is the one who removes the veil of the letter from the word of God and uncovers its interior parts which are members of spiritual understanding. He does not put these members of the Word which are known inwardly in some base place but in a high and holy one, that is, he places it 'upon the altar' when he explains the divine mysteries not to unworthy men who are leading a base and earthly life but to those who are the altar of God, in whom the divine fire always burns and the flesh is always consumed.[43]

Origen describes Christian teachers, such as himself, as priests because of their access to divine things and because of the mediating role they play between, in this case, sacred knowledge, and community of polluted believers who are not worthy having such direct access. As we saw in *HomLev* 4, the divine fire is a refernce to education and study, so the privileged priests in this passage refers to those teachers who teach advanced students who clearly dedicate themselves to advancing in Christian wisdom. Origen similarly elevates teachers through describing them as priests in *HomJos* 17:

> And if it is proper to venture into such things and unveil a profound secret, let us see what the figure of priests or Levites secretly discloses, in case there is something. For among every people - I speak of those who are saved - the great majority are no doubt those who please the Lord through good works, honest ways, and acceptable deeds because they simply believe in and fear God. But there are a few persons, exceedingly rare, who give attention to wisdom and to knowledge, keep their mind

---

[43] *HomLev* 1.4 (SC 286, 78-80).

clean and pure, and cultivate noble virtues for their souls. Through the influence of teaching, they can then illuminate the way for the other more simple ones to walk to and arrive at salvation. These persons are probably designated here under the name of Levites and priests, whose heritage is said to be the Lord himself, who is wisdom, which they dearly loved above all other things.[44]

As Origen was speaking theses words, it would have been clear to his auditors that very few people could meet the description they had just heard. One who clearly *did* meet that description was the one speaking and perhaps a handful of advanced students. Being a Christian did mean being set apart from all non-Christians, but it also meant being subordinate to Christian intellectuals.

Seeing as how often Origen uses the analogy of the priest, not only for Christians in general, but especially for teachers, it is no surprise that Origen does not use sacrificial language to discuss the Eucharist as does Cyprian, but instead applies it to

---

[44] *HomJos* 17.2 (SC 71, 374-76).

See also, *HomNum* 4.3 (SC 415, 108), " So now let us return to that tabernacle of 'the church of the living God,' and see how these details are to be observed in the church of God by Christ's priests. If someone is truly a priest, to whom the sacred vessels, that is, the secrets of the mysteries of wisdom, have been entrusted, let him learn from these things and take heed to guard these things inside the veil of his conscience. He should not be too ready to show them in public. But if circumstances demand that he show these things to the inferior, that is, to transmit them to the ignorant, he should not show them uncovered. Let him not display them in an open and completely exposed way; otherwise, he commits murder and 'destroys the clan.' For everyone is cut off who touches the secret things and the ineffable sacraments. He has not yet been transferred into the order and rank of priesthood by his merits and knowledge. For it is only to the sons of Aaron, that is, to priests, that it has been granted to see in a bare and revealed fashion the very ark of testimony and the table and the candlestick and anything else of those things we have summarized above. But others should look at these things covered up, or rather, they should carry them on their shoulders as these things that have been veiled over." See also, *HomNum* 5.1 (SC 415, 120-22).

the death of Christ, to the death of martyrs, and, more importantly for the majority of his audience, to the daily actions of living a moral life according to Christian standards. Robert Daly summarizes the variety of ways Origen argued that Christians could still benefit from sacrifice, so long as sacrifice was properly understood in allegorical terms:

> Against the complaint that those under the Old Dispensation were more fortunate in having many sacrifices by which sin could be forgiven, he counters that we also have many ways in which to enjoy the benefits of sacrificial atonement; and then he proceeds to list seven of them: baptism, martyrdom, almsgiving, readiness to forgive, converting a brother, fraternal charity, penance. In other places he also mentions chastity, self-denial, prayer and meditation as performing the same sacrificial service of forgiveness.[45]

With the acts of sacrifice being good works, Origen is able to apply his analogy of any Christian living a good life as being a priest. The ritual concerns of the bishop and presbyter are important, but they do not have the atoning function of sacrifice, which Origen appropriates for those whose lives match their understanding, i.e. for Christian philosophers. Origen shared the Stoic notion that perfectly good actions required both a morally right action and also a rational understanding and choice of that action.[46] This type of self-reflexive morality was achieved only

---

[45] Robert J. Daly, "Early Christian Influences on Origen's Concept of Sacrifice," in *Origeniana: premier colloque international des études origéniennes, Monsterrat, 18-21 Septembre 1973* (ed. Henri Crouzel, Gennar Lomiento, and Josep Rius-Camps; Bari, Italy: Instituto di letteratura Cristiana antica,1975), 318. Theo Hermans also talks about the priesthood in Origen and discusses how Origen has a spiritual understandings of ritual language. *Origene Theologie Sarificielle Du Sacerdoce Des Chretiens* (Theologie Historique: Collection Fondee par Jean Danielou Dirigee Par Charles Kannengiesser 102; Paris: Beauchesne, 1996).

[46] See, for example: *HomLev* 5.2 (SC 286, 214), "Since, therefore, you see that you have everything that the world has, you ought not doubt that you

after much spiritual progress and was the special purview of the philosophical virtuoso.

Living a virtuous life was something that could only be achieved by well educated philosopher whose life matched his doctrines. This was not the only aspect of philosophy that Origen described in sacrificial terms, however. He also used sacrifice to allegorically refer to scriptural interpretation, his primary activity within the church. In *HomGn* 10.3, scripture becomes the meat that is consumed after a lamb is sacrificed: "Christians eat the flesh of the lamb every day, that is they consume daily the flesh of the word. 'For Christ our pasch is sacrificed.'"[47] As Christ is the content and author of scripture, the consumption of scripture through study is comparable to the consumption of Christ as a sacrificial lamb. In *HomLev* 4, Origen makes it clear that casual attendance at church and a passing knowledge of scripture is not enough to be a participant in the hermeneutical sacrifce:

> Therefore, when different Prophets or different apostles should give to those who sin the counsel by which they can correct or amend the sin, they rightly will seem to have sold rams to them for sacrifice. But how much do they charge the buyers? It is, I think the cost of reading zealously, of hearing with vigilince the word of God, and above all, I think, the most diligent obedience, about which the Lord says, 'I prefer obedience to sacrifice; and hearing what I say rather than whole burnt offerings.[48]

---

also have within you animals that are offered for sacrifices and from these you ought to offer sacrifices spiritually."

HomLev 5.7 (SC 286, 234), "But since it is not for us now to offer the sacrifices according to the letter, let us inquire who among us is of such measure and kind to offer to God 'salutary sacrifices' and 'a sacrifice of praise.' I believe that one to be he who praises God in all his actions and fulfills through him what our Lord and Savior says: 'That men may see your good works and praise your Father who is in heaven.' Therefore, this one offered 'a sacrifice of praise,' for whose deeds, doctrine, word, habits, and discipline, God is praised and blessed."

[47] *HomGn* 10.3 (SC 7, 264).
[48] *HomLev* 4.5 (SC 286, 178-80).

As we have seen, Origen does not use the 'priest' and 'sacrifice' to refer to 'presbyter' and 'the eucharist' in a straitforward manner. Instead, in his philosophically oriented rhetorical hermeneutics, he uses them to assert the primacy of the philosophical life as the Christian ideal.

4.3 Conclusion: Symbolic Labor

Origen was a virtuoso when it came to constructing a Christian mythic system, connecting that system into the revered Christian scriptures, and reinforcing the hierarchies of that system through discursive and non-discursive practices. He drew on the pedagogical values and practices of his day and creatively Christianized these through his interpretations of scripture. This labor constituted his symbolic labor and round out our analysis of his scripturalizing activities. Origen's symbolic labor allowed him, to the extent that he was successful, to connect his social formation with Christian myth and to exercise a form of symbolic violence that would continue in the perpetuation of a scholastic hierarchy within some parts of the church for centuries to come.

CONCLUSION

The goal of this study has been twofold: to provide an ontological model for the bundle of activities I am referring to as "scripturalizing" and to offer a reading of Origen's works in light of that theory. This reading is intended to highlight the ideological nature of Origen's theology and to explore the various strategies he employs in order to frame the social hierarchies embedded in that theology as culturally and divinely authoritative. In my opening chapter, I synthesized the works of various social theorists in order to construct a model of scripturalizing. This model is intended to give scholars of religion a basis for studying the ways in which scriptures are used in communities. This sociological approach to scriptures takes us away from the traditional search for the content meaning of scriptures and moves us into the realm of the social and the political, a goal spurred in part by the works of W. C. Smith, Vincent Wimbush, and Bruce Lincoln, among others. Relying heavily on the Pierre Bourdieu, I developed a model of scripturalizing that I separated into three topics for analysis: social formation, mythmaking, and symbolic labor.

In the remaining three chapters I used one of these subtopics in each chapter in order to study the life and works of Origen, both to provide an ideologically critical study of Origen and to demonstrate the utility of this ontology of scripturalizing. In Chapter Two, I analyzed Origen's social formation, situating him within the field of Greek philosophers based on what we know of the intellectual and educational practices in which he engaged. In Chapter Three, I showed how the values of this field thoroughly penetrate Origen's theology, or, better put, his mythology. In my final chapter, I explored the discursive and non-discursive practices that were a part of the symbolic labor

Origen engaged in to sanction the disparities in status implicit in his mythology. These three chapters together show Origen to be a specific type of cultural producer that was readily recognizable in the Roman Empire of the third century C. E. They also show how his philosophical values pervade his notion of what it meant to be a Christian, conceptually and practically.

Although little of what I say about Origen in terms of content is new, the framing of Origen as a cultural producer whose works are thoroughly ideological is new and significant. From a historical perspective, it helps us to understand the importance of Origen's personal background in the construction of a Christian theological system, a system built on the foundation of centuries of philosophical discourse in the Greek and Jewish worlds. It moves Origen's mythology out from the realm of pure ideas and into the realm of cultural competition. Such a reading historicizes Origen's ideas not just as reflective of contemporary Platonic thought, but also of struggles for symbolic capital amongst Greek, Jewish, and Christian intellectuals in the Roman Empire.

Theoretically, the current project has taken a significant step forward in the social-scientific study of scriptures by providing a social ontology of scripturalizing. While the works of Smith, Wimbush, and others have shown the importance of studying the social life of scriptures, especially in analyzing the role scriptures have played in constructing, perpetuating, and challenging various forms of oppression, a clear theoretical model that could be applied cross-culturally has been lacking. In providing such a model, and by demonstrating the effectiveness of this model through a case study on Origen, this work has contributed to the field of religious studies and the social sciences more broadly.

That said, there are several shortcomings that stem from my present focus on a single individual for whom we have little data with which to work. As a New Testament scholar, I am already pushing the boundaries of my subfield by analyzing the ways in which the Christian scriptures (i.e. both Testaments) are interpreted and deployed in the work of a Christian teacher and scholar of the third century. I selected Origen because he is a relatively early Christian cultural producer whose writings we have a significant amount of and whose life we know something about. There is much that is missing from this picture, however, that would contribute to a more thorough study of scripturalizing.

First, it would be useful to do a more thorough analysis of the overlapping fields of cultural production in which Origen might be situated. There is much more to be said about the nature of philosophy in antiquity and more data needs to be brought into the discussion in order to flesh out the contours of the philosophical field and to situate philosophers vis-à-vis other figures such as sophists, priests, prophets, rabbis, and soothsayers. As indicated in Chapter Two, the categories employed in secondary scholarship are not clearly defined and a social history of these cultural producers has yet to be written. A full analysis of a field of cultural production cannot focus on just one individual and my present interest in Origen has prevented me from providing the full analysis of this field, which is something I plan to take up in a future project.

The process of scripturalizing is also one that requires a community, and again the present focus on Origen and his role in scripturalizing has prevented me from exploring the reception of Origen in his immediate community and in other circles beyond the Alexandrian and Caesarean churches. Since scripturalizing is, above all, a matter of group identity formation, this critical component of scripturalizing requires greater attention than I can give it here. We have no data from the lay members of Origen's Caesarean community that we can analyze in order to see the extent to which Origen was effective in persuading others that his vision of the human condition and the nature of the church were true. One might also consider Origen's influence in the development of monasticism in the fourth, fifth, and sixth centuries to see how his theology and the values imbued in that theology went on to effect the study of scriptures, the nature of asceticism, and the relationship between ecclesiastical officers and other religious virtuosi as Christianity became the dominant religion of the Roman Empire. This is a complex history, however, and Origen's voice is only one among many, but it is part of the ongoing process of reception and social formation that is a fundamental aspect of scripturalizing and thus deserves greater attention.

There is also much work left to be done in fully developing a social ontology of scripturalizing. The limited picture I have provided here deserves further research to explain, contextualize, and defend the various strands of scholarship from which I have drawn. Scholars such as Bourdieu, Schatzki, and Ricoeur are not without their challengers and detractors, nor are they lone voices for the views they espouse. In a future project, I would like to better situate my theory within various debates in philosophy and the social sciences. I would also like to expand upon the question of identity by incorporating aspects of gender, race, and class, at the very least, while leaving the theory flexible enough to incorporate forms of identity that may be more relevant for different cultural complexes.

All in all, the current project is a foray into an arena of study that is new for the field of religious studies and for the subfields of New Testament and Early Christianity. In demonstrating the significant role of interpreters in the transformation and communication of the "meaning" of scriptures, this project should, provided its message is received by others in the guild, put an end to studies that simply link historical critical readings of texts to identity. Such studies fail to appreciate the importance of reader reception both for the immediate audience and for the various audiences who continue to read and interpret scriptures in new times and places. As I have shown, scriptures can take on meanings that venture far afield from what we perceive to be their "original meaning," meanings that are reflective and supportive of the social formations of later interpreters. Only when we take this into account and analyze the political nature of scriptural interpretation can we start to answer the question "What is scripturalizing?"

BIBLIOGRAPHY

Origen Texts in Greek and Latin

Contre Celse. Introduction, critical text, translation and notes by Marcel Borret. SC 132, 136, 147, 150 and 227.

Homélies sur Ezéchiel. Latin text, introduction, translation and notes by Marcel Borret. SC 352.

Homélies sur Jérémie. Translation by Pierre Husson and Pierre Nautin, introduction and notes by Pierre Nautin. SC 232 and 238.

Homélies sur Josué. Latin text, introduction, translation and notes by Annie Jaubert. SC 71.

Homélies sur la Genèse. Introduction by Henri de Lubac and Louis Doutreleau; Latin text, translation and notes by Louis Doutreleau. SC 7.

Homélies sur l'Exode. Latin text, introduction, translation and notes by Marcel Borret. SC 321.

Homélies sur S. Luc. Introduction, translation and notes by Henri Crouzel, François Fournier, and Pierre Périchon. SC 87.

Homélies sur Samuel. Critical edition, introduction, translation and notes by Pierre et Marie-Thérèse Nautin. SC 328.

Robinson, J. Armitage. *The Philocalia of Origen: The Text Revised with a Critical Introduction and Indices*. Cambridge University Press/New York: Macmillan, 1893.

Traité des principes. Introduction, critical text, translation, commentary and fragments by H. Crouzel and M. Simonetti. SC 252-53, 268-69, 312.

Translations

Contra Celsum. Translated by Henry Chadwick with an introduction and notes. Cambridge: Cambridge University Press, 1980.

On First Principles. Translated by G. W. Butterworth with an introduction and notes. Introduction to the Torchbook edition by Henre de Lubac. Gloucester: Peter Smith, 1973.

Origen: An Exhortation to Martyrdom, On Prayer, First Principles: book IV, Prologue to the commentary on the Song of Songs, Homily XXVII on numbers. Translated by Rowan A. Greer with an introduction and prefaced by hans Urs von Balthasar. New York; Paulist Press, 1979.

Origen: De Principiis, Letter to Gregory, and Against Celsus. Ante-Nicene Fathers IV.

Origen: Homilies on Genesis and Exodus. Translated by Ronald E. Heine. Fathers of the Church 71.

Origen: Homilies 1-14 on Ezekiel. Translated by Thomas P. Scheck. Ancient Christian Writers 62.

Origen: Homilies on Jeremiah, Homily on 1 Kings 28. Translated by John Clark Smith. Fathers of the Church 97.

Origen: Homilies on Joshua. Translated by Barbara J. Bruce and edited by Cynthia White. Fathers of the Church 105.

Origen: Homilies on Leviticus. Translated by Gary Wayne Barkley. Fathers of the Church 83.

Origen: Homilies on Luke, Fragments on Luke. Translated by Joseph T. Lienhard. Fathers of the Church 94.

Origen: Homilies on Numbers. Translated by Thomas P. Scheck. Ancient Christian Texts.

Other Ancient Writers

Diogenes Laertius. *Lives of Eminent Philosophers*, vol. 1-2. Translated by R. D. Hicks. Loeb Classical Library 184 & 185.

Epictetus. *The Discourses*, vol. 1-2. Translated by W. A. Oldfather. Loeb Classical Library 131 & 218.

Eusebius. *Ecclesiastical History*, vol. 1. Translated by Kirsopp Lake. Loeb Classical Library 153; vol. 2. Translated by J. E. L. Oulton. Loeb Classical Library 265.

Gregory Thaumaturgus. *Remerciement á Origène* and *la letter d'Origène à Grégoire*. Introduction, critical text, translation and notes by Henri Crouzel. SC 148.

Gregory Thaumaturgus. *St. Gregory Thaumaturgus: Life and Works*. Translated by Michael Slusser. Fathers of the Church 98.

Philostratus. *The Life of Apollonius of Tyana*, vol. 1. Translated by F. C. Conybeare. Loeb Classical Library 16.

Philostratus and Eunapius. *Lives of the Sophists* and *Lives of the Philosophers*. Translated by Wilmer Cave Wright. Loeb Classical Library 134.

Plutarch. *Moralia*, vol. 13, part 2. Translated by Harold Cherniss. Loeb Classical Library 470.

Porphyry. *The Life of Plotinus and the Order of His Books*, vol. 1. Translated by A. H. Armstrong. Loeb Classical Library 440.

Quintilian. *The Orator's Education*, vol. 1. Translated by Donald A. Russell. Loeb Classical Library124.

Secondary Literature

Algra, Keimpe, Jonathan Barnes, Jaap Mansfield,and Malcolm Schofield, eds. *The Cambridge History of Hellenistic Philosophy*. Cambridge: Cambridge University Press, 1999.

Althusser, Louis. *On Ideology*. Radical Thinkers 26. London: Verso, 2008.

Arnal, William E. "Why Q Failed: From Ideological Project to Group Formation." Pages 67-87 in *Redescribing Christian Origins*. Edited by Ron Cameron and Merrill P. Miller. Society of Biblical Literature Symposium Series 280. Atlanta: Society of Biblical Literature, 2004.

Arnal, William E., and Willi Braun. "Social Formation and Mythmaking: Theses on Key Terms." Pages 459-67 in *Redescribing Christian Origins*. Edited by Ron Cameron and Merrill P. Miller. Society of Biblical Literature Symposium Series 280. Atlanta: Society of Biblical Literature, 2004.

Asad, Talal. *Genealogies of Religion: Discipline and Reasons of Power in Christianity and Islam*. Baltimore: Johns Hopkins University Press, 1993.

Austin, John L. *How to Do Things with Words*. Cambridge: Harvard University Press, 1975.

Bell, Catherine. *Ritual Theory, Ritual Practice*. New York: Oxford University Press, 1992.

Bell, Duncan S. A. "Mythscapes: Memory, Mythology, and National Identity." *British Journal of Sociology* 54 (2003): 63-81.

Berchman, Robert M. *From Philo to Origen: Middle Platonism in Transition*. Brown Judaic Studies 69. Chico: Scholars Press, 1984.

Berlinerblau, Jacques. "Ideology, Pierre Bourdieu's *doxa*, and the Hebrew Bible." *Semeia* 87 (1999): 193-214.

Berner, Ulrich. *Origenes*. Darmstatt: Wissenschaftliche Buchgesellschaft, 1981.

Betegh, Gábor. " The Transmission of Ancient Wisdom: Texts, Doxographies, Libraries." Pages 25-38 in *The Cambridge History of Philosophy in Late Antiquity*, Vol. 1. Edited by Lloyd P. Gerson. Cambridge: Cambridge University Press, 2010.

Bielo, James S. *The Social Life of Scriptures: Cross-Cultural Perspectives on Biblicism*. Signifying (on) Scriptures 2. New Brunswick: Rutgers University Press, 2009.

Biernacki, Richard. "Language and the Shift from Signs to Practices in Cultural Inquiry." *History and Theory* 39 (October 2000): 289-310.

Blosser, Benjamin P. *Become Like the Angels: Origen's Doctrine of the Soul*. Washington: Catholic University of America Press, 2012.
Bond, George Clement, and Angela Gilliam, eds. *Social Construction of the Past: Representation as Power*. London: Routledge, 1997.
Bourdieu, Pierre. *Outline of a Theory of Practice*. Cambridge Studies in Social and Cultural Anthropology 16. Translated by Richard Nice. Cambridge: Cambridge University Press, 1977.
_____*Distinction: A Social Critique of the Judgment of Taste*. Translated by Richard Nice. Cambridge: Harvard University Press, 1984.
_____*The Logic of Practice*. Translated by Richard Nice. Stanford: Stanford University Press, 1990.
_____"Genesis and Structure of the Religious Field." *Comparative Social Research* 13 (1991): 1-44.
_____ *Language and Symbolic Power*. Edited and Introduced by John B. Thompson; Translated by Gino Raymond and Matthew Adamson. Cambridge: Harvard University Press, 1991.
_____ *The Field of Cultural Production*. Edited and introduced by Randal Johnson. European Perspectives. New York: Columbia University Press, 1993.
Bourdieu, Pierre, and Jean-Claude Passeron. *Reproduction in Education, Society and Culture*. Translated by Richard Nice. London: SAGE Publications, 1977.
Bourdieu, Pierre and Loïc J. D. Wacquant. *An Invitation to Reflexive Sociology*. Chicago: University of Chicago Press, 1992.
Bowersock, G. W. *Greek Sophists in the Roman Empire*. Oxford: Clarendon Press, 1969.
Boyer, Pascal. *Religion Explained: The Evolutionary Origins of Religious Thought* New York: Basic Books, 2001.

Boys-Stones, George R. *Post-Hellenistic Philosophy: A Study of its Development from the Stoics to Origen*. Oxford: Oxford University Press, 2001.

Braun, Willi and Russell T. McCutcheon, eds. *Guide to the Study of Religion*. London: Cassell, 2000.

Buell, Denise Kimber. *Why This New Race: Ethnic Reasoning in Early Christianity*. New York: Columbia University Press, 2005.

Butler, Judith. *Gender Trouble: Feminism and the Subversion of Identity*. New York: Routledge, 1990.

Calhoun, Craig, Edward LiPuma, and Moishe Postone, eds. *Bourdieu: Critical Perspectives*. Chicago: University of Chicago Press, 1993.

Cameron, Averil. "Ascetic Closure and the End of Antiquity." Pages 147-161 in *Asceticism*. Edited by Vincent L. Wimbush and Richard Valantasis. Oxford: Oxford University Press, 1998.

Cameron, Ron, and Merrill P. Miller, eds. *Redescribing Christian Origins*. Society of Biblical Literature Symposium Series 280. Atlanta: Society of Biblical Literature, 2004.

Castagno, Adele Monaci. "Origen the Scholar and Pastor." Translated by France Cooper Leiden. Pages 65-87 in *Preacher and Audience: Studies in Early Christian and Byzantine Homiletics*. Edited by Mary B. Cunningham and Pauline Allen. A New History of the Sermon 1. Boston: Brill, 1998.

Clark, Elizabeth A. *The Origenist Controversy: The Cultural Construction of an Early Christian Debate*. Princeton: Princeton University Press, 1992.

Coates, Delman L. "Origen of Alexandria." *Union Seminary Quarterly Review* 59 (2005): 107-12.

Collins, Randall. *The Sociology of Philosophies: A Global Theory of Intellectual Change*. Cambridge: Belknap Press, 1998.

_____. *Interaction Ritual Chains*. Princeton Studies in Cultural Sociology. Princeton: Princeton University Press, 2004.

Cox, Patricia. *Biography in Late Antiquity: A Quest for the Holy Man.* Berkeley: University of California Press, 1983.

Cribiore, Raffaella. *Gymnastics of the Mind: Greek Education in Hellenistic and Roman Egypt.* Princeton: Princeton University Press, 2001

Cronk, Lee. "Behavioral Ecology and the Social Sciences." Pages 167-86 in *Missing the Revolution: Darwinism for Social Scientists.* Edited by Jerome H. Barkow. Oxford: Oxford University Press, 2006.

Crouzel, Henri. "Origène est-il un systématique?" Pages 179-215 in *Origène et la philosophie.* Paris: Aubier, 1962.

——— *Origen.* Translated by A. S. Worrall. San Francisco: Harper & Row, 1989.

Daly, Robert J. "Early Christian Influences on Origen's Concept of Sacrifice." Pages 313-26 in *Origeniana.* Edited by Henri Crouzel, Gennaro Lomiento, and Josep-Rius-Camps. Quanderni di Vetera christianorum. Bari, Italy: Instituto di letteratura Cristiana antica, 1975.

Dawson, John David. *Christian Figural Reading and the Fashioning of Identity.* Berkeley: University of California Press: 2002.

Deal, William E. "Toward a Politics of Asceticism: Response to the Three Preceding Papers." Pages 424-42 in *Asceticism.* Edited by Vincent L. Wimbush and Richard Valantasis. Oxford: Oxford University Press, 1998.

de Haas, Frans A. J. "Late Ancient Philosophy." Pages 242-70 in *The Cambridge Companion to Greek and Roman Philosophy.* Edited by David Sedley. Cambridge: Cambridge University Press, 2003.

Derrida, Jacques. *Of Grammatology.* 2d ed. Translated by Gayatri Chakravorty Spivak. Baltimore: Johns Hopkins University Press, 1998.

Dillon, John. "Philosophy as a Profession in Late Antiquity." Pages 401-18 in *Approaching Late Antiquity: The Transformation from Early to Late Empire.* Edited by Simon Swain and Mark Edwards. Oxford: Oxford University Press, 2004.

Dively Lauro, Elizabeth Ann. *The Soul and Spirit of Scripture within Origen's Exegesis*. Bible in Ancient Christianity 3. Atlanta: Society of Biblical Literature, 2005.

Eagleton, Terry. *Ideology: An Introduction*. London: Verso, 1991.

Edwards, Mark Julian. "Precursors of Origen's Hermeneutic Theory." Pages 232-7 in *Studia Patristica XXIX: Historica, Theologica et Philosophica, Critica et Philologica*. Leuven: Peeters, 1996.

―――― *Origen against Plato*. Ashgate Studies in Philosophy & Theology in Late Antiquity. Burlington: Ashgate, 2002.

Engler, Steven, "Modern Times: Religion, Consecration and the State in Bourdieu." *Cultural Studies* 17 (2003): 445-67.

Esler, Philip Francis. *Conflict and Identity in Romans*. Minneapolis: Augsburg Books, 2003.

Flood, Gavin. *The Ascetic Self: Subjectivity, Memory and Tradition*. Cambridge: Cambridge University Press, 2004.

Geertz, Armin, and Jeppe Sinding Jensen, eds. *Religious Narrative, Cognition and Culture: Image and Word in the Mind of Narrative*. Relgion, Cognition and Culture. Sheffield: Equinox, 2011.

Geertz, Clifford. "Religion as a Cultural System." Pages 87-125 in *The Interpretation of Cultures*. Edited by Clifford Geertz. New York: Basic Books, 1973.

Gerson, Lloyd P., ed. *The Cambridge History of Philosophy in Late Antiquity*. Cambrdige: Cambridge University Press, 2010.

Grafton, Anthony, and Megan Williams. *Christianity and the Transformation of the Book: Origen, Eusebius, and the Library of Caesarea*. Cambridge: Belknap Press, 2006.

Guy, Laurie. *Introducing Early Christianity: A Topical Survey of Its Life, Beliefs, and Practices*. Downders Grove, Ill.: InterVarsity Press, 2004.

Hadot, Pierre. *What is Ancient Philosophy?* Translated by Michael Chase. Cambridge: Belknap Press, 2002.

Halbwachs, Maurice. *On Collective Memory*. Chicago: University of Chicago Press, 1992.

Halliwell, Stephen. "Philosophy and Rhetoric." Pages 222-43 in *Persuasion: Greek Rhetoric in Action*. Edited by Ian Worthington. London: Routledge, 1994.

Hanson, R. P. C. *Allegory and Event: A Study of the Sources and Significance of Origen's Interpretation of Scripture*. Richmond: John Knox Press, 1959/2002.

Harnack, Adolph von. *History of Dogma, Vol. 2*. 3d Edition. Translated by Neil Buchannan. New York: Russell & Russell, 1958.

Harpham, Geoffrey Galt. *The Ascetic Imperative in Culture and Criticism*. Chicago: University of Chicago Press, 1987.

Harris, Carl Vernon. *Origen of Alexandria's Interpretation of the Teacher's Function in the Early Christian Hierarchy and Community*. New York: The American Press, 1966.

Hawkes, David. *Ideology*. 2d ed. The New Critical Idiom 26. London: Routledge, 2003.

Heine, Ronald E. "Articulating Identity." Pages 200-221 in *The Cambridge History of Early Christian Literature*. Edited by Frances Young, Lewis Ayres, and Andrew Louth. Cambridge: Cambridge University Press, 2004.

_____ *Origen: Scholarship in the Service of the Church*. Christian Theology in Context. Oxford: Oxford University Press, 2010.

Hermans, Theo. *Origène Théologie Sacrificielle du Sacerdoce des Chrétiens*. Théologie Historique 88. Paris: Beauchesne, 1996.

Hoffmann, Philippe. "What was Commentary in Late Antiquity? The Example of Neoplatonic Commentators." Pages 597-622 in *A Companion to Ancient Philosophy*. Edited by Mary Louise Gill and Pierre Pellegrin. Blackwell Companions to Philosophy 31. Oxford: Blackwell, 2009.

Holmberg, Bengt. "Understanding the First Hundred Years of Christian Identity." Pages 1-32 in *Exploring Early Christian Identity*. Edited by Bengt Holmberg. Wissenschaftliche Untersuchungen zum Neuen Testament 226. Tübingen: Mohr Siebeck, 2008.

Holstein, James A., and Jaber F. Gubrium. *The Self We Live By: Narrative Identity in a Postmodern World*. Oxford: Oxford University Press, 2000.

hooks, bell. *Teaching to Transgress: Education as the Practice of Freedom*. New York: Routledge, 1994.

Hughes, Aaron. "Presenting the Past: The Genre of Commentary in Theoretical Perspective." *Method and Theory in the Study of Religion* 15 (2003): 148-68.

Kaplan, David M. *Ricoeur's Critical Theory*. SUNY Series in the Philosophy of the Social Sciences. Albany: State University of New York Press, 2003.

Kassam, Tazim R. "Signifying Revelation in Islam." Pages 29-40 in *Theorizing Scriptures: New Critical Orientations to a Cultural Phenomenon*. Signifying (on) Scriptures 1. Edited by Vincent L. Wimbush. New Brunswick: Rutgers University Press, 2008.

Lamberton, Robert. *Homer the Theologian: Neoplatonist Allegorical Reading and the Growth of the Epic Tradition*. The Transformation of the Classical Heritage 9. Berkeley: University of California Press, 1986.

Laurance, John D. *'Priest' as Type of Christ: The Leader of the Eucharist in Salvation History According to Cyprian of Carthage*. American University Studies: Theology and Religion, 5. New York: Peter Lang, 1984.

Lieu, Judith M. *Christian Identity in the Jewish and Graeco-Roman World*. Oxford: Oxford University Press, 2004.

Lincoln, Bruce. *Authority: Construction and Corrosion*. Chicago: University of Chicago Press, 1994.

———. *Theorizing Myth: Narrative, Ideology, and Scholarship*. Chicago: University of Chicago Press, 1999.

Lyman, J. Rebecca. *Christology and Cosmology: Models of Divine Activity in Origen, Eusebius, and Athanasius*. Oxford Theological Monographs. Oxford: Oxford University Press, 1993.

Mack, Burton L. *Who Wrote the New Testament? The Making of the Christian Myth*. San Francisco: HarperSanFrancisco, 1995.

———. "Social Formation." Pages 283-96 in *Guide to the Study of Religion*. Edited by Willi Braun and Russell T. McCutcheon. London: Cassell, 2000.

———. *The Christian Myth: Origins, Logic, and Legacy*. New York: Continuum, 2001.

———. *Myth and the Christian Nation: A Social Theory of Religion*. Religion in Culture: Studies in Social Contest and Construction. London: Equinox, 2008.

Mailloux, Stephen. *Rhetorical Power*. Ithaca, N.Y.: Cornell University Press, 1989.

Malina, Bruce. "Pain, Power, and Personhood: Ascetic Behavior in the Ancient Mediterranean." Pages 162-77 in *Asceticism*. Edited by Vincent L. Wimbush and Richard Valantasis. Oxford: Oxford University Press, 1998.

Marrou, H.I. *A History of Education in Antiquity*. Translated by George Lamb. Wisconsin Studies in Classics 3. Madison: University of Wisconsin Press, 1956.

Martens, Peter W. *Origen and Scripture: The Contours of the Exegetical Life*. Oxford Early Christian Studies. Oxford: Oxford University Press, 2012.

Martin, Craig. *A Critical Introduction to the Study of Religion*. Bristol: Equinox, 2012.

Marx-Wolf, Heidi. "High Priests of the Highest God: Third-Century Platonists as Ritual Experts." *Journal of Early Christian Studies* 18 (Winter 2010): 481-513.

McCartney, Dan G. "Literal and Allegorical Interpretation in Origen's *Contra Celsum*." *Westminster Theological Journal* 48 (1986): 281-301.

McCutcheon, Russell T. *Critics Not Caretakers: Redescribing the Public Study of Religion*. Albany: State University of New York Press, 2001.

———. "Myth." Pages 190-208 in *Guide to the Study of Religion*. Edited by Willi Braun and Russell T. McCutcheon. London: Cassell, 2000.

———. *The Discipline of Religion: Structure, Meaning, Rhetoric*. London: Routledge, 2003.

McGinn, Bernard. "Asceticism and Mysticism in Late Antiquity and the Early Middle Ages." Pages 58-74 in *Asceticism*. Edited by Vincent L. Wimbush and Richard Valantasis. Oxford: Oxford University Press, 1998.

McGuckin, John Anthony, ed. *The Westminster Handbook to Origen*. Westminster Handbooks to Christian Theology. Louisville: Westminster John Knox Press, 2004.

Mohler, James A. *The Origin and Evolution of the Priesthood: A Return to the Sources*. Staten Island: Alba House, 1970.

Morgan, Teresa, *Literate Education in the Hellenistic and Roman Worlds*. Cambridge Classical Studies. Cambridge: Cambridge University Press, 1998/2007.

Most, Glenn W. "Philosophy and Religion," Pages 300-322 in *The Cambridge Companion to Greek and Roman Philosophy*. Edited by David Sedley. Cambridge: Cambridge University Press, 2003.

_____ "Hellenistic Allegory and Early Imperial Rhetoric." Pages 26-38 in *The Cambridge Companion to Allegory*. Edited by Rita Copeland and Peter T. Struck. Cambridge: Cambridge University Press, 2010.

Nardoni, Enrique. "Origen's Concept of Biblical Inspiration." *The Second Century* 4 (1984): 9-23.

Pyysiäinen, Ilkka. *How Religion Works: Towards a New Cognitive Science of Religion*. Leiden: Brill, 2003.

Reale, Giovanni. *A History of Ancient Philosophy, Vol. 1-4*. Translated by John R. Catan. Albany: SUNY Press, 1987-90.

Rey, Terry. "Marketing the Goods of Salvation: Bourdieu on Religion." *Religion* 34 (2004): 331-43.

_____ *Bourdieu on Religion: Imposing Faith and Legitimacy*. Key Thinkers in the Study of Religion. London: Equinox Publishing, 2007.

Ricoeur, Paul. *Hermeneutics and the Human Sciences: Essays on Language, Action, and Interpretation*. Translated, edited, and introduced by John B. Thompson. Cambridge: Cambridge University Press, 1981.

_____ *Oneself as Another*. Translated by Kathleen Blamey. Chicago: University of Chicago Press, 1992.

_____ *Figuring the Sacred: Religion, Narrative, and Imagination*. Edited by Mark I. Wallace. Translated by David Pellauer. Minneapolis: Fortress Press, 1995.

Roitto, Rikard. "Behaving like a Christ-Believer: A Cognitive Perspective on Identity and Behavior Norms in the Early Christ-Movement." Pages 93-114 in *Exploring Early Christian Identity*. Edited by Bengt Holmberg. Wissenschaftliche Untersuchungen zum Neuen Testament 226. Tübingen: Mohr Siebeck, 2008.

Rombs, Ronnie J. "A Note on the Status of Origen's *De Principiis* in English," *Vigiliae Christianae* 61 (2007): 21-29.

Runia, David T. *Philo in Early Christian Literature: A Survey*. Minneapolis: Fortress Press, 1993.

Sanders, James A. *Canon and Community: A Guide to Canonical Criticism*. Philadelphia: Fortress Press, 1984.

_____ *Torah and Canon*. Second Edition. Eugene: Cascade Books, 2005.

Schatzki, Theodore R. *Social Practices: A Wittgensteinian Approach to Human Activity and the Social*. Cambridge: Cambridge University Press, 1996.

_____ "Introduction: Practice Theory" Pages 1-14 in *The Practice Turn in Contemporary Theory*. Edited by Theodore R. Schatzki, Karin Knorr Cetina, and Eike Von Savigny. London: Routledge, 2001.

_____ *The Site of the Social: A Philosophical Account of the Constitution of Social Life and Change*. University Park, Pa.: The Pennsylvania State University Press, 2002.

Scott, Alan. *Origen and the Life of the Stars: A History of an Idea*. Oxford Early Christian Studies. Oxford: Clarendon Press, 1991.

Shin, Daniel. "Some Light from Origen: Scripture as Sacrament." *Worship* 73 (1999): 399-425.

Sidebottom, Harry. "Philostratus and the Symbolic Roles of the Sophist and Philosopher." Pages 69-99 in *Philostratus*.

Edited by Ewen Bowie and Jaś Elsner. *Greek Culture in the Roman World*. Cambridge: Cambridge University Press, 2009.

Smith, J. Z. *Imagining Religion: From Babylon to Jonestown*. Chicago: University of Chicago Press, 1982.

Smith, Wilfred Cantwell. "The Study of Religion and the Study of the Bible." *Journal of the American Academy of Religion* 39.2 (June 1971): 131-40

_____ *What is Scripture? A Comparative Approach*. Minneapolis, Minn.: Fortress Press, 1993/2005.

Snyder, H. Gregory. *Teachers and Texts in the Ancient World. Religion in the First Christian Centuries*. London: Routledge, 2000.

Somers, Margaret R., and Gloria D. Gibson. "Reclaiming the Epistemological 'Other': Narrative and the Social Construction of Identity." Pages 37-99 in *Social Theory and the Politics of Identity*. Edited by Craig Calhoun. Cambridge: Blackwell, 1994.

Stowers, Stanley K. "Mythmaking, Social Formation, and Varieties of Social Theory." Pages 489-96 in *Redescribing Christian Origins*. Edited by Ron Cameron and Merrill P. Miller. Society of Biblical Literature Symposium Series 280. Atlanta: Society of Biblical Literature, 2004.

_____ "The Ontology of Religion." Pages 434-449 in *Introducing Religion: Essays in Honor of Jonathan Z. Smith*. Edited by Willi Braun and Russell T. McCutcheon. London: Equinox, 2008.

_____ "The Concept of 'Community' and the History of Early Christianity." *Method & Theory in the Study of Religion* 23 (2011): 238-56.

Swartz, David. "Bridging the Study of Culture and Religion: Pierre Bourdieu's Political Economy of Symbolic Power." *Sociology of Religion* 57 (1996): 71-85.

_____ *Culture & Power: The Sociology of Pierre Bourdieu*. Chicago: The University of Chicago Press, 1997.

Theissen, Gerd. *The Religion of the Earliest Churches: Creating a Symbolic World*. Translated by John Bowden. Minneapolis: Fortress Press, 1999.

Torjesen, Karen Jo. "'Body,' 'Soul,' and 'Spirit' in Origen's Theory of Exegesis." *Anglican Theological Review* 67 (1985): 17-30.

_____ *Hermeneutical Procedure and Theological Method in Origen's Exegesis*. Patrsiticsche Texte und Studien 28. Berlin: De Gruyter, 1986.

_____ "The Rhetoric of the Literal Sense: Changing Strategies of Persuasion from Origen to Jerome." Pages 633-44 in *Origeniana Septima: Origenes in den auseinandersetzungen des 4. Jarhunderts*. Edited by W. A. Bienert and U. Kühneweg. Leuven: Peeters, 1999.

Trapp, Michael. "Philosophy, Scholarship, and the World of Learning in the Severan Period." Pages 466-84 in *Severan Culture*. Edited by Simon Swain, Stephen Harrison, and JaśElsner. Cambridge: Cambridge University Press, 2007.

Trigg, Joseph W. "The Charismatic Intellectual: Origen's Understanding of Religious Leadership." *Church History* 50 (March 1981): 5-19.

_____ *Origen: The Bible and Philosophy in the Third Century*. Atlanta: John Knox Press, 1983.

_____ "Was Origen Systematic: A Reappraisal," Pages 258-64 in *Studia Patristica XLI: Orientalia, Clement, Origen, Athanasius, The Cappadocians, Chrysostom*. Edited by F. Young, M. Edwards, and P. Parvis. Leuven: Peeters, 2006.

Tripolitis, Antonia. *Origen: A Critical Reading*. American University Studies Series VII: Theology and Religion 8. New York: Peter Lang, 1985.

Tzamalikos, P. *Origen: Philosophy of History and Eschatology*. Supplements to Vigiliae Christianae 85. Leiden: Brill, 2007.

Ullucci, Daniel C. *The Christian Rejection of Animal Sacrifice*. Oxford: Oxford University Press, 2012.

Urban, Hugh B. "Sacred Capital: Pierre Bourdieu and the Study of Religion." *Method & Theory in the Study of Religion* 15. 4 (2003): 354-89.

―――― "Spiritual Capital, Academic Capital and the Politics of Scholarship: A Response to Bradford Verter." *Method & Theory in the Study of Religion* 17. 4 (2005): 166-75.

Urbano, Arthur, Jr. "'Read It Also to the Gentiles': The Displacement and Recasting of the Philosopher in the *Vita Antonii*." *Church History* 77 (December 2008): 877-914.

―――― *The Philosophical Life: Biography and the Crafting of Intellectual Identity in Late Antiquity*. North American Patristics Society Patristic Monograph Series 21. Washington: Catholic University of America Press, 2013.

Valantasis, Richard. "A Theory of the Social Function of Asceticism." Pages 544-52 in *Asceticism*. Edited by Vincent L. Wimbush and Richard Valantasis. Oxford: Oxford University Press, 1998.

Verter, Bradford. "Spiritual Capital: Theorizing Religion with Bourdieu against Bourdieu." *Sociological Theory* 12. 3 (2003): 150-74.

―――― "Bourdieu and the Bāuls Reconsidered." *Method and Theory in the Study of Religion* 16 (2004): 182-92.

Wall, Robert W. "Canonical Criticism." Pages 291-312 in *A Handbook to the Exegesis of the New Testament*. Edited by Stanley E. Porter. Boston: Brill, 2002.

Wall, Robert W., and Eugene E. Lemcio, eds. *The New Testament as Canon: A Reader in Canonical Criticism*. Journal for the Study of the New Testament Supplement Series 76. Sheffield: Sheffield Academic Press, 1992.

Watts, Edward J. "The Student Self in Late Antiquity." Pages 234-52 in *Religion and the Self in Antiquity*. Edited by David Brakke, Michael L. Satlow, and Steven Weitzman. Bloomington: Indiana University Press, 2005.

―――― *City and School in Late Antique Athens and Alexandria*. The Transformation of the Classical Heritage 41. Berkeley: University of California Press, 2006.

Wijeyesinghe, Charmaine L, and Bailey W. Jackson III, eds. *New Perspectives on Racial Identity Development: A Theoretical and*

Practical Anthology. New York: New York University Press, 2001.

Williams, Rowan D. "Origen: Between Orthodoxy and Heresy." Pages 3-14 in *Origeniana Septima: Origenes in den auseinandersetzungen des 4. Jarhunderts.* Bibliotheca Ephemeridum Theologicarum Lovaniensium 137. Edited by W. A. Bienert and U. Kühneweg. Leuven: Leuven University Press, 1999.

Wimbush, Vincent L., ed. *African Americans and the Bible: Sacred Texts and Social Textures.* New York: Continuum, 2000.

_____ "Introduction: TEXTures, Gestures, Power: Orientation to Radical Excavation." Pages 1-20 in *Theorizing Scriptures: New Critical Orientations to a Cultural Phenomenon.* Edited by Vincent L. Wimbush. Signifying (on) Scriptures 1. New Brunswick: Rutgers University Press, 2008.

_____ "Talking Back." Pages 284-285 in *Theorizing Scriptures: New Critical Orientations to a Cultural Phenomenon.* Edited by Vincent L. Wimbush. Signifying (on) Scriptures 1. New Brunswick: Rutgers University Press, 2008.

Winter, Bruce W. *Philo and Paul among the Sophists: Alexandrian and Corinthian Responses to a Julio-Claudian Movement.* 2d Edition. Grand Rapids: William B. Eerdmans, 2002.

Wright, Robert. *The Moral Animal: Evolutionary Psychology and Everyday Life.* New York: Vintage Books, 1994.

Young, Frances M. *Biblical Exegesis and the Formation of Christian Culture.* Peabody: Hendrickson Publishers, 2002.

Young, Frances, Lewis Ayres, and Andrew Louth, eds. *The Cambridge History of Early Christian Literature.* Cambridge: Cambridge University Press, 2004.

Index

Primary Sources

Origen Texts

CCels
   I.4 - 101
   I.7 - 103 n. 98
   I.9 - 104, 106 n. 111
   I.12 - 82
   III.30 - 140 n. 46
   III.50-51 - 105 n. 109
   III.58 - 104
   IV.26 - 140 n. 46
   V.61 - 103 n. 99
   VI.16 - 105 n. 108
   VI.48 - 140 n. 46
   VII.60 - 106 n. 110
   VIII.73 - 169 n. 41

EpistAfr - 143

EpistGreg
   1 - 105
      2 - 103 n. 100

ExhMart

HomEx
   4.6 - 103, 160-161

HomEz
  1.11 - 146 n.66
      2.1 - 121
      2.2 - 120 n. 167, 149
      5.4 - 156-157
      9.2 - 111-112

HomGn
  1 - 140 n. 48
  2.3 - 147 n. 69, 163-164
  2.4 - 164
      6.2 - 102
  6.3 - 139 n. 42
  8.6 -- 167 n. 31
  8.9 - 167
  10.1 - 115
  10.3 - 174
      14.3 - 102

HomJd
  2.3 - 103 n. 102
  2.5 - 167 n. 30
  3.3 - 136

HomJos
  1.7 - 115 n. 152
  2.1 - 139 n. 42
  3.5 - 139 n. 44
  4.1 - 167 n. 30
  5.6 - 161
  6.1 - 161-162
  7.1 - 162, 168
  7.3 - 168 n. 37
  7.6 - 167 n. 30

9 - 170
10.1 - 120-121
17.2 - 147, 171-172

HomJr
  4.2 - 139 n. 42
  12.3 - 167 n. 30
     27.4 - 103 n. 102

HomLc
  16.6 - 70 n. 8

HomLev
  1.4 - 171
  4 - 171
  4.5 - 174
  4.6 - 168 n. 36, 169
  5.2 - 173 n. 46
  5.3 - 167 n. 30
  5.5 - 145 n. 63
  6.3 - 168
  6.5 - 170
  7.1 - 158 n. 14, 168
  9.9 - 169 n. 39

HomNum
  4.3 - 172
  5.1 - 172 n. 44
  10.1 - 167 n. 30

PArch
  I.1.4 - 138 n. 39, 138 n. 40
  I.2.2 - 133
  I.2.10 - 133
  I.3.1 - 141-142

I.3.5 - 133-134
I.4 - 135 n. 22
I.6.3 - 136-137
II.9.3 - 138 n. 38
III.4.2 - 137
III.4.4 - 137 n. 35
IV.1 - 143 n. 57
IV.1.6 - 138 n. 40
IV.2.2 - 147 n. 68
IV.2.4 - 145
IV.4.2 - 138 n. 37

Other Ancient Texts

Diogenes Laertius
    LCL 184, 6-8 - 80-81

Epictetus
  LCL 131, 31 - 95
      LCL 218, 375-391 - 90 n. 61

Eunapius
  LCL 134, 347 - 92

Eusebius
  LCL 265, 11 - 155 n. 9
      LCL 265, 13 - 107 n.116
  LCL 265, 15 - 107 n. 117
  LCL 265, 17 - 109 n. 124
  LCL 265, 18-20 - 119-120
  LCL 265, 19-21 - 109 n. 122
  LCL 265, 23-27 - 109 n. 126
  LCL 265, 27-29 - 109 n. 123
  LCL 265, 51 - 109 n. 126
  LCL 265, 55 - 110 n. 128

LCL 265, 63-65 - 111 n. 136
LCL 265, 71 - 111 n. 137
LCL 265, 83 - 113 n. 140

Gregory Thaumaturgus
  76 - 114 n. 145
  79 - 114 n. 146
  116 - 114
  135 - 114
  151-152 - 114

Philostratus
  LCL 16, 47 - 92
    LCL 134, 7 - 83 n. 41

Plutarch
  LCL 470, 413 - 89

Porphyry
  LCL 440, 3 - 95 n. 77
  LCL 440, 7 - 107 n. 117
  LCL 440, 57 - 92 n. 67
    LCL 440, 59 - 97
    LCL 440, 71 - 92

Quintilian
  LCL 124, 59 - 84 n. 43
  LCL 124, 14 - 84

General Index

Abimelech - 102
Abraham - 138
Academy, Plato's - 98
Acts of the Apostles - 168
Acts of Paul - 143
Adam - 138
Aelius Aristides - 85
Aeschines - 89
Alexander, bishop of Jerusalem - 111
Alexander Severus - 111
Alexandria - 72, 80, 103, 106-107, 109, 111-112, 131, 155, 165, 179
Althusser, Louis - 20, 40, 45
Ambrose of Alexandria - 155
Ammonius Saccas - 110
Analogy - 32, 159-160, 163, 169, 172
Angel - 129, 131, 136-137
Antioch - 111, 131
Apocalypse of Peter - 143
Apollonius of Tyana - 91-92, 95 n. 78
Apostles - 168-169
Arabia - 110
Aristotle - 94, 118
Arnal, William - 19, 20, 23
Arrian - 95, 97
Asad, Talal - 27-28
Asceticism/ascetic practice - 68, 78, 87-89, 92-93, 106, 120, 156, 170, 180
Astrologer - 82, 103
Astrology/astronomy - 105, 113

Athenodoros - 113
Athens - 94
Austin, J. L. - 153
Baptism - 134, 170, 173
Barnabas, Epistle to - 143
Bell, Catherine - 44 n. 21
Bell, Denise Kimber - 15
Bell, Duncan - 55-56
Bellatores - 140
Berchman, Robert M. - 70 n. 10
Berlinerblau, Jacques - 123 n. 172
Berner, Ulrich - 128 n. 6
Betegh, Gábor - 94
Bible - 35, 60
Bielo, James S. - 3 n.5,
Blosser, Benjamin P. - 71
Bond, George Clement - 64
Bourdieu, Pierre - 4, 9, 30-31, 39-40, 44-50, 52, 53, 67, 73-75, 123, 126, 151-154, 177, 180
Bowersock, G. W. - 82 n. 40, 85
Boys-Stones, George R. - 123 n. 171
Braun, Willi - 20
Butler, Judith - 42
Butterworth, G.W. - 131 n. 12
Caesarea (of Pontus) - 113
Caesarea Maritima - 32, 70, 103, 111, 113, 117, 155-156, 164, 179
Canonical criticism - 2 n. 3
Capital - 9, 45-46, 50-51
  Cultural - 46-47, 122
  Political - 47
  Philosophical - 78, 94, 96-98, 100, 146, 154
  Religious - 47-48
  Salvific - 146
  Symbolic - 9, 31, 39, 45-47, 49-50, 73-74, 77, 80, 82, 85, 93, 97, 99-100, 108, 117-118, 122, 125, 127, 151, 153, 155, 157, 163, 166

Castagno, Adele Monaci - 140, 166 n. 28
Castricius - 107 n. 117
Catechumen - 103, 134
Celsus - 101, 103, 105
Chaldea/Chaldean - 81
Chadwick, Henry - 130
Christ - see Jesus Christ
Chryssipus - 98, 100 n. 90
Clark, Elizabeth A. - 69 n. 5
Clement of Alexandria - 109
Clement, First Epistle of - 16
Coates, Delman L. - 159
Collins, Randall - 76-77
Commentary (textual) - 63, 65, 94, 98, 108, 118, 121, 129, 131, 155, 159
Commentary on Romans- 130
Contra Celsum - 100
Cosmos/cosmology - 14, 39, 83
Counter-intuitive agents - see gods
Cox, Patricia - 78-79, 87, 91, 97 n. 84, 106 n. 118, 106 n. 119
Cribiore, Raffaella - 80, 92 n. 68, 92 n. 69, 108
Criticism
    Historical - 36
    Textual - 17, 99, 157
Cronk, Lee - 50-51
Crouzel, Henri - 70, 128, 135, 137 n. 36, 141, 145 n. 64
Cultural producer - 31, 48, 76, 127, 151-153, 160-161, 178-179
Cynics - 105, 160-161
Cyprian - 166, 172
Daly, Robert J. - 173
Daniel, Book of - 143
Dawson, John David - 29
De Haas, Frans - 98
Deal, William - 88
Demetrius, bishop of Alexandria - 110-113, 155

Demiurge - 132
Democritus - 97
Demon/daemon - 129, 131, 136-137
Depth semantics - 58
Derrida, Jacques - 63
Devil - 111-112
Didache - 16
Dillon, John - 98 n. 86
Diogenes Laertius - 80, 82
Diogenes of Sinope - 78
Distanciation - 58-59
Dively Lauro, Elizabeth Ann - 68 n. 4, 115-116, 119, 145-146
Doctor (medical) - 82
Doxa - 73
Droge, Arthur J. - 7
Durkheim, Emile - 40
Eagleton, Terry - 20
Ecclesiology - 14, 68 n. 4, 139
Edwards, Mark Julian - 70, 144 n. 61
Ehud - 136
Egypt/Egyptian - 81, 103, 106, 160-162
Empedocles - 13
Emplotment - 53
Engler, Steven - 44 n. 21
Epictetus - 90, 94-95, 97, 148
Epicureans - 161
Esler, Philip - 24-25
Ethics - 24, 77, 83-84, 101-102, 108, 121
Eucharist - 172, 175
Eucleides - 97
Eudaimonia - 91, 95, 97
Eunapius - 84, 91-92
Euphrates of Tyre - 95 n. 78
Eusebius of Caesarea - 106-108, 119, 131, 167 n. 30
Evolutionary psychology - 50-51

Exegesis - 29, 69, 94, 99
Father - see god
Favorinus of Arelate - 95 n. 78

Field
    Cultural production - 31, 45-46, 67, 73-75, 125, 151, 153, 179
    Christian - 127
    Educational - 47
    Intellectual - 75
    Literary - 74
    Philosophical - 67-68, 73, 75-76, 78, 80, 89-93, 96-97, 99-101, 105, 108, 122, 127, 179
    Political - 47
    Power - 75, 83, 85, 92
    Religious - 47-49
    Rhetorical - 83

Flood, Gavin - 88
Gadamer, Hans-Georg - 57
Geertz, Armin W. - 52 n. 52
Geertz, Clifford - 25-27
Geometry - 105, 113, 121
Gerson, Lloyd P. - 76 n. 26
Gibson, Gloria D. - 54
Giddens, Anthony - 30
Gilliam, Angela - 64
Gnostics - 132, 138, 141, 146, 159
God(s) - 35, 48, 85, 101-104, 114-115, 119, 121, 129, 131-139, 141-142, 144-145, 147, 149-150, 157, 165, 169-171, 174
Gospel of Thomas - 16
Grafton, Anthony - 72, 94 n. 72, 96 n. 79, 111 n. 136, 117-118
Grammatikos - 107-108, 113, 116
Greece - 111
Gregory Thaumaturgus - 104, 106, 113
Gubrium, Jaber F. - 54

Guy, Laurie - 111 n. 136
Habermas, Jürgen - 57
Habitus - 45, 49, 53, 73-75, 88, 116, 125
Hadot, Pierre - 77-78, 90 n. 60
Halbwachs, Maurice - 55
Halliwell, Stephen - 82 n. 40, 83
Hanack, Adolf von - 69
Hanson, R.P.C. - 119 n. 162
Harris, Carl Vernon -72, 100 n. 91, 115
Hawkes, David - 21
Hebrews, Epistle to the - 167
Hegel, G. W. F. - 40
Heine, Ronald E. - 72 n. 21, 108, 116, 118, 130 , 157 no. 11, 158 n. 13
Heliodorus - 97
Heraclas - 109-110, 155
Hermans, Theo - 173, n. 45
Hermeneutical Method - 32, 69, 131
Hermeneutical Idealism 60-61
Hermeneutical Realism - 60-61
Hermeneutics, rhetorical - 61-62, 159
Hermeneutics, theory of - 57-58
Hexapla - 116-117
Hippolytus - 67 n. 1
Hoffmann, Philippe - 91 n. 62, 94
Holmberg, Bengt - 25
Holstein, James A. - 54
Holy Spirit - 129, 131-136, 138, 140, 142-143, 147, 149
Homer - 117-119, 158
Homilies on Genesis - 130
Homilies on Numbers - 130 n. 9
Hooks, bell - 9, 10
Hughes, Aaron - 63-64
Iamblichus - 166
Identity - 4, 5, 14-16, 23-25, 27-30, 32, 42, 52, 59, 87, 162

    Class - 9
    Ehnic - 7-9
    Formation of - 4, 8, 14-15, 23, 54, 64, 127, 179
    Gender - 42
    Group - see Social
    Idem - 53
    Ipse - 53
    Narrative - 30, 31, 32, 52, 54, 60, 127, 138, 151
    Racial - 7-8
    Religious - 7, 9, 14-15, 24, 127
    Social - 8, 13, 24-25, 28, 55-56, 64-65, 127, 139, 151, 179
Ideology - 14-15, 20-21, 48, 56-57, 123, 125, 150, 151
Ignatius -16
Illusio - 74
India/Indian - 81-82
Infirmiores - 140
Institute for Signifying Scriptures - 2
Interpretation - 28-29, 31, 49, 57, 59, 62-65, 93-94, 99, 116, 119, 121, 126-127, 129, 131, 148-149
Isaac - 167
Jackson III, Bailey W. - 8 n. 7
James - 168
Jericho - 162-163, 169
Jerome - 130
Jerusalem - 111
Jesus Christ - 104, 119, 121, 129, 131-135, 138-140, 142-144, 148-150, 157, 160, 165, 167-168, 171, 174
John - 168
Jude - 168
Julia Mamaea - 111, 131
Julius Africanus, Epistle to - 143
Kaplan, David M. - 54 n. 44
Kassam, Tazim - 38
Laity - 48
Lawyer - 82

Lamberton, Robert - 71, 99 n. 89
Laurence, John D. - 166 n. 29
Lemcio, Eugene E. - 2 n. 3
Leonides - 106-107, 109, 112
Lieu, Judith - 28
Lincoln, Bruce - 6, 11, 13, 20, 56, 125-126, 150, 154, 177
Logos - see Jesus Christ
Luhmann, Nicklas - 40
Luke - 168
Lyman, Rebecca - 70, 110, 132 n. 14, 133 n. 18
Mack, Burton L. - 6, 11, 13-14, 16-24, 126
Mailloux, Steven - 60-62, 64, 158
Malina, Bruce J. - 88 n. 54
Malinowski, Bronislaw - 40
Marcion - 16, 138
Marcionites - 143
Marrou, H. I. - 86 n. 48
Martens, Peter W. - 100 n. 91, 105 n. 107. 116, 148 n. 71
Martin, Craig - 141 n. 51
martyrdom/martyrs - 7, 173
Marx, Karl - 40
Marxism - 45
Marx-Wolf, Heidi - 166
Mathematics - 121
Matthew - 168
McCartney, Dan G. - 158 n. 12
McCutcheon, Russell T. - 5-6, 11-13, 20-22, 56, 126
McGinn - Bernard - 78 n. 29
McGuckin, John Anthony - 109-110, 117 n. 157
Memory
Misrecognition - 47, 151
Mohler, James A. - 166 n. 27
Morgan, Teresa - 79
Moses - 138
Most, Glenn W. - 158 n. 12

Myth/mythology - 4, 9, 13-14, 16-24, 28, 31-32, 48, 56-57, 64-65, 67-68, 82, 113, 125-132, 135, 137, 149-150, 151, 154, 159-160, 165, 175, 178

Mythmaking - 4, 13, 15, 16, 18, 19, 20, 21, 22, 24, 31, 32, 57, 65, 67, 125, 127, 150, 152-153, 155, 162, 177

Nardoni, Enrique - 144 n. 58

Narrative - 9, 20-23, 28, 53-55, 58-60, 65, 87-88, 123, 125-129, 150, 151, 159-160

    Conceptual - 54-55
    Meta- - 32, 54-55, 132
    Mythic - see myth
    Ontological - 54-55
    Personal - 32
    Public - 4, 31-32, 54-57, 68 n. 4, 73, 121, 127
    Shared - 8
    Theological - 32

New Testament - 16-17, 24, 138, 143-144, 147, 178, 180

Noah - 138, 164

Nun - 168

Nussbaum, Martha - 86

Objectivism - 40

Old Testament - 138-139, 143-144, 163, 165

On First Principles - 32, 128-132, 143-144

Ontology - 30-31, 36, 39, 177

    Individualist - 40
    Practice - 52
    Site - 41-42
    Social - 31, 41, 180
    Socialist/wholist - 23

Orator - see sophist

Oratory - see sophistry

Orders - 41-42, 44

Origen - 3-5, 9, 13-15, 29-32, 67-69, 75, 82, 100-123, 125, 127-151, 153-175, 177-180

Othniel - 136

Palestine - 111
Pantaenus - 109
Parsons, Talcott - 40
Passeron, Jean-Claude - 45
Paul, apostle - 22, 24-25, 149, 158, 168
Paul of Antioch - 107
Performativity - 42
Persia/Persian - see Chaldea/Chaldean
Peter, apostle - 149, 168
Peter, First Epistle to - 169
Philosopher - 31, 67-73, 75-78, 80, 83-100, 102-103, 105, 110, 113, 115, 118-119, 121-123, 127, 132, 137, 146, 151, 155, 157, 159-160, 162, 166, 173-174, 177, 179
Philosophy - 69-72, 75-80, 82-87, 89-90, 92-97, 100-106, 108, 110, 114, 119, 121-123, 179-180
Philostratus - 81-82, 84-85, 91, 111
Physics - 113, 121, 131
Pindar - 13
Plato - 13, 17, 94, 98, 117, 144 n. 61
Platonism/Platonists - 70, 135, 178
Plotinus - 92, 95, 98, 107 n. 117
Plutarch, disciple of Origen - 109
Plutarch of Chaeronea - 89
Polemo - 95 n. 78
Porphyry - 78, 91-92, 97, 166
Practical intelligibility - 43
Practical understandings - 43
Practice theory - 40, 52
Practices, social - 4, 9, 13, 24, 27-28, 30-31, 38-42, 44, 49, 52, 65, 67, 71-74, 76-78, 82, 85, 93-95, 97, 99-100, 103, 106, 121-123, 175, 177
Presbyter, Origen as - 111, 154-156, 166-167, 173
Priest/priesthood - 112, 157, 165-171, 172, 175
Proclinus - 97
Prophet - 103, 121, 138, 174, 179

Prototype - 25, 28
Public narratives - see narratives
Pythagoreans - 144
Pyysiäinen, Ilkka - 48 n. 38
Q - 16
Quintilian - 84
Rabbi - 179
Rahab - 163
Rational choice theory - 40
Reale, Giovanni - 76 n. 26
Rey, Terry - 44 n. 21
Rhetoric - 83-84, 86, 92, 99, 122, 149, 159
Ricoeur, Paul - 52-54, 57-60, 180
Ritual - 18, 22, 24, 37
Roitto, Rickard - 26
Roman Empire - 17, 67, 72, 75, 79, 85, 94, 110, 117, 122-123, 178, 180
Romans, Epistle to the - 25
Rombs, Ronnie J. - 128 n. 5
Rome - 80, 110
Rufinus - 130-131, 161, 167 no. 30
Rules - 43, 52, 65, 73
Runia, David T. - 128
Sacrifice - 139, 167, 172-174
Sanders, James A. - 2 n. 3
Schatzki, Theodore - 30, 39-42, 49 n. 41, 180
Scheck, Thomas P. - 166 n. 26
School, philosophical - 70, 77-78, 88, 92-95, 99-100, 103, 108-110, 113
Scott, Alan - 101 n. 92
Scripture - 1, 2-4, 7, 11-12, 30, 35-38, 49, 57, 63, 65, 70, 103, 105, 108-109, 111, 116-117, 119, 121, 127, 131-132, 138-139, 142-144, 146-149, 155-159, 162, 166, 171, 174-175, 177-180
Scripturalizing - 3-5, 19, 30-33, 35-39, 49, 64-65, 67, 169, 177, 179-180, 181

Second Sophistic - 83, 117
Self-control - see self-mastery
Self-mastery - 68, 89-90, 94, 97, 118, 123, 136
Septuagint - 116
Shepherd of Hermas - 143
Shin, Daniel - 144
Sidebottom, Harry - 83 n. 40, 86 n. 51, 95 n. 78, 96, 97 n. 83
Simpliciores - 116, 140-141, 159
Smith, Jonathan Z. - 19, 62
Smith, Wilfred Cantwell - 1, 30, 35-36, 40, 177-178
Snyder, H. Gregory - 93 n. 70, 71
Social formation - 4, 13, 15-24, 31, 55, 64-65, 67, 72, 75, 123, 126, 159, 177
Social identity - see identity
Social location - 4, 6, 14, 15, 140-141, 154-155
Social network theory - 40
Socrates - 78, 83
Somers, Margaret R. - 54
Son - see Jesus Christ
Soothsayer - 179
Sophist - 82-86, 96, 161, 179
Sophistry - 84-85
Soteriology - 132, 135, 149, 169
Speech act - 153
Stoicism/Stoics - 95, 119, 157-158, 173
Stowers, Stanley K. - 8, 23, 39
Structuralism - 40, 49
Subjectivism - 40
Sulla, Lucius Cornelius - 94
Swartz, David - 44 n. 21, 45 n. 24, 45 n. 25, 46 n. 29, 46 n. 30, 47 n. 33, 47 n. 35, 48 n. 37, 50 n. 46, 53 n. 54, 74 n. 23, 74 n. 24, 125 n. 1, 151 n. 1
Symbolic capital - see capital
Symbolic labor - 4, 31, 32, 48, 65, 67, 151-155, 157, 159, 163, 175, 177

Symbolic power - 39, 45, 47-48, 152
Symbolic violence - 4, 14, 31, 45, 47, 74, 88, 125, 152, 158, 175
Tajfel, Henri - 24
Teleoaffective structures - 43-44, 86, 91, 99, 101
Telos - 91, 93
Theissen, Gerd - 26-27
Theoctistus, bishop of Caesarea Maritima - 111
Theologian - 70-71
Theology - 14-15, 24, 57, 68 n. 4, 70, 101, 122, 129, 131, 133, 177, 179
Thrasyllus - 144
Torjesen, Karen Jo - 68 n. 5, 69, 119 n. 163, 130-132, 134, 135 n. 21, 141-142, 144, 145 n. 62, 146, 147 n. 67, 148-149, 150 n. 74, 158-159
Trapp, Michael - 98 n. 87
Trigg, Joseph Wilson - 107 n. 115, 128-129, 165
Tripolitis, Antonia - 71, 110 n. 132, 110 n. 133, 111 n. 135, 135 n. 24, 139 n. 43
Turner, John C. - 24
Tzamalikos, Panayiotis - 71
Ullucci, Daniel C. - 167 n. 33
Urban, Hugh B. - 44 n. 21
Urbano, Arthur P. - 67 n. 2, 122
Valantasis, Richard - 87-88
Valentinus - 16, 138
Verter, Bradford - 44 n. 21
Wall, Robert W. - 2 n.3
Watts, Edward J. - 79, 110
Weber, Max - 45
Williams, Megan - 72, 94 n. 72, 96 n. 79, 111 n. 136, 117-118
Williams, Rowan D. - 112-113, 142 n. 55
Wimbush, Vincent - 2, 11-12, 38, 40, 62, 177-178
Wijeyesinghe, Charmin L. - 8 n. 7
Winter, Bruce W. - 86 n. 49
Word - see Jesus Christ

Wright, Robert - 51
Young, Frances - 29
Zeno of Citium - 94
Zenodotus - 116
Zephyrinus - 110
Zeuthus - 107 n. 117

www.ingramcontent.com/pod-product-compliance
Lightning Source LLC
Chambersburg PA
CBHW020354170426
43200CB00005B/164